Madeleine Slade

THE SPIRIT'S
PILGRIMAGE

Coward-McCann, Inc.

New York

Illustrations will be found following page 158.

An Appendix of important dates will be found on page 317.

FOREWORD

by Vincent Sheean

THE Odyssey of Miss Madeleine Slade will not be forgotten, I think, so long as mankind can still keep the chronicle.

Many in the western world will be able today to remember how we first made her acquaintance, from afar, by means of our daily newspapers. It was during the Round Table Conference in London in 1931, when Mahatma Gandhi was more photographed than ever before. He had already become one of the most familiar visual phenomena to which the art of photography had made the masses accessible. From 1921 onwards the pictures of this small, snaggle-toothed man had become constantly more familiar to the entire world until, in 1930, he marched across India to make salt out of sea water. At that moment, when the whole world seemed to hang upon his footsteps, his pictures seemed to appear upon every page of newsprint. He became more familiar than one's own mother or father, because one saw him everywhere. There was only a single rival to Gandhi at that time in the visual repertoire of our small planet (its mind's eye, if one can use that term for photography), which was, oddly enough, the Prince of Wales. Either one could have been recognized almost anywhere by almost anybody because of photography alone, with no other significance attached.

3

Then, as a result of the Salt March, the great empire of modern history began its noble acknowledgment of responsibility, its grand and thrilling liberation of those whom it had once held to the dust. The first step was the Round Table Conference in London, in 1931, called to devise some method of constitutional self-government for India. At this conference Gandhi was the only representative of the Indian National Congress, the party of independence—the only party that counted for anything in India. As such he undertook his historic journey to Europe, during the course of which the bewildered West learned to know him for the first time in every detail of his daily regime, his food and clothing, his language and cast of mind. Those familiar with Indian affairs had known him for a long time, and had known others akin to him, but I am speaking here of the widest mass of our own people, the Americans most of all, who had looked upon him as semilegendary until then. He grew and grew and grew upon our newspapers until there was a period, shortly before his return to India, when he really seemed to dominate the press here. The very slightest of his doings merited the closest attention; every word was recorded; in some mysterious way, although what he was, what he meant and what he was doing were not understood, he himself commanded the attention and to some degree the imagination of our country.

It was just then that we all began to notice the constant attendance of a rather statuesque figure just behind him in most of the photographs which abounded. Who was this? It was a woman not Indian, obviously European of some sort, dressed in Indian clothing, head bowed, eyes cast down, never speaking, always there. The man himself was small, the woman large. Some rudimentary information was provided with these innumerable photographs. It was Miss Madeleine Slade, "the daughter of a British admiral." She was called "a follower of the Mahatma." How? Why? The important affairs of the day were numerous; Gandhi himself spoke without ceasing; events crowded in; this hooded, silent figure never gave interviews, had nothing to say— she was simply there, always there. When the tremendous three-ringed circus of the Round Table Conference was over, and the

4

Mahatma returned to India, there were many of us in the United States who retained as a most abiding recollection of the whole business this silent and noble figure in the background, this enigmatical Veronica.

We all knew much more about India afterwards, as events moved on to their climax during the next two decades. We did not, however, learn much more about Miss Madeleine Slade. She never again appeared in our newspaper photography with such constancy; she was never again in such constant attendance on the Mahatma; she took her constancy to the fields, to the villages, to the hills; we of the West seldom heard her name. When she was arrested, it was known, but then so many were arrested. She seemed to come and go through the complicated flames and shadows of the revolutionary period almost in silence and very nearly unexplained. A solid and comminatory phantom to many of us, she was there like a natural phenomenon—let us say a mountain in the form of a cross, or a rainbow bent in upon itself—to shock and bewilder the conscience of western man.

And without a doubt Mahatma Gandhi knew this—knew the irresistible symbolism of Mira behn (Miss Slade's Indian name). He knew it with that extrasensory apparatus of his which thought in symbols and created in symbols, but he also knew it with his brain. Readers of this book will readily perceive that its author was and is a woman of the utmost simplicity. It was not within her nature to comprehend more than a fraction of the superb intellect which directed her life and those of so many others. What she understood was the magnitude of the little man's heart and soul, how he felt for all beings and was all beings, how he warmed and soothed and encouraged and brought forth life, how death shrank from his shadow. She knew the beauty and splendor of a Man of the Lord. What she did not know—and this book is the plainest evidence of it—is that her saint and hero, embodiment of all that is best and truest in human nature, had a first-class brain as well, and was in almost every respect the intellectual superior of those with whom he had to deal from birth to death. Few persons really understood this highly significant detail because the spiritual phenomenon was too much for them. In a

5

sense, the light from Mahatma's spirit and ethics—his sheer good-
ness—gave his qualities of mind little chance to shine. A very
few in the highest places (Halifax and Smuts in public life, Shaw
in contemplation) perceived the fact. Professor Einstein also perceived it. Some of those who were closest to Gandhi, leading off
with Jawaharlal Nehru, never really knew, until after he was
dead, what a great and indomitable mind had inhabited that frail,
small body, along with its exalted spirit. Jawaharlal's printed
work on the subject shows chiefly bewilderment over a crucial
period of years, although he, too, knows by now. The lucidity
and altitude of Gandhi's intellect were expressions of the Hindu
phenomena of time and place, attributes of the universal, with
a strong kinship to such other expressions as Socrates and
Confucius.

Mira behn, or Mira as she was most often called, came out of
the blue to the Indian movement as an expression of life's aware-
ness of its own shortcomings. In the mode of thought set going
by Dr. Carl Jung one might say that she was the western world's
acknowledgment of guilt and of the will to atone. This was not
at all in her own consciousness, but in that which put her forth.
Gandhi did not evoke her. The most he did was to tell her she
could come if she wished. She came as a daughter not only of the
western mind but, specifically, of that class which had made and
governed the British empire of India. Her father had been the
naval commander-in-chief there. During all the years she spent
in Mahatma's service she loomed against the sky as a configura-
tion of the grave, sincere and honorable elements in that against
which she had revolted.

We find no hint of such things in her own story, which is told
within the precise limits of her own individuality. She attributes
nothing general, nothing social or historical, to her own yearn-
ings and fulfillments. She longed for something which she found
in part, as it were afar off, in the piano sonatas of Beethoven,
which in turn led her to Romain Rolland, who in turn led her
to Gandhi. Now that the long, hard struggle is over, she begins
to hear the music of Beethoven again in the wind as it stirs the
trees in the high Himalaya. She tells her story with the absolute

6

simplicity of a child and with no effort to relate it to any other. I, Madeleine Slade, she says—I, Madeleine Slade. It is left to us to see, if we do, how this I connects with all others in a world which is trying, as she has been trying, to get itself born. To me it is and will always remain a story with terrifying undertones and dark, concealed reproaches, but touched into glory now and then by the pure shimmer of hope.

There are few of us who could have endured as Mira did under conditions so inimical to physical welfare. She was not constitutionally suited to the rigors of Indian climate in the plains; she had malaria every year for twenty-five years, along with numerous other ailments; her work was hard, her hours long, her rewards only now and then a letter or a kind word from the Mahatma. Her very first job after she knelt at his feet and he accepted her was the scrubbing of latrines. This and other hard manual labor were her lot for many years. She had no talent for language and yet had to toil at her Hindi lessons endlessly. Mahatma was deeply disturbed by her attachment to him, and for fear of it he kept her at a distance for decades. His letters to her, published some years ago here as *The Love Letters of Mahatma Gandhi,* bear down heavily upon the theme that her devotion should be to "the cause we serve," and not to any one of its servants. Mira learned this lesson so well that when Mahatma was killed she did not even go to Delhi. She stayed in her village in the foothills and heard his voice in the wind, saw his eyes in the stars. She has gone higher into the mountains since then.

Hard and even cruel as Mira behn's life may seem to us, it has bestowed upon her the kind of recompense which comes in the end to saints and anchorites. She can talk to the birds and the beasts and they understand; in a way they talk back, they are her familiars. They come to her from far and near and not always, perhaps, for food alone. She hears stirrings in the hills and the valleys, sees the light on the peak, listens to the slumberous murmurs of the night on the mountain. It is her custom to keep silence, in the Gandhian manner, for a day or a week or more (this is what the Mahatma called "disciplinary resolutions"). Why should she speak, when so much speaks to her? And she has done great good to human beings. In village after village she has taught the women to spin and weave, to take care of the cattle, to fertilize and irrigate the soil and make it yield green shoots from the barren dust. What she has sacrificed must seem to her very little—after all, it is only the world—in comparison to these results. If she ever has time to look at her toil-worn hands and her feet hardened by the roads of India she has there the evidence of the offering she has made. It is the maximum offering: her life.

IT was a lonely spot on the shore of the Arabian Sea. I was standing there in the spray of the breaking waves, and gazing out on the vast stormy ocean, when a solitary, pure white bird passed over the waters. To me, at that moment, it was as a symbol of the Soul passing over the Ocean of Life—detached and peaceful. For is not that what the soul within us is—and which we realize in the rare moments when we become conscious of our inmost selves?

That feeling comes clear and simple in one's early years, without one's knowing what it is. And then, with God's grace, it may begin to come even clearer in later days, now with something of conscious understanding, as the joys and sorrows of life fall into their true perspective. It runs through life like a thread strung through a row of beads, the two ends of which are finally joined together.

CHAPTER I

MY earliest recollections belong to the end of the last century, as I was born in 1892. I had one sister, Rhona, three years older than myself, who died some time ago, and no brothers. But my mother's youngest brother was only three years older than Rhona, and we grew up together as brother and sisters. We never addressed him as uncle, but by his pet name, Alec.

My father, a naval officer, was often away in distant waters for two years or more at a stretch, so my mother took us to Milton Heath, her father's country home, and all my earliest recollections center around that place. The house stood in some twenty acres of land on high ground, beautifully laid out in gardens, paddocks for the cows, and a rich collection of shrubs and trees. Motorcars did not exist in those days, so there were stables full of fine horses, some for the carriages and some for riding and hunting. At the bottom of the sloping paddocks was a cowshed with four or five Jersey cows, chicken house and pigsties.

The house had a beautiful view up the Dorking Valley with the North Downs to the right and the Lieth Hill Range to the left. If there was one thing my grandfather loved it was a "good prospect," and he had especially bought Milton Heath, many years before, for its charming view. The day nursery was on the top floor, so I got the best view of all, and the night nursery was on the middle floor, looking out over the stableyard, which, of course, pleased me much.

At a very early age my sister went to a boarding school, as it suited her temperament better, so I was the only child in the house. But from the beginning I enjoyed solitude, and was perfectly happy playing all by myself under the trees in the garden. My grandmother, thinking I ought to have other children to play with, arranged accordingly. I have a definite recollection of being quite upset at this plan, which was soon dropped. I was very devoted to my mother and my nurse, Bertha, and a special pal was my grandfather. Though there must have been about fifty years difference between us, we had a quiet natural understanding like old friends. We used to play regularly on the floor together. It was always the same old picture puzzle, but I never got tired of it, and felt the same delight each time that my grandfather would say, "Now you finish it off by putting the hoopoo right in the middle"; and I would take the little hoopoo, well worn with fingering, and place him in the empty hole in the center of the picture. From this we advanced to building with wooden "bricks" of all lengths. Sometimes we would achieve an openwork edifice three or four feet high, in the middle of which my grandfather would place a lump of sugar for Snatcher, the old white fox terrier, who understood the game perfectly; namely, that the moment he grabbed the sugar, the whole castle would come tumbling down on his head. But the sugar was worth it and he played his part each time, to my utmost delight.

Out of doors the twenty acres were a whole world for adventurous exploration. I got to know every nook and corner, and from the beginning I had a feeling of fellowship with the trees and plants. There were some trees for which I had a special affection and some I was not very fond of, but one and all were for me personalities. Later on, as a young girl, I can remember throwing my arms around trees and embracing them, and to this day that feeling remains.

I did not care much for toys, and as for dolls, I could not bear them. But I had two special playthings—a little monkey made of hairy leather filled with stuffing, and a little squirrel of the same material. I called them Nippy and Squilly, and got Bertha to make clothes for them. Nippy was the husband and Squilly the wife. They had a little house, and a servant, Impy (also made of leather), and they became such defined characters that even now I can clearly recall with what interest and respect I regarded them.

It was during this period that one day my elders explained to me that I had to be a bridesmaid at some family wedding. When I managed to understand the implications of the proposition—that I should be dressed up in fine clothes and have to follow the bride to the altar, holding up her train along with other bridesmaids—I did not like it at all. I protested strongly, and finally stipulated that if I *must* go I should at least have the support and consolation of Nippy and Squilly's company. I was told that the clergyman would disapprove of such a thing, and that it would not be done. But I was adamant. Then Mother and Bertha hit on the idea of hiding Nippy and Squilly in the basket of flowers which I was to carry with the rest of the bridesmaids. I felt this was rather disrespectful to Nippy and Squilly, but at last agreed. However, that was not the end of the problem. I said if I was going to have special clothes, they must also. I remember being very particular about this part of the business, and Bertha had to make a black satin suit, with lace frills, for Nippy, and a green satin dress for Squilly.

The untrammeled child mind seems to have unique power to create things of the spirit, for what else was this? Out of two little bits of stuffed leather I had created companions that I not only loved but respected! Even now I cannot think of them without a sense of respect, and I have just been hesitating several times before writing the words "little bits of stuffed leather." It is the feeling of pure affection that becomes enshrined in an inanimate thing which gives it such value, just as it is the adoration of pure-hearted worshipers that gives sacredness to an image. The truth of that belief that "God made man in His own image" is really the other way round. It is man who had made (conceived of) God in *his* own image throughout the ages, and since God allows man to find Him through that image, it can, in a sense, be said that "God made man in His own image."

CHAPTER II

In those early years life was quite regular, and there were definite "rules." During the day I would be in the day nursery with Bertha, or playing in the garden. There were also walks of about a mile out and a mile back for which Bertha used to take me, either toward the town, toward the village, or up the lane, and whenever I was asked which of these walks I would like to take, I invariably replied "Up'e lane." That way there was a pond with swans, a farmyard, then fields, and a coppice full of primroses in the spring. Who would want to go along the high road toward ugly, smelly, human habitations when such joys lay "up'e lane"?

Then there were definite times for meeting my elders. After nursery "tea" Bertha would tidy me up, dress me in a simple silk smock, and then bring me downstairs where I would either play games with my grandfather or be taken to the drawing room, where my grandmother, who was of Scotch stock, would be sitting knitting. The only meal I attended downstairs was Sunday lunch, when I sat next to my mother, who kept careful control over everything I had to eat. I was only allowed the simplest food, and if there was nothing simple enough on the table, something special was brought for me. It never occurred to me to beg or cry for the rich things I saw others eating.

Out of doors also there were "rules" and I remember that I was not allowed to pick flowers in the garden. There was, however, one exception to this, and that was a rosebush by the side door, from which I was allowed to pick the lovely sweet-smelling pink roses. I am sure I got more delight in gathering and smelling those special roses than I ever should have felt in ransacking the whole garden.

Though my life was carefully regulated I never felt any monotony, for the world was new and full of interests and surprises. Even the after-tea visits to the drawing room could be fruitful. I remember one such evening when I was with my grandmother and her sister, Aunt Carrie, who were sitting together on the sofa quietly knitting. Suddenly, to my utter astonishment, the two old ladies screamed and leapt up onto the sofa, where they stood with their long Victorian skirts gathered tight around their ankles. What was the matter? I could not make it out. "Don't you see—Oh! take care, there is a spider in the middle of the floor." There was a spider, right enough, and quite a big one, but I was more interested than alarmed. The bell was rung, and, after a few tense minutes, the butler came into the room, and was told to remove the spider immediately. "Yes, ma'am," he replied with immovable gravity, and went out to return again in a minute or two with a glass tumbler and a stiff sheet of paper. The glass tumbler he popped over the spider before it realized what was happening, and the stiff piece of paper he then slid underneath. There was the spider properly caught, and the butler solemnly walked out of the room with it. My grandmother and aunt heaved sighs of relief, and descended from their place of safety. I had watched the butler's performance with immense interest and admiration, and then and there made a mental note of this excellent way of dealing with such a situation.

Quite a number of things I can recall of those early years which helped to lay the foundations of one's common sense. Some were chance incidents like the catching of the spider and some were definite occasions when I was shown how things were done.

As I grew a little older, there was the carpenter's shed which my father used to work in as a hobby when he was home on leave. Here I learned all about the correct uses of saws, hammers, screwdrivers, planes and chisels. But the place I loved most was the stable. I watched and watched the horses being groomed—the brushing and rubbing down, the picking out and washing of their hoofs—not a detail escaped my child eye. The head coachman, seeing my interest, taught me the how and why of everything, including the saddling and bridling of riding horses and harnessing of carriage horses, and many a time has this training stood me in good stead.

During winter holidays, when Alec and Rhona were home from school, there used to be quite elaborate indoor games in which I, being much the youngest, had to play a properly subordinate part. Two of these games I remember. One was for Alec and Rhona to be King and Queen and for me to be their slave, and the other was for me to be a wild bear in a cave—which was the underside of the nursery table with the cloth hanging down all around. My part was to be very fierce, and to try and come out of the cave, and theirs was to keep me inside. This sometimes led to genuine remonstrances on my part when I was kept in too long.

One very great occasion was when we decided—it must have been Alec's plan—to act "The Mad Tea Party" from *Alice in Wonderland,* and to invite all the elders from downstairs to attend the performance. Bertha, about twenty, was to be Alice, Alec, about eleven, the Mad Hatter, Rhona, about eight, the March Hare, and I, about five, the Dormouse. My part, though very short, was particularly important for a successful and dramatic ending, as I was to repeat the verse: "Twinkle twinkle little bat, how I wonder what you're at," and then go on murmuring "twinkle twinkle twinkle" until I fell asleep and was to be put into the teapot. As this last dramatic gesture by the Mad Hatter and the March Hare was obviously not possible to perform, it was decided that Bertha should let down the curtain just as I was being seized hold of. We held very serious rehearsals in which Alec and Rhona did their best to drum that verse into my head.

On the appointed evening grandparents, parents, and others came up to the nursery and sat on a row of chairs arranged for them. The curtain was pulled up, not without difficulty, and the performance began. Bertha was rather shy, and the suppressed laughter in the audience made her much worse. Alec and Rhona did bravely, and the whole thing was passing off quite well when it came to my turn. Alec and Rhona nudged me from both sides, and I at once began saying "twinkle twinkle twinkle." I had forgotten the verse, to the consternation of the others, who kept

16

prompting me in loud whispers, but I had got wound up, and just went on repeating "twinkle twinkle twinkle" till in despair Alec and Rhona seized hold of me to put me in the teapot, and Bertha rushed to the curtain, but it refused to drop. We felt terribly crestfallen, and I had an uncomfortable feeling that it was all my fault. But the members of the audience seemed to have enjoyed the show immensely, no doubt much more than if it had gone according to plan.

CHAPTER III

MY grandfather's father was still alive at over ninety when I was a tiny child, and I can just remember being taken to Clifton to be shown to him. He was very like my grandfather, so I felt quite at home when he sat me on his knee, and I looked up into his old face and wondered at the black skullcap he was wearing. Then he stuck pieces of stamp paper on his fingernails and played a little game of "Fly away Jack! Come again Jill!" and we at once became chums.

Another early recollection of that kind was of being taken to see my Great-uncle Edmond, on my father's side—Dr. Warre, Provost of Eton. My parents used to go every year to Eton on the 4th of June for the celebrations, and on one occasion they took me. I can see as if it were yesterday, the imposing figure of Uncle Edmond sitting in his study. I was led up to him, he looked at me with a kindly smile, and put his hand on my head in gentle blessing. But with him I felt a little shy, not as with my great-grandfather in his skullcap. I was sensing the difference between my mother's and my father's families. My temperament harmonized more with Mother's family and my sister's with Father's.

In Mother's family there was an unusual strain which had come down through several generations. A great-great-grandfather, while he was on duty abroad, had fallen in love with a dark gypsy-like beauty who was possibly of Eastern European origin. He married her and brought her home to England. Her exotic characteristics passed into the succeeding generations of that English family, showing sometimes more, sometimes less—but there it was, and it had come again strongly in my mother, and from her it has come to me in many a blessing. Mother's family was unusual and never a slave to convention, but Father's family was decidedly conventional, with an aristocratic society touch about it which did not quite suit my temperament.

Though Father's father was in the Church, his grandfather had belonged to the Army—General Sir John Slade—and many a story had passed down in the family about "The Little General." He married twice, the second time a girl of sixteen when he was sixty, and his youngest daughter was born when he was eighty. I remember her well—Aunt Gertrude—a perfectly charming old lady, unmarried, very cultured, and most witty. She had traveled extensively in Europe all on her own, and spoke French and Italian as fluently as her mother tongue.

The Little General seems to have had extraordinary vitality and lived, like my maternal great-grandfather, to be well over ninety. One of his hobbies was to roll the lawn with the garden roller, regardless of the fact that there were plenty of gardeners. This was all very well in the beginning, but as he got older and older his sons became seriously concerned. They dared not say anything, for he would brook no interference. Nevertheless something *had* to be done. So they secretly got another roller made, exactly like the one in use, even to the scratches and worn appearance, only several pounds lighter in weight. Then one night, in fear and trepidation, they exchanged the rollers. The next morning the old gentleman did his rolling, and said afterwards he felt wonderfully fit. He never found out.

This hobby of doing manual work in the garden was a characteristic of my maternal grandfather also. Besides the more gentlemanly jobs of grafting roses and the like, he delighted in sweeping the garden paths with a long besom broom, to which my grandmother strongly objected. But objection was of no use. He just loved fiddling around in the garden doing odd jobs on his off days. He was the director of a London company, and went to the City regularly. This meant an early drive to the station, usually driving the horse himself, and then an hour's run on the trundling old South-Eastern Railway to Charing Cross, where in those days hansom cabs and four-wheelers stood in rows ready for hire.

London without motorcars! That was what it was as I first remember it. When Mother used to take me for those shopping visits, what I looked forward to most was to get a drive in a hansom cab, because of the close proximity of the horse. It was considered rather "fast" for ladies to go in hansoms, but of course I did not understand or care about any such ideas. When my grandmother went to town she invariably hired four-wheelers, which I looked upon as stodgy to the last degree. Another pleasure I always petitioned for during a day in London was a ride in one of the front seats on top of an omnibus—they were never called buses—next to the coachman, looking down over the horses' backs and seeing all the world around, with horses of all kinds going along the streets. Those coachmen, too, in their great overcoats, mufflers, and folds upon folds of rug, were often jolly fellows, like Sam Weller's father, and hearing my child voice prattling away about the horses to my mother, would make a few friendly observations to which I would listen with glowing interest.

The anguish that the coming in of motorcars caused my grandmother has remained imprinted on my mind. One day at Milton Heath a number of people were in the drawing room discussing something very seriously. I was trying to make out what was the matter when I suddenly beheld my grandmother throw herself down in an armchair and almost burst into tears. "I'll never go out again in my carriage—never!" she exclaimed. This is awful, I thought to myself, what has happened? By listening and inquiring I discovered that the law, which made it illegal for engines of any kind to go along the highroads without a man walking some way ahead with a red flag, was going to be repealed, so that these new things called motorcars, which had begun to be heard of, might go along the roads at the terrific speed of 15 to 20 miles an hour! It certainly was an alarming idea, and I felt very sympathetic toward my poor grandmother, who was in the habit of going out for a drive almost daily in her victoria with a pair of horses, and coach-men and footmen on the box in good old style. But regardless of what agonies it might cause grandmothers—or granddaughters for the matter of that—the law was repealed by an act of Parliament, and to go out along the roads, either in a carriage or on horseback, became a nightmare. No horses had ever seen such things as these outrageous-looking contrivances pop-pop-popping along the roads without animals to pull them, and they became absolutely terrified at the sight and sound. I remember one day when we were out riding and met a motorcar, one of the horses jumped clear over the hedge. When the monstrous machine had gone by the poor creature was streaming with sweat, every vein on its body standing out in ribs. After a few years, of course, the horses began to settle down. But the quiet English country roads had lost forever their former charm.

While I was still very small, five or six years old, in spite of the happy and loving surroundings in which I lived, my mind began to search in the region of the *unknowable* and was stricken with awe. I heard my elders talk about the stars and the infinite space which was beyond. I tried to think it out for myself, and a sicken-ing dread would come over me, so that I would hurriedly seize on some mundane interest to drive away the horror. I never spoke of this to others, but silently tried to live it down. It lasted for years! In the same way I dared not think about eternity, and used to dread being taken to church, where I should have to listen to things like the repetition of the prayer termination: "As it was in the beginning, is now, and ever shall be, world without end— Amen." People seemed to repeat these sorts of phrases quite glibly, and I felt it was useless to say anything of what troubled me. The church attitude about Heaven and Hell also worried me a lot. How could people be fixed up for eternity as the fruits of one short life, especially as no two people had the same opportunities for winning through? What about people who died young, and what about poor colored people, who, I heard, were all heathens? Obviously something was wrong. It was an impossible puzzle. I

20

could not make it out, and would again seek escape in the happy life around me.

But there was something which every now and then wafted me far away. It would come at quiet moments, and always through the voice of Nature—the singing of a bird, the sound of the wind in the trees. Though this was the voice of the unknown, I felt no fear, only an infinite joy.

CHAPTER IV

AS I grew older, I was given live pets with which to play. One of the first was Junix, the goat. He was a tiny kid when he was given to me, and I used to be able to carry him about in my arms. Before long, however, the tables were turned, and he became so big that he could take me around the garden in a little cart which was specially made for him.

When I was about eight years old, Father came home from abroad to an appointment in London, and we moved to a rented house in Cheyne Walk, Chelsea. Junix, of course, had to be left at Milton Heath, but a new pet arrived in the form of a delightful puppy—Scotch terrier with a dash of dachshund. We called him Rags. I played endless games with him, and his response was almost human.

A totally new experience came to me in Cheyne Walk—something solemn and awesome such as I had never known before.

In those days there was a law that newspaper sellers might not shout the news as they went along the streets. But one evening, when I was with Mother and Father in the drawing room, there came the sound of muffled voices calling news. What was it? I saw my parents listen, and as they listened their faces changed to a dread solemnity. I ran to my mother, and holding on to her, gazed into her face. The muffled voices were calling: "Death of the Queen, death of the Queen." Mother whispered: "Childy, Queen Victoria is dead."

Something had passed out of England at that moment. Yes— the Victorian Age had closed. No one could picture England without Queen Victoria. Even at my age I could sense the feeling of blankness which filled the air.

The next thing I remember was seeing the royal funeral from a distance, as it passed slowly through Hyde Park. I believe practically all the potentates of Europe were there—and there were plenty of them in those days.

It was during this Cheyne Walk period that I was introduced to the very troublesome job of learning to read and write, and worst of all, to struggle with arithmetic, of which I never have got the better. A young cousin, Lucy Saunders, sister of Arthur, my doctor cousin, joined the family as my governess. I was already eight years old, and thoughts and feelings had, as it were, developed in a free and easy way, so that lessons felt very irksome. As may be imagined, I was no brilliant scholar. However, since the lessons had to be done, I did my best and gradually became interested, especially in history and geography.

Thanks to Mother's insight I was never forced to go to school. It certainly would have been a dismal failure if the experiment had been tried out. I had a positive horror of the idea of schools, not because of the work, but because of the noisy crowd of other children, and the regimented life.

The sojourn in London brought many new experiences. As our house was close to Battersea Bridge, across which we could enter the park, I did not feel shut in, and the daily routine was for me to go either with Lucy or Bertha—and Rags of course—for a walk in Battersea Park. It must have been during this period that I went to my first theatre. It was Shakespeare's *Tempest*, produced by Beerbohm Tree, with all the realistic scenery and splendor characteristic of his productions. I gazed in wonderment.

However I was not taken often to the theatre, as the excitement and the stuffy air almost always resulted in my having a sick attack afterwards.

CHAPTER V

WHEN Father again went to sea, we returned to the country. We did not always remain now at Milton Heath, and I think it was just at this time that Mother rented a farmhouse from a farmer who was not in need of it, as his son, who was looking after the land, was unmarried. This was Phoenix Farm, on the high land above Great Bookham, a village in Surrey. It was perfectly unspoiled country in those days, with rolling open fields in one direction, and a mixture of fields and woodlands in the other. The farm buildings were just at the back of the house, with their cowsheds, and stables for the farm horses. Then came the rickyards, and all around were the meadows and cultivated fields. It was an ideal place for a child to live and learn. Perhaps we were not there for more than three or four years, but the place, and the life there, have stuck as a landmark in my memory. All the time, except for the lesson periods, I was out and about watching, learning, and growing in experience.

Then the weekends were a thing I especially looked forward to, when "the boys" used to come down from London, and we all went out for long rambles on the North Downs. In the evenings we had sing-songs in "the smoking room," an old room in an outhouse, with a log fire, a settle, and plain chairs. "The boys" were young men, some fifteen or twenty years older than I—Arthur Saunders, my doctor cousin, Robert Buxton, an artist, and usually one or two of their friends. Mother, Lucy, and sometimes one of Lucy's sisters completed the party. Those were grand days, ram-

23

bling through the sweet-smelling woods and over the glorious downs from morning till evening, when we would all come in tired and hungry, ready for a good supper, and the sing-song afterwards. As I was too small to be able to keep up with the others walking, I had a donkey, called Spartan.

As Mother and Lucy were enthusiastic botanists, I soon learned, on these rambles, to look intelligently at the flowers in the woods and fields, and was always on the watch for rare specimens. With the birds it was the same thing. All their different songs and other characteristics I got to know, and the hearing and seeing of a rare bird was a thrilling event. Then Arthur, being a doctor, initiated me into the mysteries of anatomy while dissecting dead mice or other small creatures. I did not quite like this, but sheer interest held me, and I stuck it out and watched the whole process, made specially interesting by Arthur's detailed explanations. Rob's companionship, in turn, helped to develop my understanding of the artistic and beautiful. In this way the weekends became an education through direct experience.

The sing-songs at night were of a different nature. They awakened in me emotions mostly jolly and romping, but sometimes a little serious. Rob played the guitar and was the principal singer. The others had their special songs, and many a song, of course, had its chorus in which everyone joined. Quite a number of old English hunting songs and drinking songs I can still remember. Then there was one quite different song, which Lucy could sometimes be persuaded to sing, in spite of the fact that the boys always made fun of the German words. It was an old German folk song about lovers parting. I was as yet unacquainted with any German music, and this folk song struck a new note in my feelings —I wanted to hear it over and over again.

It was while we were at Phoenix Farm that one of those very early motoring expeditions was carried out on the road from London to Brighton. As the route passed along near Great Bookham, we all went down to have a look. We chose a section of the road where there was a gentle incline followed by a rise. The scheduled time was long past when the first competitors made their appearance. With anxious faces they put on their brakes as they came down the incline, and then, with much accelerating and pop-popping of their little engines, they leaned forward over their driving wheels in their efforts to get up the rise. One of them failed right there, and many, we heard afterwards, collapsed on the way, only a few ultimately reaching Brighton. In appearance they were like converted carriages, with the man at the wheel sitting up on a kind of coach-box. There were no windshields as yet, for they had only just emerged from the red-flag period, and their speed was still very mild.

The rapidity with which motorcars were developed must have been extraordinary. Before we left Phoenix Farm a very "advanced" friend of Mother's visited us with her car. I think it was a two-cylinder De Dion Bouton—still a funny upstanding little conveyance, but nevertheless a great advance in every way over what we had seen a year or two previously on the London-Brighton road. This friend took Mother and me on a little tour. I felt apprehensive. The noise, the smell, the speed at which the thing went, all upset me. However, seated as I was between Mother and her friend at the wheel, I just had to grin and bear it. And it was a hair-raising experience. Nobody on the roads was able to calculate the pace at which we were approaching, and there were horrible moments when the brakes had to be jammed on just in time to prevent our running over someone. All horses were frightened of us, and dogs got wildly excited, at great risk to their lives. Then, when we reached the city we had been making for, there were tram lines, and, as there had been a shower of rain, our car with its smooth tires began skidding in all directions.

The joys of the old days at Milton Heath were now fast disappearing. My grandfather replaced the beautiful carriage horses with motorcars; the riding horses also dwindled. Then a telephone was installed in the house—and so it went on. In a few short years we had switched over to the Machine Age.

Then on top of everything else came the airplanes. The papers were full of news about W. Wright and his repeated attempts to fly across the English Channel. I remember well the secret satisfaction I felt each time he failed. I realized it was only a postponement but at least for the time being it was delayed. Not for long however. The Channel was crossed, and just as with the motorcars, the airplanes began to increase rapidly. One day when we were playing tennis in the garden at Milton Heath someone shouted "Airplanes!" Down went our rackets, and we rushed to the big open lawn. There they were, making the same trial trip from London to Brighton that the motorcars had done a few years previously, only up in the sky this time. "What is this!" I said to myself. "Is there to be no privacy left in the world?"

CHAPTER VI

IN about 1903 Father was appointed Captain of the Royal Naval College at Greenwich. Here another lot of new experiences were in store for me. The architectural design of the buildings had been carried out by Sir Christopher Wren, and the place was originally intended as a palace for Charles II. It had a wonderfully dignified repose about it, and coming to live in such surroundings soon awakened in me the meaning of architecture as a fine art. I used to hear my elders discussing the artistic qualities and values of the palace, and my ideas began to form into an understanding which was further developed by visits to other important buildings in and around London, both Renaissance and Gothic.

The Admiral's and Captain's quarters were on the river front, so our windows commanded a full view of the Thames, which, in those lower reaches, was always alive with shipping of all descriptions. As the walls of the palace were four feet thick, there were lovely deep window seats in every window. My bedroom, which was next to my parents', had one looking straight out over the river, and I used to spend hours sitting there, gazing at the new world spread out before me.

An endless procession of vessels of all kinds passed up and down with each tide. There were cargo steamers of many nationalities, some of them quite large; there were busy little tugs towing long strings of heavily loaded lighters or bringing in handsome four-masted sailing vessels which could not manage such a crowded thoroughfare under their own sail; there were schooners of all sorts, some sailing and some being towed; and everywhere and at all times there were the russet-colored sails of the barges, and the old Thames lighters with no sails at all, drifting along with the tide precariously guided by two men with long oars and looking for all the world like enormous water beetles.

I was enthralled. I learned from Father the names of all the different rigs of the sailing vessels, and the names of the sails—quite a difficult job. I invested in a book which illustrated the flags of the nations and the various house flags and funnel marks of the shipping companies. My parents had given me a Zeiss monocular, and with it I was able to read the names and ports of registration of the vessels as they passed. Before long I got to know all the principal steamers, and when they came and went. The Thames opposite the college was particularly broad, which allowed for anchorage of small sailing vessels near the embankment under our windows. Among these too I got to know various regular visitors.

But my riverside window seat was not my only interest in those days. I was passing out of childhood into early youth. Nursery days were past and gone, and new emotions, thoughts and feelings were steadily growing. I do not think they tended to make life happier. On the contrary they created restlessness and an inexplicable dissatisfaction with myself and my environment. Though I was surrounded by the greatest affection, and was devoted especially to my mother, there was something unanswered always there. However, I was not depressed or gloomy, and threw myself with zeal into the things which interested me. That those things were often not what would usually interest girls of my age resulted in my being different from others, and inevitably conscious of it, as it gave me a feeling of aloofness in serious matters. And serious matters for me meant not only intellectual ones, but also things like horses and ships.

Art now began to stir me. Architecture was already there all around, and visits to museums and picture galleries introduced me to sculpture and painting. But music was still a closed book, as there was no one in the family who played any musical instrument, or who was much acquainted with classical music. Lucy was the only one who had some idea of the great composers, but she had no gift for playing, and the book remained closed.

A naval officer's appointment is usually for two years in one place, so we were continually moving, and wherever we went Mother made a perfect home, as if we had lived there always and were going to go on living there for the rest of our lives. It was the direct outlet for her self-expression, and, as she had a quiet genius for house decoration and furniture, the homes she made us, one after another, bore the stamp of her nature. And who can describe that nature? It is as impossible as it was for an artist to paint her or for a photographer to photograph her. She came and went, a beautiful, unique and unknown spirit—unknown, I think, to herself as well as to others. We came very near to one another, but I was young and restless, and she in her deep affection watched, and let me go my way.

With Father it was quite different. He was a bit strict and correct in his nature, though at the same time affectionate in that reserved English way. Physically too he was unlike Mother, who was thin and quick in her movements, whereas he was solidly built with an impressive mien. My earliest recollections of Father were with a rather loose beard, but as the years went by Mother so groomed him that by the time he was Captain of Greenwich College his beard had become neatly trimmed, his cheeks clean-shaved, and the mustaches short and smartly waxed at the tips. His dress, too, Mother watched and guided in every detail, and certainly the resulting ensemble was quite striking.

After Greenwich I cannot remember exactly what happened, because there were so many moves—seven homes in thirteen years. But I think at this stage there was again an interval at Milton Heath while Father was away on another appointment abroad.

I was now twelve or thirteen years old, so my grandfather allowed me to start riding full-sized hunters, and before long I was actually going hunting. This became a regular passion with me. It did not occur to me to think about the unfortunate fox. I took all that as a matter of course. What thrilled me was the rough riding across country, to the sound of the hunting horn and the voices of the hounds. The horses too used to be as thrilled as their riders. What a fine feeling it was to have been out riding all day in the open country, and to return home well splashed with mud, hungry and delightfully tired! Here was a new bond between my grandfather and myself. We had advanced from toys on the floor to real hunting, and now, in the evenings, we started playing cards together. He loved a quiet game of bezique, and as soon as I was old enough he taught me.

Alec and Rhona were growing up, but we usually foregathered during their vacations, and sometimes they brought along with them college and school friends, when games and country walks were the order of the day. Rhona however spent more and more of her holiday time at the homes of her school friends, which meant that Alec and I were the only young people at Milton Heath. There was, of course, six years difference in our ages, but that did not matter. I remember that one of the enterprises we decided on together was to learn milking. We thought it better not to say much about it in the beginning to the rest of the family, in case there might be objections for one reason or another. So we made advances to the cowman direct. But even this line of approach was not as easy as we had hoped. Truelove, the cowman, was sure that the milk yield would go down, and that there would be complaints at the house. He explained that cows did not like new hands, and then too, not only were we new, but we were ignorant. This was very baffling. We had not taken the cows' opinion into our calculations. However we did not give up. We assured Truelove we would be very quiet and very gentle, and do everything he told us. Finally he agreed, on the understanding that we milked only one cow between us in turns, whose milk yield was in any case beginning to go down, and who was of an understanding temperament. We felt triumphant, and started our lessons in real earnest. We went quietly and regularly to the cowsheds, and by the time the family came to realize what we were doing, we were able to say that we were becoming quite good milkers. So instead of reproof we won approval and even admiration.

CHAPTER VII

FATHER'S next appointment in England was at the Naval Training College at Portsmouth, and we settled into a furnished country house nearby at Fareham. I cannot remember exactly how long we stayed there but I suppose it was two years, that being the usual duration of a naval appointment. It was a quiet country life, and might well have been expected to be uneventful. But into those peaceful surroundings there came something which awakened me as from a slumber.

Father was fond of light music and, regretting that neither he nor any of the family could play the piano, decided to purchase an "Angelus" pianola, which was the latest and best form of mechanical player-piano and gave a certain amount of scope to the player, as one could make it loud or soft and fast or slow as desired. The Angelus Company also had in its library of music rolls a very varied selection of music including that of the best classical composers.

There was a grand piano in the drawing room, to which the Angelus was attached when it arrived, and various members of the family tried their hand at playing it. I watched and listened, and finally tried my hand at it too. A selection of pieces by various composers had been sent along with the Angelus, some light and some classical. I played and listened, but nothing interested me particularly except one piece which held me from the moment it began. It was Beethoven's Sonata Opus 31 No. 2. I played it over and over again.

Now I searched in the Angelus library, and procured one Bee-

30

thoven sonata after another. I went on playing and listening, and my whole being stirred and awoke to something which had remained unknown to me consciously till then. Yes, unconsciously I had known it in nature, but now it came to me through the medium of another human soul. Though I had never had any musical training whatever, yet I *heard*. I was finding something far beyond the music as such; I was contacting the spirit speaking through sound, the spirit of Beethoven. Yes, I had found *him*. But now an anguish seized me—oh, what an anguish! I threw myself down on my knees in the seclusion of my room and prayed, *really* prayed to God for the first time in my life.

"Why have I been born over a century too late? Why hast Thou given me realization of him and yet put all these years in between?"

But this was all deep down in the inner being, of which I spoke to no living soul. All that people saw outwardly was my devotion to Beethoven's music. For the rest, my life went on as usual. Of course I wanted to learn to play the piano with my own hands, and fumblingly started on scales and exercises.

Then suddenly there came a complete break in the routine of our family existence. Father, who had become an admiral, was appointed Commander in Chief of the East Indies Station, and this meant that we were to go to India for two years. What an upheaval! My feelings were terribly mixed, because of the thought of losing contact with Beethoven's music, but at that age—only fifteen—I got swept into the flood of preparations and the general excitement. Mother was alarmed on account of the climate, especially for us young girls, but the wife and daughters, if any, of a commander in chief are an essential part of his entourage because of the social side and the tremendous amount of entertaining involved.

The news must have come sometime in the summer, and we were to get ready to sail in a P & O liner at the beginning of November. Father, Mother, Rhona and I, along with Bertha, who had evolved from nurse to lady's maid, were to make up the party. Father had served on the China Station as a young man, otherwise none of us had any idea of the East. Friends and acquaintances who had ever been there volunteered all sorts of advice. Double felt hats, anticholera belts, double sunshades, special-colored spectacles, clothes like this, clothes like that, and medicines of all sorts. Father's uniforms had to be put into the best possible order and plain clothes also. As for us, we had to have best new evening dresses, afternoon party frocks, fashionable hats, tennis clothes and what not. I, of course, made a special point of good riding clothes, and even had saddle and bridle all ready for the horse I hoped to get.

Trunks, hatboxes, and wooden cases of all sizes were filled and the time came for saying our goodbyes. We might have been departing on a lifelong expedition for the amount of feeling aroused in our farewells. For me especially it meant parting with Lucy, who had been not only my governess but devoted companion since I was eight years old. And this too meant the end of lessons, but for that I was glad enough.

What I was not so glad about was the sudden approach of society life, with the prospect of dinner parties and balls, things I had had practically nothing to do with up to then. For Rhona it was a different matter. She loved dancing and parties, and was just at the age to enjoy to the full the kind of life we were going to enter.

We went around all the way by sea, and Mother and I, being very bad sailors, did not enjoy ourselves at all, especially in the Bay of Biscay. I do not remember much about the voyage except that Rhona, being very attractive, was sought after for games and dances by young men, who took me to be the elder daughter on account of my serious manner, and were nervous about approaching me—which I enjoyed as a good joke, especially as I did not want to dance.

Rhona and I could hardly be taken for sisters by outsiders. Her complexion was much fairer than mine, and her hair blacker; yet her eyes were not dark like mine, but hazel brown with a soft bewitching look in them. The most striking difference, however, was in our noses, hers being small and almost snub, the very opposite of my sharply aquiline one.

32

ONCE we had arrived and settled down, the round of social duties began in earnest. When I look back on those times I marvel at the strictness of the segregation which was practiced by the British high officials. I can't remember exactly the rules, but the impression which is left with me is that we mixed only with the Governor, the General, and any other high British officials, while of Indians we saw only the princes, and a very few big financiers and the like, chiefly Parsees. The sort of weekly routine that I remember was tennis two or three times a week at Government House, and on other days tennis at Admiral's House, frequent dinner parties at Government House alternating with dinner parties at Admiral's House. All this I could have managed and even enjoyed, if it had not been so perpetual! But when it came to the dances and balls, I was nowhere. I had never learned to dance, and never wanted to, but I was persuaded to try, and Rhona used patiently to go round and round with me in our bedroom. The effort was not very successful as can well be imagined, and when I found myself at real parties with young men coming and asking me for dances, I felt awkward and indignant. Why should I be dragged around the ballroom by young men I hardly knew and for whom I cared nothing? I thought it was a repulsive form of entertainment, especially in that hot perspiry climate. But the men did not seem to think so, and were always pestering me to dance. I avoided those parties as much as I could, but it was not possible, as Commander in Chief's daughter, to escape altogether.

It was not long before I had a horse, and one of the things I enjoyed most was the early morning ride around Back Bay, which had not yet been spoiled by modern improvements. Rhona also did some riding, but she did not take the same pleasure in it that I did, nor did she have any interest in horses.

In the midst of all these activities the thought of the music I had left behind was always there, and I now started seriously on piano lessons, but made painfully slow progress.

Government House at that time was altogether without ladies, as the Governor, Sir George Clerk, later Lord Sydenham, had lost both his wife and daughter. This made entertaining difficult enough for him in any case, but when it came to the time for the Purdah Party, which had to be given at Government House each year for the maharanis, ranis, and other grand ladies of the land, what was to be done? He could not receive them himself, nor could any of his staff of secretaries or ADCs show their faces. So Mother and we two girls had to be requisitioned, Mother to do the receiving, and Rhona and I to do the job of ADCs. A pretty busy job it was, with only two of us to see to everything. The carriages went on arriving one after another, and as each one drew up at the entrance, a long piece of dark blue silk would be produced by the coachman, who would fasten one end of it to the carriage and hand us the other end, with which we would run up the red-carpeted steps and, holding it aloft at the top, make a covered way. Then as soon as the coachman had hidden himself behind the porch, the maharani, attired in richest silk and priceless jewels, would step out of her carriage and pass up under the silken veil. Many of the less important ladies did without this contrivance, but none would emerge from their closed carriages till the coachmen had hidden themselves. All this made the ADC's job much more complicated than at non-purdah parties, and we were continually running up and down the red carpet, besides announcing the guests and trying to see to the refreshments. The Government House orchestra was there in its usual place, playing away, but that too had to be screened from view so that the players should not be able to set eyes on the purdah ladies.

A predicament of this kind did not, however, arise again, for before long Bombay city experienced a unique event, a governor's wedding! The first we knew of it was when Sir George Clerk confided in Father that he was contemplating remarriage. It so hap-

34

pened that the lady of his choice was a bosom friend of a cousin of my father's, and this helped to ease the position. There was a problem, however, as the bride would have no one to give her away at the wedding. It was finally decided that Father should undertake this office.

The romance was, I believe, an old attachment of years gone by, which Fate so far had frustrated, and now that they were to meet again at last, free to marry, the Governor and his bride were as emotional as young lovers. The wedding was to take place immediately on her arrival, but the Governor said he must be allowed to see her for a short while before the ceremony—how could they face having their first meeting in the Cathedral itself under the eager gaze of crowds of people! So, as soon as she arrived at our house from the ship, the news was passed to Government House, and the Governor quietly stepped into his carriage, without retinue, and drove straight over.

We had decided that the little boudoir at the end of the drawing room would be the ideal place for their meeting, so we seated her there on the sofa, drew the entrance curtains and closed the door. Soon the sound of the carriage-and-pair could be heard on the drive. Mother and Father were at the front porch to receive the Governor, and I waited at the top of the stairs outside the outer door of the drawing room. As Sir George was rather fond of me, and would feel more at ease in my youthful company, it had been decided that I should conduct him alone through the drawing room. Accordingly, as he arrived at the outer door with Mother and Father I took charge, conducted him across the drawing room, opened the boudoir door, and saying, "You will find her behind the curtain," closed the door and ran back to the stairs to report "all's well."

Bombay society was agog, and the Cathedral was packed to capacity. For many days there had been speculation on two things: what the bride would look like, and whether the Bishop would get through the marriage service without stuttering. His impediment of speech was well known, and what was more, "r" was one of his worst difficulties, and the bride's Christian name began with "r." So the congregation was holding its breath when the Bishop came to the words *Roseline, wilt thou* . . . etc. But he carried it off splendidly, and not a word went wrong.

When the summer came we went to Ceylon, where there was a naval camp in the middle of the mountains to which the British crews of the warships were taken up turn by turn for change of air. Deyatalawa was its name, and it lay in the midst of rolling grasslands at about 4,000 feet, with the higher mountains all around on the distant horizon. A fine place it was, and what pleased me, good for riding. I had become the proud possessor of a little Australian mare whom I had chosen with great care at the horse dealer's in Bombay, and I wanted to train her for the yearly Bombay Horse Show in the coming winter. Here was the very place for the job, and I was delighted.

On these open grasslands my mare Delta and I had lots of exercise together and she improved greatly in her paces and general behavior. She had been quite raw when I had first got her, looking about everywhere, shying at things, and neighing at the top of her voice whenever she got excited. Such behavior had to be changed before the horse show, otherwise the judges would turn her out of the ring. If I remember correctly, it was after our return from Bombay that the Horse Show took place. I entered Delta in three classes: Ladies' Mounts, Hacks and Hunters. We carried off respectively one first prize, one second and one third.

Besides riding, at Deyatalawa there was golf—of a sort. I tried my hand at it, but never grew to like the game. Rhona, on the contrary, enjoyed it more than riding. I loved a solitary ride and she loved a social game. A girl friend, Mona Halliday, had now joined us, and this gave Rhona a companion at the parties and games. I soon discovered that Mona was fond of music and could play the piano a little, so I was equally pleased at her arrival.

Our life at Deyatalawa was quite countrified. The Admiral's House was a single-storied bungalow situated at some distance from the camp, with a garden, and beyond it open country. We even had a cow of our own. She was an Australian of Jersey type, and a good milker. In order that the milk should be clean and unadulterated, I undertook to do the milking morning and evening. So those lessons of the old days at Milton Heath now stood me in good stead.

I can't remember whether it was at the beginning or end of our stay on the island that we paid a short visit to Trincomali, and on the way went to see the ruins of Anuradhapur. The enjoyment of the wonderful natural harbor at Trincomali, and the luxuriant tropical scenery, were outweighed for me, and I think for most of us, by the hot damp climate. I did not enjoy the time there a bit. Then there were snakes on land and sharks in the sea, unpleasant unless you are used to such things, and we were not used to them at all. One night at dinner the fish course was very much delayed. Inquiries were sent as to what was the matter, and the message came back that a snake had passed under the legs of the man who was bringing it across from the outside kitchen, which had caused him to jump into the air with such violence that the fish had gone flying.

It was during this visit that there was a romantic episode in the domestic staff. Bertha was the only woman among the domestics, and being of a cheery, attractive nature, she was very popular. The rest of the staff consisted of an English steward, a Goanese valet and Goanese butlers, etc., and there was the bandmaster too, who was a middle-aged Sicilian with upturned mustaches and a gallant air about him. The English steward, a married man of about forty, considered Bertha his special charge and was very jealous if any one of the others so much as looked at her. One evening there was a sudden uproar in the back quarters, and Bertha came running to Mother, indignant but laughing. "What's happened?" said Mother. "Oh!" exclaimed Bertha. "The bandmaster has just proposed to me. He went down on his knee and started making a fine speech when the steward saw him—and I think there is going to be a murder," she added in alarm. Mother quickly reported the news to Father, who intervened before any blood was spilt. "What an old rascal!" said Bertha afterwards. "They tell me he has a wife in every port, just look at that!"

In the autumn we returned to Bombay and the eternal round of social functions. Music was always there in my mind, and I went on with my piano lessons. Now that I had Mona's companionship, there was someone to help me along at home, and we started playing duets together. I could only manage the bass, and that very inadequately.

CHAPTER IX

IN this second winter there was a pleasant break in the routine when, at Christmastime, we went for a trip up the Persian Gulf. Rhona accompanied Mona to her relatives in Calcutta, but Father's cousin, Dorothy Eyre, who had come out with the Governor's bride, went with us up the Gulf, and what's more, this resulted in her meeting her future husband. We traveled in the flagship to the top end of the Gulf, and there we changed into a paddle boat, which could pass up the Shat-el-Arab. The plan was to go all the way to Baghdad, but "Turkish susceptibilities," we were told, made it advisable not to go beyond Basra. On the way up the Gulf we called at Bandar Abbas, Lingah, and Bushire, where we stayed at the British Residency with Sir Percy and Lady Cox. Our visit there coincided with the arrival of a warlike and wild-looking tribe from the mountains, which encamped itself in a big empty building in the open country at a short distance from the Residency. The Chief had come to have talks with the Resident about some matter or other. Whenever one went out one would meet groups of these fiery tribesmen, galloping along on their horses and every now and then firing a rifle into the air just as an expression of their general feelings. One day, for some especial occasion which I can't remember, the flagship fired a salute from her guns. The tribesmen evidently felt this needed a suitable response, so a whole party of them dashed up onto the flat roof of their big house and fired off their rifles together into the air.

There was plenty of riding at Bushire. Sir Percy Cox used to take Dorothy and me out sometimes on white Arab horses and sometimes on camels. Dorothy was considerably older than I, but she was of slight figure and full of energy and enterprise. We found these rides quite nice, but rather formal, as the Resident was, after all, the Resident, and had three or four mounted Lancers riding along behind. Dorothy and I felt we should like to get out sometimes informally on our own. We thought the matter over, and decided that the ideal thing would be to get hold of donkeys. So we went to Sir Percy and told him. "Donkeys!" he said. "What on earth do you want to go out riding on donkeys for?" We persisted, and he finally said he would procure us our mounts. But on account of wild tribesmen all around, we were told we could on no account go out alone, and a Lancer would have to be in attendance. This rather took the shine out of our hoped for simplicity, but as there was no alternative, we agreed with thanks. The next day two little donkeys came up to the British Residency. We scrambled onto their backs and rode off, followed by a magnificent turbaned Lancer on a white horse, with lance in hand and pennant flying. Our donkeys proved excellent, and nearly galloped us off their backs at times. On these rides we, of course, met batches of the tribesmen every now and then. They used to glance at us with considerable curiosity, but with one eye on the Lancer, and then, galloping away, would fire off a shot or two over their heads.

From Bushire we went via Mohammerah to Basra, and then back down the other side of the Gulf, calling at Kuwait, Bahrein, and Muscat. Everywhere there was ceremonial drinking of black coffee in tiny cups, and Father had long serious talks with the Sheikhs, as he was tackling the problem of gunrunning by local dhows which had reached serious proportions. At each place Mother and we girls used to be introduced after the talks were over, and it was all very dignified and solemn, but at Muscat things took an unexpected turn. While Father was having his talk through an interpreter with the Sultan, at one end of a big room in the fort, we all sat a little way off, waiting. The Sultan, who evidently had an eye for ladies, could be seen glancing every now and then in our direction. When the time arrived for introductions, he came across the room with Father and the interpreter and shook hands with each one of us in turn. I, being the youngest, came last, and when he took me by the hand he did not let go but went on shaking my hand and saying something. We looked toward the interpreter, but he was blushing and confused, and would not explain. The Sultan, seeing that his meaning had not been interpreted, spoke with yet more emphasis, still holding onto my hand. At last the interpreter mumbled out something and the Sultan let go of my hand, smiling sweetly. The interpreter afterwards explained to Father that the Sultan had been warmly expressing his desire to have me in his harem. Just as we were leaving the harbor, a beautiful little gazelle and some china were sent on board, and of course I claimed them as mine, particularly the gazelle.

The period of Father's appointment was drawing to a close when news came that, in recognition of his successful handling of the gunrunning problem in the Persian Gulf, his term was to be extended to last over the visit of the King and Queen to India for the Durbar of 1911. It was then decided that Mother and we girls should return to England for the summer, and come out again in time for the Durbar celebrations. I was delighted to think of getting away—the coming back I kept out of my mind—for India had meant nothing to me but a life of social functions and formalities in a very restricted society which did not appeal to me at all. The real India, which was to draw me to herself in the days to come, I had neither seen nor even sensed.

We returned to Milton Heath. Very soon the preparations for the coming Durbar began, and I was to go to London with Mother and Rhona to select dresses of all kinds. I was in a fix. I did not want to go back to India, but how to tell Mother so quickly? I began to hint at my feelings, and the choosing of my clothes was put off for a little, with the hope, perhaps, that I should change my mind. Friends and relatives reasoned with me: "Think what a unique occasion it is going to be. It will be something to remember all your life. Just imagine! We hear that the Commander in Chief's party will be in the Royal Camp. Others would give anything to get to the Durbar even among the camp followers, and you are going to have a tent of your own with your name on it right near Their Majesties!" But such arguments did not attract me. Mother saw it was no use going on pressing me, so she wrote and told Father, and finally I was allowed off. The others left for India in the autumn, and I remained at Milton Heath.

I devoted myself to music and reading. I went riding, and played bezique with my grandfather of an evening, but I don't recollect any more hunting. He was growing too old, and I had lost my taste for it. Alec had become an Oxford man and was busy with his studies. So I was pretty well left to myself. I had the Angelus attached to an upright piano in a room upstairs, and there I played and listened to Beethoven day after day, following the music in the score. Being untrained I could not analyze what I was listening to, but I imbibed, more surely than if there had been words, a sense of fearlessness, strength and purity passing, especially in the slow movements, to those regions of the spirit which lift one into that which can only be felt but never spoken.

I became more and more aware of the limitations of the mechanical player, and the longing to be able to play with my own hands became intense. Yet, in spite of all my efforts, I could make no real headway. It was as if Fate said *"No."* I felt desperate. Was there no way in which I could be of service? And my prayers to God, which had never ceased, throbbed passionately in my heart—"Guide me, guide me!"

The East Indies appointment had now come to an end, and the family returned. For some time we all stayed at Milton Heath. Rhona had become engaged while at the Durbar to an officer in the Indian Civil Service, Harold Vernon, and the wedding took place from the house, in the same little church at Westcott village in which the family weddings of the old days had been solemnized.

By now I had begun going to concerts in London whenever I saw especially good programs in which Beethoven's music predominated. One day my eye caught the announcement of a Beethoven recital by a pianist called Lamond. I found out on inquiry that he was well known for his renderings of Beethoven's sonatas, and I decided at once that I must go. I had heard very few good pianists up to then, and when listening to them I had had the feeling that their own personalities stood in the way. So I was full of hope that now I was going to hear something different, and my heart beat fast as the pianist stepped onto the platform—a man of medium stature, thick-set, clean shaved, and with a lofty forehead. From the moment he struck the piano I felt a directness of expression, strength of rendering, and fullness of tone that I had not heard before.

As the days went by my longing to do something more than merely listen gave me an idea. Let me at least arrange a recital by Lamond here in Dorking. Could it be done? I was not sure. But once the idea had come to me I would not drop it. I went to see the concert agent in London, and managed to come to terms. Then I had to hire the Town Hall and arrange for the printing and selling of tickets, as well as the advertising. A Beethoven recital would have been too much for the local public, so it had to be a mixed program.

I felt very agitated and nervous when the day of the concert came. I had only seen Lamond at a distance on the platform of the concert halls, and I had never in my life come in close contact with a man of his caliber. I met him at the front door when he arrived from the station, and conducted him upstairs. His manner was quite unaffected and in fact a little shy, and when he spoke with a delightful Scotch accent my own nervousness quickly disappeared.

I showed him the piano in my room and told him that the butler would bring him some lunch, and that I would come again to take him to the concert hall. When I came back just before 3 o'clock the little piano was pouring out glorious sound, and I hardly dared to knock on the door. Would he be annoyed at being disturbed? But it was no good hesitating. We had to reach the Town Hall on time. So I knocked fairly loud, the music stopped, and I heard him say "Come in." I opened the door in trepidation. Was he annoyed? No, he greeted me with a smile as he wiped perspiration from his forehead.

We drove together to Dorking, I showed him into the artist's room behind the platform, and then went through to the hall to see that the audience was all in order.

After the recital, which proved quite a success, Lamond went off by the next train to London, and so back to the Continent. He was in the habit of coming to England only occasionally, for he had long since made the Continent his field of activity, and his home was in Berlin, where his wife, an Austrian tragic actress, was also well known in the world of art.

CHAPTER X

WE stayed on at Milton Heath till Father was appointed to a post at the Admiralty, when we all moved up to London. Mother had found a quite unusual old house in Church Street, Kensington, and she soon turned it into a delightful home. At this period of my life the idea of living in London naturally appealed to me, because of the artistic and intellectual interests, and above all because of the music. The old house even turned out to have artistic associations, as Mendelssohn, the composer, had been wont to visit it in the old days while he was courting the daughter of the household.

We thought we had settled down peacefully to our London life, but the world was drifting toward eruption. Nobody, however, anticipated anything very serious, and so unsuspecting were we that Mother, Mona and myself, at my urgent request, all went off to Bayreuth in the summer of 1914 to hear the *Ring* and other Wagner operas. We were enjoying ourselves there thoroughly when a telegram arrived from Father saying we had better return without delay. We could not quite see why he should be impatient for us to go back, and as there was one more opera of the series to hear, we thought we could stay on for it. Our German not being

43

at all good, we had not been able to make much out of the newspapers, beyond that there was some international tension. Now
another telegram came saying RETURN AT ONCE, and we sensed
that something really serious must be developing. So we packed
up, and lo and behold, the tone of the people around us became
more unpleasant hour by hour. At the station the German porters
were insulting and rough, and when we reached the Dutch frontier
all the passengers were turned out of the railway carriage by
soldiers with fixed bayonets. It looked as if we might get held up,
but we just got through on August 1st, and were met at the London station by Father, who was in a perfect fever of anxiety.

Only then did we begin to realize the magnitude of the danger
we had been in by delaying our return. London was seething with
excitement. The tension grew worse and worse, and on August
4th, war was declared with Germany. Thousands upon thousands
of people turned out into the streets and trooped toward Buckingham Palace. We all turned out too. It was a spontaneous surging
of the emotions, and carried all classes on a single wave toward
their Monarch. By the time we reached the front of the Palace, a
huge crowd had already collected, and when the King and Queen
came onto the balcony, the multitude burst forth with one voice
singing the grand old hymn "Oh God, Our Help in Ages Past."
In measured tones, and full voice, they sang it through verse by
verse, and after it "God Save the King." Then the King and
Queen retired into the Palace, and we slowly wended our way
back home. It is a marvelous thing how, at times of intense feeling,
thousands of untrained people can sing together without anyone
to lead them. At that moment, on that evening, hate, revenge,
and all the degrading feelings that develop during a war had not
yet entered people's hearts. There was just one single feeling of
unavoidable peril to be faced, and as the people sang their hearts
—and therefore their voices—united in prayer to God.

So we had entered on World War I. It being still the pre-
Atomic Age, the tempo took time to work up. The first air raids,
if I remember rightly, were made by Zeppelins. They did comparatively little damage, but themselves went down in flames one after
another. Then the airplanes began coming, but how mild they

44

were! It was unpleasant of course, and they killed quite a number of people and damaged buildings, but each bomb just made a hole in what it fell on, nothing much more. The first time they came over London was a Saturday afternoon in broad daylight. The rest of the family had gone down to the country for the weekend, and I was alone in the house with the servants. Suddenly people began shouting "German airplanes!" and we all dashed out into the street to look at them. They were flying fairly high for those days, but clearly visible, and right overhead. They must have dropped very few bombs, I don't know why, and my recollection is that there was hardly any attempt to fire at them with anti-aircraft guns. I think London was taken completely by surprise that Saturday afternoon.

Later on of course the whole thing became well planned on both sides. The Germans used to come at night, and as soon as the news reached London that they had crossed the coast, the police would ride along the streets on bicycles, blowing whistles and calling out "Take cover, take cover." Those whose houses were very small would dash to the underground railway stations, and others would descend to their basements. That is what we used to do. No bomb ever dropped near our house, but the noise of the anti-aircraft guns was deafening, and the shrapnel from their shells used to fall all over the place. The next morning after a raid we would go onto the roof to pick up the pieces, and some of them were stuck into the tiles like spears.

CHAPTER XI

I HAD been conscious for some time of both my grandfather and my parents discreetly watching to see whether there was not some young man on my horizon, but I paid no attention. Some of the officers whom I had met in India I had liked well

45

enough as good friends, but nothing more, and I took it that none of them were seriously attached to me. So when a young naval officer whom I knew well contacted me on my return from India in the spring of 1911, I thought nothing of it. I remember his inviting me to view the Royal Procession of King George V's Coronation from the windows of his club. Then I recall lunch sometime later at Scott's Restaurant on the corner of Bond Street and Piccadilly, to meet his sister and others. Still I took it as a matter of course. But when at the beginning of the war he took me to tea at his home, and I found that the only other person present was the aristocratic old viscountess his mother, I suddenly realized that I was being inspected, and if she approved—! Next time he met me, without his having said anything direct, I somehow made it clear that my interests and thoughts were elsewhere. I felt very sorry to pain him, as we had been good friends, and I blamed myself for not having realized sooner what was developing. Not very long after he was appointed to a ship destined for a dangerous mission. Later came the news that the vessel had been sunk in action and not a soul had survived. Those were grim days.

We were entering on the terrible dark days of the war. The physical side was bad enough, but the mental side was even worse. The shooting and bombing maimed and killed the body, but the hate propaganda maimed and killed the sanity of the mind.

That frightful hate machinery was now being put into action with amazing results. Before long the kindest and sweetest people on earth began talking as if the opponents were not human beings at all, but just so much vermin to be trampled underfoot. My heart sickened. I had, in the beginning, joined parties of ladies who sat and prepared bandages, etc., but the kind of hate talk I had to listen to was so shocking that I could not bear it. I left off going altogether, and said that if I must do something, then let me go to the country and work on a farm from time to time, when there was pressure of work. Mona usually joined me and, along with Bertha to cook for us, we used to go to a farm where we already knew the people. Park Farm was its name, and it lay in the Dorking Valley amid lovely surroundings. Here the atmosphere was quite different. The country people had not been so poisoned

46

by the hate propaganda. In fact when, toward the end of the war, some German prisoners were brought to work on the farm, the local people were kind and gentle with them. The poor men were country folk like themselves, with no political or city thoughts. Why should they hate them?

The periods at Park Farm were not of very long duration, and much of my time, during the war, was spent in London. However, I never went back to those bandage parties, and, as the days went by, I somewhat withdrew into myself. I had a small sitting room of my own with piano and books at the top of the house, and I would usually avoid coming down except just at meal times, so as to escape, as far as possible, having to listen to "war talk." My emotions were all the more harassed because the music for which I lived had all come out of Germany and Austria. My parents realized my feelings and were patient with me.

I went on doggedly with my studies, and since I could make no appreciable headway with the piano, I thought I would try singing. I much preferred instrumental music to vocal music, but seeing that my fingers would not work, I hoped perhaps my voice would. However, I was doomed to disappointment in this also. Fate's "No" was there, and there seemed no getting round it.

As time passed, the strain of the war became greater and greater. Rationing intensified, and the nightly blackout for air raids was complete. I remember one evening the police came knocking at the door to say that some light was showing from our house. How could that be, we said, we had shut up everything tight. We went out into the street with the police to look, and there was, sure enough, a tiny ray of light coming out of the bathroom ventilator! So that was blocked up too.

Father's job at the Admiralty was to organize "Protection of Trade Routes." The German submarine menace grew to such proportions that this was one of the hardest of jobs, and at the same time of vital importance, as England's very existence depended on her supplies from overseas.

What with working at the Admiralty all day, often late into the evening, and then many a time sitting up most of the night in the basement during air raids, Father was having a tough time, and

47

Mother's whole thought was concentrated on keeping him well, in spite of the strain and the bad food.

When at last hostilities drew to a close, and the day of Armistice arrived, again, as at the declaration of war, the masses poured out into the streets, but this time in joyous mood. We all trooped out of our house in Church Street, class distinctions were completely forgotten. Everyone rejoiced and laughed with everyone else, and my recollection is that even Father did a round or two in the middle of the street, after Mother had egged him on to dance with the chauffeur's wife.

So the war was over—at least the shooting part of it—and gradually the world began to open up again.

CHAPTER XII

THERE were quite a lot of people in those days who boycotted German music, and the German musicians, of course, must all have been back in Germany. But Lamond, being Scotch, had got out of Germany with his wife and daughter, and was now staying in Holland, from where it would be possible for him to come over to give concerts. By cutting themselves off from everything connected with Germany, the English had reduced their concert halls to a monotonous mediocrity. I was thirsting for the real thing and felt sure that many others must be silently feeling the same way. So I went to Lamond's concert agent and urged him to organize some recitals. As I found him not very efficient, and, as I thought, lacking in imaginative ideas, I started helping him in various ways, including the designing of posters, etc. At the same time I got in touch with Lamond himself and explained the situation. He was hesitant to come. Finally the family agreed that he should be invited to stay with us in the old Church Street house, and he accepted.

48

The recitals, when they came off, were fairly well attended, but the English as a people—putting aside the Celtic elements of the island—are not very musical, and then too, blind prejudices were still running high. It was just at this time that a London newspaper published insinuations that Lamond was a nationalized German, which, if it had been true, would have meant, in those tense days, that his concerts would have been ruined. So he risked a libel action and won the case, with the result that at the next Beethoven recital the tickets were sold out.

This was a tide to be taken at the flood, but the agent did not seem capable of it. My enthusiasm was unbounded, and, by helping from outside, I had already gained considerable knowledge of concert management. Why then should I not take up the work myself? Why not indeed! And I did take it up, registering myself as a full-blown concert agent and renting rooms just off Bond Street, which made a good address for the office. I managed the work all by myself, and as the concerts came only for a short period once or twice a year, it was not too hard.

Outwardly everything went well, but before long an ordeal of inner turmoil developed. The joyous association of friendship with Lamond in the cause nearest my heart was developing into something else, something I had never pictured to myself. Now I came face to face with it. I never ceased to pray to God with all my heart and soul for guidance, not in the orthodox way, but as the spirit moved me. Time and again I would enter a church or cathedral, if I found it empty or with only a few other seeking souls in prayer, and there pour out my heart in silence. It could be Church of England, Roman Catholic or Greek Church. I was not concerned with the denomination, but only with the spirit. I said not a word to any human being about all this. It was a sacred communion in which I trusted all alone—and not in vain.

I think there was a fairly long period now without concerts, and when Lamond came over again he brought his wife and daughter with him. I arranged lodgings for them, and did what I could to make them comfortable. For the rest the concert work went on as usual.

My grandfather's death came about this time. Though he was

over eighty he had kept well and active to the last, and just a few days' illness took him at the end. My grandmother had passed away before the war. So now they were both gone. I got to Milton Heath in time for the funeral. The coffin had been closed and was placed in the middle of the drawing room, that room where my grandmother had sat knitting in the old days, and which was so full of early recollections. As I stood contemplating the coffin my heart was very full, for my grandfather had been the companion of my childhood. Now he was gone, and with him the link with those fresh early days had vanished.

Milton Heath itself now passed out of my life, because with the changed conditions after the war it was too big for anyone of the family to keep up. A house which required nine servants indoors, and as many more in the stables and gardens, was an impossibility. So Milton Heath was sold.

I am rather hazy about the exact sequence of events, but I think this was the period when we went to stay in the country for a time in a rented house near Warnham. It was Field Place, where Shelley was born.

Sketching in pastels had become a soothing outlet in those days, and many a quiet time I spent in the woods and fields, accompanied by Billy, a donkey I then had. He used to come along by my side like a dog, without having to be led, and would carry on his back my sketching materials, rug and lunch. When I sat down to sketch he would graze around nearby, but as soon as ever I opened my lunch packet he would come up squeaking gently and touch me with his soft white nose, asking for the piece of chocolate which he knew for sure I had waiting for him. He enjoyed these outings as much as I did, but he held very strongly to the opinion that "Two's company, three's none," and if anyone else happened to be with me, he would be sure to come up from behind as we walked along, put his head in between us and give a little nip with his teeth to the other person—not a regular bite, but just a pulling of the clothes.

I looked after Billy entirely myself, fed him, groomed him, and even clipped him in the summer. Donkeys are terribly maligned

50

creatures. If they are handled properly, and looked after with care and affection, they make the most delightful companions.

Father had by now retired from the Navy, after which he had become a director of the Anglo-Persian Oil Company. The house in Church Street had been given up, and Mother and Father had settled down in a smaller, quieter, and more convenient house in Bedford Gardens. Another nice thing about this place was that Rob Buxton, the old artist friend of my childhood, was living just opposite in a charming little house with a studio in the back garden.

CHAPTER XIII

TRAVELING abroad was still not easy at that time, and the crossing of frontiers was a great trial. But these things did not deter me, for there were two pilgrimages which only the war had prevented me so far from accomplishing. One was to Bonn and the other to Vienna.

I had managed to learn a little German and I went all alone, for I was entering into the deep down recesses of the heart which could be opened only in solitude with the spirit I was seeking. I reached Bonn and, avoiding all guides or other people, slipped silently into the little house where Beethoven was born. How long I stayed there I do not know. So profound an emotion filled me, that time had no meaning. Of all the relics which are treasured in that little house, the one that affected me most deeply was the piano with its keys worn by the continual touch of his fingers as he played and composed long, long ago. Yes, it was long ago, and yet—and yet, he has not gone. And my mind lost contact with the material—but when it returned, there I was alone in that little room, and my heart felt as if it would break.

Later I went to Vienna. Silent and alone I entered the cemetery at the time when no people were about. I walked, searching along the paths till I came to a grave a little apart. There it was—*his* grave. I felt I could not take it all in. I did not try. I just stood there lost in an infinite longing. As in the little house at Bonn, I lost all sense of time.

I do not remember how I went away, but the next thing I recall is walking up the little valley leading out into the country where he was said to have passed when he used to go for those long, solitary walks across the fields and through the woods.

Silently I gathered some tiny leaves from the bushes, and they have remained with me ever since.

CHAPTER XIV

BACK in England I again entered on my life of activity, but an inner searching had begun. My dreams of service had gone wrong, and what was I to do? It was just at this time of growing restlessness that I heard of an epic novel in ten volumes by a French writer which, people said, was a great work. It was partly based on Beethoven's life. This straightaway caught my attention. I immediately made more inquiries and was told that the book was called *Jean Christophe,* and that the author, Romain Rolland, was a profound admirer of Beethoven, of whom he had also written a short and very fine biographical sketch. I knew very little French at that time, but I got the first volume of *Jean Christophe* and the little *Vie de Beethoven.* I started to try to read them, and as I tried, my desire to understand properly grew. I made hardly any headway, as at that time I was too busy to find an opportunity to learn French, but what little I was able to glean made it clear to me that I *must* read those books, and in French, for there was a spirit speaking in them that I must come to know.

I had by now reached the decision to give up my concert work, but before finally closing down the agency there was one last thing I wanted to do. The prejudice against German and Austrian musicians was still strong, which meant that the musical public was deprived of hearing the great conductors, while the London Symphony and the London Philharmonic orchestras were languishing for want of inspiration. I wanted to break the ice by bringing over Weingartner, and having two symphony concerts with the London Symphony Orchestra. I knew it was a risk, but I was determined to take it. There were to be two Beethoven Symphonies, two Beethoven Pianoforte Concertos and a selection of other classical music. When I contacted Weingartner, he agreed and came over in time for two rehearsals. The moment these began the orchestra stirred to life as in the old days. When the opening evening came, the Queen's Hall was not quite sold out, but there was a thrill of expectation in the air, and the audience greeted Weingartner with a grand welcome as he came onto the platform. He was on his mettle, and gave of his best. How the orchestra played under his magic baton! And how the audience applauded at the end! The ice of prejudice was broken.

The expense, of course, had been heavy, and I was out of pocket by a good bit, but I sold my piano and managed to pay off my debts.

Shortly after the Symphony concerts, while I was still in London winding up my agency affairs, I chanced to see in the newspapers that Romain Rolland had come to London at the invitation of the Pen Club. My heart leapt into my throat. Without my realizing why—for the call of Fate was still hidden—he had become an objective which drew me with such force and urgency that at this moment I began trembling all over. I dashed to the telephone and rang up a member of the Pen Club whom I knew, and asked him, with such voice as I could command, whether he knew of any reception or other function where I might at least set eyes on Romain Rolland. He replied that the receptions were over and that probably Romain Rolland had left for Paris, but he had been staying at the Cecil Hotel and might still be there. I did not stop to think about anything. Perspiration was standing out on my

53

forehead as I hung up. I immediately telephoned the Cecil Hotel. A man in the reception office answered. "Could you tell me," I somehow managed to say, "if Monsieur Romain Rolland is still staying at your hotel?" "Yes," he replied. "Hold on, he is standing right here by the telephone." My heart nearly stopped beating. "Oh," I gasped, "don't ask him to the telephone, I only wanted to know if he was there." "It doesn't matter. He is right here by the telephone. I'll call him," the man again said. "No, no," I cried. "Don't, don't! I can't speak French, and I don't want to disturb him." "Very well," said the voice, "his sister is here too, she can speak to you." And before I knew where I was, she was on the telephone. I tried to excuse myself and explained that I had only been inquiring as to whether her brother was staying at the hotel, and whether there might be any occasion where I might possibly be able to see him, and so on. She replied very sweetly, saying she was so sorry but they were all packed up and just then waiting to leave for the station, and that if they had only known a little sooner she was sure her brother would have been willing to meet me.

When I put down the telephone receiver I leaned back in the chair quite exhausted, and wiped my perspiring brow. It took me some time to collect my thoughts. After a few days I decided I must write to Romain Rolland, excuse myself for having broken in upon him on the telephone unintentionally, and explain more clearly how I had been drawn to him through Beethoven. This I did, not expecting any reply, but one came, in which he expressed his readiness to see me if I happened to come over to Switzerland any time. My joy knew no bounds.

I realized he did not speak English, and I felt that to go to him without being able to converse in his own language would be wrong. I must learn French properly and without any further delay.

I decided to go to France, as that was the only way really to master the language. But where to go? I knew no one in France. So Father wrote to a friend in Paris, who recommended an old comtesse who took in paying guests. It was not quite the sort of thing I would have chosen, but I thought it better to make a start

54

and find my way. So I went to her. She lived in a little flat in a semifashionable quarter. Unfortunately the other paying guest was an English girl, and the old comtesse also spoke excellent English, all of which was very bad for the progress of my French. I did not stay many months.

Now I hunted for a pension where English was not likely to be spoken. I found a somewhat suitable one in the Latin Quarter and took a room there. Then I bought the remaining nine volumes of *Jean Christophe*, and a large French-English dictionary, and sat down to it in real earnest.

This pension was rather too crowded, with always several nationalities at the table, which again resulted in the French not being of the best. I, therefore, began looking out for something better, and as luck had it, I found the ideal place in the rue Nôtre Dame-des-Champs, at the little flat of a cultured old lady who lived alone with her granddaughter who was studying at the Sorbonne. I was the only paying guest and the grandaughter, Arlette, a delightful girl, agreed to give me French lessons. Now I began to make good progress. I worked away at my lessons and reading, and during off times, walked in the Luxembourg Gardens, or visited the museums, picture galleries and beautiful Gothic churches.

It must have been around this time, during a summer holiday in Switzerland, that I first met Dr. Axel Munthe, the author of *The Story of San Michele*. I remember I was standing looking at some little marmots in a wire enclosure in the hotel garden at Argentierre, where I was spending the summer with my parents, when I heard a quiet voice asking me over my shoulder if I did not think it rather cruel to keep those little creatures shut up like that. I looked around, and there was a tall thin man with tousled gray hair and beard, wearing dark glasses. There was something very strange about him. I had the feeling that he had not spoken to me by chance, but that he had been watching me perhaps for days. I was not sure whether I liked that, but his quiet and unconventional manner attracted me. The marmots had been a good introduction, for they put us immediately in contact with a common interest—animals and birds. But there was much more to him than that, which I could not exactly size up even after many days, for though he talked freely of many things, in a sense he was reticent—reticent over things that would have enabled me to understand him fully.

He looked me up again in London, and our friendship grew. But even so there was always something left unknown about him, an unexpressed melancholy. Though he had many friends, he seemed to be strangely lonely. I never met a single one of those friends and, for all I know, none of them ever heard of me.

His eyesight in those days had become so bad that he had great difficulty in traveling about alone, and I remember one day his telling me he wanted to pay a visit to Bruges—or rather to his special friend the old Town Clock—and would I come along with him? So off we went and stayed in a hotel from which he could see and hear his friend the clock, who plays a long tune at every quarter, so long, indeed, that he is playing most of the time.

CHAPTER XV

MY French was now becoming manageable, and I began to think seriously of approaching Romain Rolland. My first step was to stay in a village on the Swiss-French frontier just opposite Villeneuve, called St. Gengolph. I could see Romain Rolland's little villa across the lake, and I found out a local school mistress with whom I continued my French. It was summertime, and I used to take long, solitary walks in the nearby mountains.

I was still feeling very shy of writing to Romain Rolland and telling him that I had come there and was hoping to be allowed to visit him. Every time I thought of writing, I felt my French was not yet good enough. But the summer was passing, and write I must. An inexplicable conviction possessed me that *all* depended on my meeting him. I did not try to explain anything to myself in

56

detail. Something was working in me which was beyond the realm of reasoned thought. I wrote, and a friendly reply came inviting me to tea. I bicycled around the end of the lake, and arrived on time in a state of intense inner suspense. *It is all or nothing* was the only sensation I had. I rang the bell, the door was opened by a maid who showed me into a small sitting room and said that M. Rolland would be there in a minute or two. I sat down mechanically. I heard steps and a hand on the door handle. I stood up. Romain Rolland entered—tall and pale and clad in black. He greeted me gently, almost shyly, and sat down on a small chair by the door. As I sat opposite him I could think only of the quiet all-embracing penetration of his blue eyes, holding me in their gaze. I tried to express myself, but my words were halting and awkward. He listened and replied patiently, but it was as if an invisible veil separated me from him. After a little the door opened and his sister came in and suggested that we go to the dining room for tea. We went. The time passed, I must get up and go, but that "something" which I knew was there I had not been able to reach. Somehow I rose and said thank you and goodbye. I bicycled back to my lodgings at St. Gengolph in blind despair.

During the next few days I wandered like a lost soul in the mountains, returning to my room late, sometimes after dark or in wind and rain, which harmonized with my inner feelings. The landlady became anxious and asked why I stayed out so late all alone.

Perhaps three or four days had passed like that when, coming downstairs in the morning, I saw a big yellow envelope lying on the hall table. Was it possible? Yes—it was from Romain Rolland. I opened it with trembling fingers—a book on music, with a friendly inscription on the front page. The light came back into my heart. He had not forgotten me, and perhaps he would let me come and see him again if I asked, and then that something which I knew was there would open up to me. I wrote, and again came a friendly reply. He said his sister had gone to Paris, but if I would like to come and have tea with him we could have another talk, adding that if I felt like opening my heart I could, and if I did not, it would not matter.

I moved to another village nearer Villeneuve, just up the Rhone Valley, and on the day he had suggested I bicycled to his villa. We met again in that little sitting room. Within a few minutes the former embarrassment had disappeared, the veil separating us lifted, and I could speak freely. We talked for some time, and then went to the dining room for tea. He sat opposite me at the table and we talked on and on. It seemed as if we had always known one another. His thoughts flowed forth as if he were thinking aloud. He advised me to travel, and spoke of Austria and other places. Then he mentioned India, not with any suggestion that my travels should take me there but in connection with a small book he said he had just written, and which was on the press, called *Mahatma Gandhi*. I looked blank.

"You have not heard about him?" he asked.

"No," I replied.

So he told me, and added: "He is another Christ."

Those words went deep, but I stored them away without thinking that they had any special significance for me personally.

The evening was drawing in, and I must depart. He said, "It will be getting dark, and you have to bicycle back to that village."

We rose from the table. I stood before him. What could I say? He had given me that something for which I had sought, though neither of us knew in so many words what it was. I was silent, but he understood and, smiling gently, put his hands on my shoulders, kissed me a blessing on each cheek, and sent me on my way.

As I bicycled back to the little village in the Rhone Valley my heart was overflowing with a sense of peaceful joy. Everything was going to be all right. How, I did not have any idea, but it would be all right, I knew. When I entered the little inn where I was staying, I found a letter waiting for me from Dr. Axel Munthe, suggesting that I should accompany him to Egypt, where he had never been but much wanted to visit while he still had a little eyesight left. I said to myself: "Romain Rolland has just now told me I should travel, then let me start with this trip to Egypt." I wrote by the next post agreeing to the suggestion. The Doctor, in his usual happy-go-lucky way, had given me very short notice, and it was going to be a rush to get ready in time. I telegraphed to Mother asking her to send me a few clothes suitable for the Egyptian climate, as I had nothing but Swiss-climate clothes with me. Then I dashed on my bicycle to Montreaux and got my passport put in order. The clothes arrived just in time, and off I went to Naples via Rome. I cannot quite remember the sequence of events, but I think it was on this occasion, before going to Egypt, that I went to Capri, where Dr. Munthe showed me his beloved San Michele. He wanted me to learn Italian and even found me a teacher, but I had no zest for learning another language at that time.

The voyage to Alexandria was rather rough, and as I started a bad tooth at the same time, I felt wretched. On reaching Cairo I had to go to the dentist in spite of the Doctor's impatience to get on to Thebes. Once we got there he became all absorbed in the ancient ruins. However, he didn't want to stay very long, and as he met some acquaintances who were returning to Europe, he said he would go with them. For I was in no mood to return so soon. I wanted to bask in the wonderful sunlight which harmonized with my own feelings.

CHAPTER XVI

I THINK it was October when I finally returned to Europe. I stayed only a day or two in Naples, and then went straight to Paris. I was impatient to get that little book of Romain Rolland's which was due to appear, and the very next day after reaching Paris I went to the publishers. The shop window was entirely filled with a small orange-colored book bearing the title *Mahatma Gandhi* in bold black letters. I entered the shop and bought a copy.

I started reading it that morning, and once having begun there was no stopping. In the middle of the day when I went out to a restaurant for lunch I took the little book with me, then back I went to my room, and by evening I had finished it.

Now I knew what that "something" was, the approach of which I had been feeling. I was to go to Mahatma Gandhi, who served the cause of oppressed India through fearless truth and non-violence,* a cause which, though focused in India, was for the whole of humanity. I did not weigh the pros and cons or try to reason *why* this was the outcome of my prayers. The call was absolute, and that was all that mattered. I went back to London and reserved a berth in a P & O liner. I told my parents. They sensed the magnitude of my inspiration and did not argue with me. I soon realized, however, that I was being altogether too hasty. I must put myself through severe training before I could hope to be accepted. So I returned to the P & O office and exchanged my booking for one twelve months later.

It was necessary to think out in real earnest how to set about my year's training. Without any doubt I should learn spinning and weaving, but most especially spinning, because Mahatma Gandhi had made this the pivot of his constructive program for the masses, which in India meant the villagers—millions and millons of them who, since the introduction by the British of Lancashire cloth, had lost their age-old subsidiary occupation of cloth production and consequently remained unemployed for several months in the year, as the Indian climate is such that agriculture has long off-seasons. Another reason why he fastened on cotton spinning was that it could touch every house in the village. Weaving was the job of only a few, but spinning had been the job of all the women and girls—it takes many spinning wheels to feed one loom. So the spinning wheel had now become the emblem of India's masses and their fight for freedom. At the same time spinning and the wearing of khadi (hand-spun and hand-woven cloth) had become obligatory for political leaders and constructive workers, making a bond of sympathy between them and the dumb millions.

Learning how to spin, therefore, was at the top of my program.

* In Gandhian phraseology this means active resistance to evil without use of physical force, and cheerful acceptance of the consequences of one's actions.

But as no one spins cotton in the West, I had to do my training with wool. For this I was very luckily situated, as right at the bottom of Bedford Gardens were "The Kensington Weavers," run by Dorothy Wilkinson and her sisters, old friends of the family. I bought a spinning wheel and carding brushes and started spinning wool at home, while for the weaving I went to the school. Then I had to become a vegetarian and a teetotaler, and start learning the language. I should likewise teach myself to sit cross-legged on the floor and sleep there also, and of course I must read all I could about India. In regard to the change of diet I decided to proceed gently, as it would be foolish to spoil one's health at such a time. First I gave up alcohol and then progressively limited my food to a purely vegetarian diet. The language was a more difficult problem. Who could teach me and what language should it be? As with the French, Father had come to my aid. He wrote to the then Permanent Under Secretary of State at the India Office, who was a friend of his, and asked his advice. We were told it should be Urdu, and an Indian student in London was recommended as teacher. So I bought the *Munshi,* an excellent Urdu grammar, and it was arranged for the Indian student to come and give me lessons. I found them extremely difficult and made very slow progress. French had been hard, for I am not a natural linguist, but this was enough to make one's hair stand on end! The sitting and sleeping on the floor developed quite well, though I am afraid it gave Mother much pain to have to remove my comfortable bed. As for the reading, I immediately subscribed to Mahatma Gandhi's weekly, *Young India,* and located a shop near the British Museum where I could get some books.

Part of this year of training I spent in Paris at my old quarters in the rue Notre Dames-des-Champs. I wrote to Romain Rolland telling him of what had come to me through the reading of his book. In Paris I also found Indian students with whom I could continue my Urdu studies. It was during this time that I first read the *Bhagvadgita* and some of the *Rigveda*—both in French.

Back in London, and right in the midst of my training, the report appeared in the newspapers that Mahatma Gandhi had started a twenty-one-day fast for Hindu-Moslem unity, and it was doubtful whether he would survive the ordeal. This was agonizing. There was nothing I could do but pray in silence. Day by day the news grew more alarming. Those twenty-one days seemed never ending, but I kept on at my studies without slackening. When at last the news came that the fast had been successfully broken, and all was well, my thankful joy was such that I could remain silent no longer. I must write and send some thanksgiving offering. But what to send? I had run out of money with those orchestral concerts and had sold my piano, but there was a small diamond brooch which my grandfather had given me on my twenty-first birthday. I would sell that and send the proceeds. I sent a letter, along with a check for twenty pounds, expressing my thankfulness for the successful fulfillment of the fast, and explaining how I had read Romain Rolland's book, how I had in the beginning wanted to come to India at once and then, realizing that I should first put myself through a year's training, I was now carrying out that task. I hardly expected an answer, but I knew the endorsed check would come back through the bank. I went on with my training with renewed vigor. Some time later, when I happened to be sitting one day at the telephone table at Bedford Gardens, someone placed a worn-looking post card in front of me. The handwriting was unfamiliar and rather indistinct. I turned it over and looked at the signature—*M. K. Gandhi.* Reverently I read it through. This is what it said:

DEAR FRIEND,

I must apologize to you for not writing to you earlier. I have been continuously travelling. I thank you for £20. sent by you. The amount will be used for popularizing the spinning wheel.

I am glad indeed that instead of obeying your first impulse you decided to fit yourself for the life here and to take time. If a year's test still impels you to come, you will probably be right in coming to India.

On the train,   Yours sincerely,

31-12-24   M. K. GANDHI.

With new confidence and joy I went on with my training, and when I was just halfway through, I wrote again asking whether I might actually join Sabarmati Ashram, and enclosed some samples of wool I had spun. In August a reply came which put all fears and suspense at rest:

148, RUSSA ROAD,
CALCUTTA.
24 JULY 1925.

DEAR FRIEND,

I was pleased to receive your letter which has touched me deeply. The samples of wool you have sent are excellent.

You are welcome whenever you choose to come. If I have advice of the steamer that brings you, there will be someone receiving you at the steamer and guiding you to the train that will take you to Sabarmati. Only please remember that the life at the Ashram is not all rosy. It is strenuous. Bodily labour is given by every inmate. The climate of this country is also not a small consideration. I mention these things not to frighten you but merely to warn you.

Yours sincerely,

M. K. GANDHI.

The heat of the summer I spent in Switzerland, working with the peasants in their fields in order to be in as good physical trim as possible, because I could see there would be a lot of hard manual work once I reached my destination.

The P & O on which my passage was booked was due to sail from Marseille on October 25th, so by the end of the summer I returned to London to make preparations. I had already written to Delhi for khadi, which now arrived and was made into plain white frocks. I kept a minimum of warm things for the voyage, and the rest of my clothes I distributed along with everything else except a certain number of books and what little jewelry I possessed. I had a nice collection of about four hundred really good books, from which I made a selection which filled two trunks. The jewelry, such as it was, I had decided to take for presentation to the Cause. Being the younger daughter, and known to have no interest in fashion and society, not much jewelry had come my way. This was the first time I felt sorry about it, as now there was so little to give.

Up to the last I pursued spinning and weaving intensively and, having achieved some proficiency, I managed to spin, dye, and weave a woolen scarf for Romain Rolland's sister. This I would take with me when I went on my farewell visit to Villeneuve.

The year of training was drawing to an end. The two trunks of books, and perhaps one other with odds and ends, were sent off to the P & O office to go around by sea, and my plan was to go to Paris and Villeneuve and so south to Marseille where I could pick up the P & O liner.

It is remarkable how the English, by tradition, are habituated to keeping their feelings to themselves, restraining an outward expression of emotion. There were, therefore, no tears or other visible manifestations of the wrench that the parting meant, especially with Mother. Everyone was quiet and gentle. Mother and Rhona saw me off at the London station, and Father, who was in Paris at the time, said goodbye to me there. From the beginning no one had ever tried to dissuade me from my decision. Everyone seemed to realize that it was a spiritual necessity and accepted it as inevitable. The only advice that Father gave me was as we separated, when he merely said, "Be careful." And it was not an easy thing for a man connected with the highest British officials and ministers to have a daughter going to join the archrevolutionary of the British Empire!

From Paris I went to Villeneuve to bid farewell to Romain Rolland and his sister. To this day remains in my memory the picture of them standing together on the doorstep of the little Villa Olga as I left them—the look in those wonderful eyes of his, and the ring in his voice as he said, "How lucky you are!"

CHAPTER XVII

I BOARDED the P & O liner on October 25, 1925, and the voyage began. The weather was fair and the moon was waxing. Each evening, as it rose in the east and shed on the ocean a path of light along which the ship traveled, I gazed upon it as an emblem of what I was approaching. And day by day I wrote down my thoughts and feelings to be posted to Villeneuve as soon as I reached India. On November 6th the ship came alongside the dock in Bombay. As had been promised, friends were there to meet me. They took me to the Nairojees' house on Malabar Hill, where the brother and sisters, grandchildren of Dadabhai Nairojee, pressed me to stay and rest for at least twenty-four hours. But I had no thought for anything but to reach Sabarmati without delay. In the afternoon, Devadas Gandhi, Mahatma Gandhi's fourth and youngest son, came in and he too pressed me to stay, but, seeing my determination to go on at once, he finally arranged for my departure by the Ahmedabad train that night.

The train steamed into the Ahmedabad station next morning, November 7th, exactly on time, and as it drew to a standstill, a smiling bespectacled person looked in at the window. In half a minute another, also smiling but of quite a different character, looked over his shoulder, and a third was in the background. They all seemed to know that I was the person they were looking for, and introduced themselves—Mahadev Desai, secretary and right-hand man of Mahatma Gandhi; Vallabhbhai Patel, later to become first Home Minister of Free India; and Swami Anand, manager of the weekly *Young India*. Even at that moment of concentrated anticipation I noted the masterful manner of Vallabhbhai, who turned to Mahadev and said, "You two look after the luggage and I'll take her off in the car." And before I knew where I was I found myself being swept away in the car, this new acquaintance sitting by my side. I looked at his clean-shaven face and was struck by its power curiously intermingled with a kindly and humorous expression. Then we turned into a courtyard and drew up in front of a house.

"This is not the Ashram, is it?" I exclaimed.

"No, no," he said, "this is the All-India Spinners' Association Office."

As he spoke, someone came out and had a few words with him through the window, all in Gujerati, and I could not understand anything. I looked inquiringly at him as we drove off again.

65

"That was the All-India Spinners' Association Secretary," he said, "Shankarlal Banker."

Now we passed out of the city and over a bridge to the other side of the Sabarmati River. I was gazing out of the window in tense suspense. I saw buildings ahead.

"Is that the Ashram?" I eagerly asked.

"Not yet," he replied, and I noticed the quizzical look in his expression. Then in a few minutes he remarked, "You see those trees and some buildings beyond? That's the Ashram."

By this time I had lost any sense of physical being. All was concentrated in the thought of what was approaching. In a minute or two the car drew up at a gate under a big tamarind tree. We got out and went along a narrow brick path which passed through a custard-apple orchard. Then a little garden gate led to a small enclosure where a simple building stood. We stepped up onto the veranda. I felt encumbered with the bag in my hand and hurriedly handed it to my companion. He took it and, standing a little to one side, ushered me into the room. As I entered, a slight brown figure rose up and came toward me. I was conscious of nothing but a sense of light. I fell on my knees. Hands gently raised me up, and a voice said: "You shall be my daughter." My consciousness of the physical world began to return, and I saw a face smiling at me with eyes full of love, blended with a gentle twinkle of amusement. Yes, this was Mahatma Gandhi, and I had arrived. He went back to his white gaddi behind a little desk, and I sat down on the floor in front of him.

People began coming in and out of the room, and I noticed everyone spoke of "Bapu." Here there was no Mahatma Gandhi, only Bapu, meaning in Gujerati, Father. But in this case it had a meaning all its own, just as he whom it described was unique.

Bapu now said, "Come along, let's go to see Ba [Mother]," and he took me onto the veranda and on into the kitchen.

Bapu introduced me jokingly in Gujerati, but I could understand he was telling Ba she would have to bring out her best English. Ba, very small and dignified, folded her hands and said sweetly, "How do you do." But she kept looking at my feet.

"She is looking at your shoes," said Bapu, "because our custom

66

in India is to take off our shoes before coming into a kitchen."

I rushed out onto the veranda and took mine off at once. Bapu laughed.

Thus my new education began.

Mahadev had by now arrived with the luggage, and I was taken away to see the room which had been prepared for me. It was the farther corner room of the first building to the right as one enters the Ashram, just opposite a well. It had a veranda, two windows, and a door at each end. A separate bathroom was also allotted me at the end of the side walk. A bed, a chair and a table had been thoughtfully procured from somewhere and placed in my room. I explained that I had been practicing sitting and sleeping on the floor for many months and therefore did not require them. So they were removed and two mats, a mattress, and a low desk were brought instead. Everyone was kind and natural, and there was no sense of stiffness or awkwardness.

Mahadev then took me back to Bapu's room and we sat down on the floor. Bapu handed me a *takli* (spindle) and some slivers, which are small rolls of carded cotton fiber, and told Mahadev to show me how to spin with them. I straightaway started trying. But the ability to spin cotton does not come in a day! There was some discussion between Bapu and Mahadev about my feeding arrangements and program of work, and it was decided that for the time being, at least, I should feed along with several other Ashramites in Ba's kitchen. As to the work, Bapu said I was to learn carding and spinning of cotton, and Tulsi Mahar, of Nepal, should be my teacher. Then there was the language question. I explained that my efforts to learn Urdu had not been very success-ful up to now. Bapu said I should not forget the Urdu, but I should make a start on Hindustani with the Devanagari script, and my teacher for this would be Surendraji, of Gorakhpur district in East U.P. And last but not least I was to join the Chinese member of the Ashram in the daily sweeping of the Ashram latrines. The hours of rising, prayer, work and retiring to rest at night were also explained to me, and I saw that I had not been mistaken when I had anticipated a busy life of hard work.

I was then taken and introduced to my teachers. Tulsi Mahar, a delightful, smiling, simplehearted man from the mountains of Nepal, with no English except for two words he had gathered up from someone: "dear sister," which he would pronounce in the sweetest way and then burst into laughter. Surendraji was equally kindhearted, but more solemn in manner, and inclined toward study and meditation. He even knew a little English. I learned afterwards that both these men had felt that irresistible call to come to Bapu which no obstacles could thwart. In the beginning they had one by one been rebuffed by Bapu, who had felt their impulses might be shallow. But they had both persistently stuck out all resistance and finally won entrance into the Ashram life, where they had now gained Bapu's wholehearted appreciation.

The next morning started with my rising at four o'clock, and prayer on the Prayer Ground by the riverbank at 4:20. After daylight the young Chinese, whose Ashram name was Shanti, came to my room and handed me a broom. He had quite a smattering of English, and we went off to our scavenging work chatting together happily. Our job was to sweep and if necessary wash the floors of the latrines after the buckets had been removed by a batch of young men and women who emptied them into trenches, cleaned them, and replaced them after our sweeping and washing down had been finished.

The carding of cotton was no easy matter, but Tulsi Mahar was an expert, and even without the help of English conveyed his meaning to me. The Hindustani was a new ordeal. I had struggled with the Persian script, and now here was a totally different one. But I soon discovered to my relief that it was less difficult, and that my teacher was very patient.

Though I had made every effort to prepare myself physically for this new life, it was hardly surprising that some disturbance in my health should take place. Bapu saw that I was not faring very well in Ba's general kitchen and so, after a few days, arranged that I should join a small quiet party consisting of Surendraji, Tulsi Mahar and Krishnadas, a Bengali intellectual in Bapu's secretarial group. This plan I liked very much, and as their kitchen and quarters were just beyond my room, it all fitted in excellently.

Surendraji set about making me large, solid *rotis,* an un-leavened bread. They looked splendid, and I ate them with relish, but unfortunately the results were disastrous. My stomach refused to digest them and I collapsed. The matter was reported to Bapu. He came to see for himself. I felt very ashamed lying on my mat-tress in the corner of the room. Poor Surendraji got a severe scolding—not unmixed with humor—for having expressed such blind affection for me in "those preposterous *rotis,*" and as a punishment that should impress upon him his folly, he was told to be my nurse until I recovered. Bapu then left us. I was feeling like vomiting and very uneasy, so Surendraji got a basin and put it by my side. He then sat down cross-legged in the middle of the room and fell into deep meditation. Here was a situation I had not foreseen! With a nurse like this, one must at all cost keep still and not disturb his meditation by vomiting. Anyway, it had the de-sired result. I lay there as quiet as a mouse, watching Surendraji out of the corner of my eye, and gradually I began to recover.

Bapu now decided that I had better learn to cook for myself. So he sent one of the young women of the Ashram to teach me. It did not take me long to pick up the Indian method of cooking on a small charcoal stove or open wood fire, and I was delighted with the simplicity.

CHAPTER XVIII

BY God's infinite blessing I had arrived, not on the outer edge of Bapu's activities, but right in the intimate heart of his daily life. The impact on my emotions was tremendous. From early morning to the last thing at night I lived for the moments when I could set eyes on Bapu. To be in his presence was to be lifted out of oneself. Not that there was anything imposing about his physical appearance, or striking about his manner of speech;

indeed it was the perfect simplicity of both which held one. Here one was face to face with a Soul which, in its very greatness, made the body and speech through which it manifested itself glow with gracious and natural humility. At the same time there was a sense of spiritual strength, quietly confident and all-pervading, while the whole presence was made intensely human and appealing by the purehearted and irresistible humor which kept peeping through like golden sunshine through the leaves of a deep forest.

I was so busy in those days with lessons, cooking, cleaning and the rest that I used hardly to see Bapu except at the morning and evening Prayers, and then for the most precious half-hour at the end of the day, when Bapu used to lie down on his bed under the open sky in the garden, and I was allowed to sit on the ground by his side while Ba rubbed oil on his head, and someone else (at that time Surendraji) rubbed ghee, the clarified butter of India, on the soles of his feet. The conversation was in Gujerati, and Bapu spoke English only when addressing me. Often some visitor who happened to be staying in the Ashram would come for a talk at that time; then the language used was sometimes Hindustani. I listened attentively but could as yet follow very little.

Though Bapu himself was all and more than all I had pictured, the Ashram proved a different matter and I had to make a big effort to readjust my expectations. I had imagined to myself that the inmates would be a compact group, wholeheartedly of one mind about Bapu's ideals. Instead of that I found a heterogeneous collection of one or two hundred people, men, women and children of all ages and all degrees of faith, from fanatical ascetics to skeptical family women. What was more, the ascetics were few in number, and the family types were in the majority. One thing that was clear was that most of the women were there not because they had themselves felt a call to join the Ashram, but because their husbands or relatives had thrown in their lot with Bapu. As to the young people and children, they of course were there because of their parents. Among the men there was considerable variety in the reasons which had led them to Bapu. Because Bapu himself was all-sided, he attracted people of the most varied types. Some were drawn especially by the revolutionary and political aspect, some by the social and economic aspect, and some by the ascetic and religious aspect. But one and all were drawn by the magnetic power of Bapu's spirit, and had thrown up everything else to join the cause.

Thus the Ashram was not at all of the monastic type, but was a miniature cross-section of the everyday world, on which Bapu was experimenting with the most lofty and drastic conceptions of moral, physical and economic reforms. Moral standards were poised at a height where the slightest wavering by an inmate from the strictest truth, honesty and rectitude was noted down and made the subject of public discussion between Bapu and the rest of the Ashramites. Physical standards regarding diet, labor, and hours of rising and going to rest were rigidly severe, and economic ideals required that everyone should use only hand-spun and hand-woven cloth, and other hand-made articles as far as possible, besides living a life of the utmost simplicity, even by Indian standards.

Naturally, the reactions on this heterogeneous group were as varied as the temperaments involved and led to high tension of the nerves, except in the case of Bapu, who usually sailed peacefully through the repeated disturbances, though even he became affected when the storms were very severe.

I did not realize all this at once, but it did not take me long to comprehend that the Ashram was composed of highly explosive material. I also sensed that my arrival had added yet another type of problem to the ones already there, and one about which the Ashramites were naturally none too sanguine. Where was I to fit in? I was myself sufficiently highly strung at that period and spontaneously joined the ascetic group with not a little fanatical zeal.

To keep things hidden from Bapu was, for me, a spiritual impossibility, and before many days were out I had explained to him, as best I could, my past life with all its strivings and blunders. The quiet and complete understanding with which he listened was in itself a revelation.

Within the first few weeks a whole rush of experiences came upon me.

For some days everything seemed to be going on as usual, then suddenly one day there was a big internal commotion. People became agitated, and the usual smiling faces looked drawn and sorrowful. Long conferences were taking place in Bapu's room, and Bapu himself, at Prayer, was sad and thoughtful. I could not follow the talk in the Ashram, or what Bapu said in the Prayer, and had to wait till someone explained what the matter was: some of the boys in the Ashram school had been detected in sexual misconduct amongst themselves. This had pained Bapu very deeply, and what was agitating the Ashramites so much was that Bapu had finally decided to atone for the boys' misconduct himself by undertaking a week's fast. The conferences in Bapu's room had been prolonged by the beseeching efforts of the Ashram inmates to persuade Bapu to change his mind. But they had been of no avail, and he had announced his resolve at the end of the Prayer.

This information came to me as a severe shock. Bapu, knowing that it would be so, called me and explained that I should remain undisturbed while carrying on my daily work as usual, and that I should share with him the peace and joy which he felt having once made the decision to undertake this penance. I promised to go on with my work, and for the rest, to do my best. That Bapu was indeed now at ease was clear from his expression and easy manner.

But though Bapu was at peace spiritually, his body suffered. By the third or fourth day nausea and exhaustion took their toll, after which the physical condition somewhat settled down. Throughout, Bapu remained quiet and smiling.

To go through this experience so soon after arrival braced me up for the long series of ordeals which lay ahead, but it also tuned up my nerves to such a pitch that the tension was not easy to control.

CHAPTER XIX

NO sooner was Bapu out of the fast and on the way to recovery, than it was time for him to prepare for the yearly visit to Wardha in the Central Provinces where the learned ascetic, Acharya Vinoba Bhave, was at that time running a Brahmachari Ashram for celibates. Bapu used to go there for about ten days' rest each year before attending the Open Session of the Indian National Congress. I was on tenterhooks as to whether I should accompany the party, and dared not think what it would be like to remain behind without Bapu. However, the final decision was that I should go. The Congress Session that year was to be at Kanpur, where the nights would be cool in the middle of winter, and Bapu asked me if I had sufficient warm rugs. As a matter of fact I had only one very thin one, so something had to be done. Bapu thought for a little, and then sent for Tulsi Mahar. "You come from Nepal," said Bapu, "and you must have a warm rug or two." "Of course," said Tulsi Mahar. "Then you give her one," replied Bapu, pointing to me. Off went Tulsi Mahar and returned with a beaming face, holding out with both hands a splendid warm, soft rug woven in black and white wool.

So far I had only seen Bapu at work in the Ashram. Now when we moved out to go to Wardha and Kanpur, a new and amazing realization burst upon me, and that was the peculiar hold Bapu had upon the masses. At every station, pressing, surging crowds thronged the platform, and the air throbbed with the cry "Mahatma Gandhi ki Jai!" (Victory to Mahatma Gandhi). The faces did not reflect the excitement of people out to catch a glimpse of a celebrity, but the eager, thirsting look of devotees seeking to set eyes on some holy person, a savior on whom they had pinned all their hopes with a faith which they would not have been able to explain or express in so many words, but which drew them irresistibly. At the smaller stations, where the peasantry from the surrounding countryside gathered, this was most striking. Their eyes had an inspired glow about them as the peasants pressed toward the carriage window with folded hands and no thought in the world but to obtain the *darshan* (sight) they were seeking. I watched in wonderment, and was deeply moved. Then I looked at Bapu to see his reaction. There he sat perfectly quiet and still, with hands folded in acknowledgment of the salutations, and with a stern look upon his face. This impressed me still more—the throbbing, surging mass of humanity on one side, and the still, small, stern figure on the other.

Up to now I had not witnessed this stern side of Bapu's nature. It was, as I came to know by continual observation, his invariable reaction to excessive expression of emotions, especially when those emotions demonstrated admiration and devotion toward himself.

When we reached the Wardha Ashram I found quite a different type of center to Sabarmati, and I could not help being enthusiastic about it, as it was very much the kind of Ashram that I had pictured to myself before reaching India. It was a small compact group of men all earnestly believing in the principles of the institution. Bapu's ideals and experiments were being carried out with great thoroughness, and onto them had been added theories and methods evolved in the austere and searching soul of Vinoba, whom the inmates looked up to as their Guru (preceptor). Quietness of atmosphere, unity of endeavor, hard work, and spiritual purposefulness were the qualities which impressed one. Bapu noticed my enthusiasm, and when I talked to him about it and asked whether we could not have more such discipline and earnestness in Sabarmati, he pointed out how he could not break up the families of the devoted co-workers who had gone through the South-African ordeal with him, how they must all strive together toward the ideal, and how it was not in his nature to pick and choose, selecting only the best and casting away the rest. On the contrary he must take all along with him, even to the weakest. Though Bapu was severe in his admission of outsiders, such was the ever-growing pressure of new aspirants that his sternness could not always hold out against his all-accepting heart. Hence Sabarmati was made up of that heterogeneous group, that miniature cross-section of the everyday world.

I began to realize that a laboratory for experimenting with theories for the betterment of the world must be comprised of such a cross-section, and not a carefully chosen selection of unusual people. I began to understand also another fundamental difference between Bapu and other spiritual leaders. Bapu would, on no account, accept anyone as a disciple, and flatly refused to be looked upon as a Guru. "The conception of Guru," he would say, "is so lofty that there is no one in these days competent to live up to the ideal. There may have been such super-beings in the past, and even today there may be some purest *Rishis* [seers] existing in unknown caves in the Himalayas who are worthy of being accepted as Gurus, but this ancient conception of Guru and disciple is not for us ordinary mortals of this degenerate age. So seek God and look to Him alone as Guru, for He will never fail you if you seek Him with a true heart."

This teaching of Bapu was fundamental and perhaps unique, because throughout Hinduism we find the practice of Guru and disciple carried on to this day. Indeed it is so deeply ingrained in the Hindu nature that most people of a religious bent feel they just cannot do without a Guru, while those ready to be Gurus are not wanting. A number of the best and most devoted workers who joined Bapu after his return from South Africa were disciples of Gurus they had already chosen for their spiritual guidance. In this case both Gurus and disciples associated themselves with Bapu's movement, keeping their own schools of thought intact, without any friction, and many of his best and most devoted workers were among these.

From the quiet, strict and austere life at the Wardha Ashram we passed straight into the hurly-burly of the Congress Open Session. Bapu himself had been the President during that year, and he was to hand over the office to the poetess of India, Sarojini Naidu.

A big old-style house, not far from the Congress camp, had

been made ready for Bapu and his party. The room prepared for him had been, according to custom, completely emptied of furniture, and in its place, against the wall on one side, had been placed a white khadi-covered *gaddi* with a small desk in front, as at Sabarmati, the rest of the floor being covered with mats and rugs.

No sooner had Bapu arrived and sat down on the white *gaddi* than this room became the focal point of the whole Congress activity, while the rest of the rooms and passages of the house became alive with people coming and going, talking in groups, and waiting in corners. Congress volunteers, stationed at all strategic points in the house and garden and especially at the entrance gate, controlled things as best they could. The one comparatively quiet spot in the whole place was Bapu's room, where only the principal actors in this great national drama could come and go.

I watched with interest. Here was a standard of life which made mixing and meeting and moving around so easy and simple—no stiffness and no botheration with the trappings and fetters of Western civilization.

The great leaders of that time—and how many there were—came and went with the gracious charm of Eastern culture. They sat on the floor with natural ease, and the only extra thing for which Bapu would sometimes call was a pillow or bolster for one or two of the elder leaders to lean against.

Perhaps it was the day after our arrival that Bapu asked me, "Have you a sensitive nose?"

"Yes," I replied, "particularly sensitive—what can I do?"

"Well," said Bapu, "they have asked me to inspect the sanitary arrangements in the Congress camp, which they have arranged according to my suggestion of trench latrines. I have no sense of smell whatever, so I want you to come along with me and do the smelling part of the inspection."

A special time had been arranged, and no doubt people must have planned to come to convey Bapu to the camp. I was new to everything, so when Bapu said to me, "Come along, let us start out a little before time and walk across," I gladly agreed without thinking twice about it. I can't imagine now how it can have happened,

76

but Bapu and I passed out of the house into the garden without anyone taking any notice, and from there out onto the public road. I began to realize that Bapu was enjoying a little experiment, testing whether he could get off on his own without all the attendants and volunteers who would otherwise accompany him. There were not many people about, so all went well for a short distance. Then one after another of the passers-by began to recognize Bapu. They rushed up to touch his feet. Then others, seeing from afar, came rushing, and before long it became impossible to make any progress. A two-wheeled carriage, called a tonga, was nearby, and we got into it. The people gave way, the horse trotted off, and we managed to reach the camp, but no sooner had we passed through the entrance gate than the cry went round that Mahatma Gandhi had come. There was a headlong rush, and in no time the tonga was surrounded by a wildly excited crowd. Whether the horse was frightened or not it could do nothing, for it was submerged in a mass of humanity. Some people seized it by the head, others climbed onto its back, one of the shafts gave way, the harness broke. Bapu and I held on to our seats as best we could, and I was just wondering what would happen if the other shaft broke and pitched us forward when some camp organizers came racing to the rescue. A car was brought as close as possible, a passage was made through the shouting, surging crowd with great difficulty, and somehow Bapu was passed into the car, I after him. With much hooting and pushing the driver managed to extricate the car, and we were taken off to the other end of the camp.

So that was the outcome of the little experiment. As far as I know it was the last of its kind!

The sanitary inspection passed off quite successfully. Bapu was satisfied with what his eyes told him, and I was able to give him an equally satisfactory report of what my nose told me.

For the first two or three days there were meetings of the Working Committee and Subjects Committee, and then finally came the Open Session. I sat behind Bapu on the dais with Mahadev, who took down notes in his sensitive and beautifully clear longhand, which he manipulated with almost the speed of shorthand. Many of the speeches were in Hindi or Urdu, but some were in English, and I listened to them greedily.

CHAPTER XX

WHEN the proceedings of the Open Session were terminated, we returned to Sabarmati, as Bapu had decided to spend a whole year in the Ashram without going on tour anywhere. People said to me, "You are indeed most fortunate to have come just at this time. Bapu is usually either touring or in jail, and this is a unique thing that he should spend one whole year at Sabarmati."

There was a sense of expectation in the Ashram and sure enough, Bapu took things in hand. He went into every detail himself: the general discipline of the inmates, the organization of the various activities, such as khadi production, the workshop, the gardening, the dairy and so on. Every day he would move about the place, looking here, looking there, and especially visiting those who were sick. When there was an outbreak of smallpox among the children, he went daily without fail to see the little patients and to console the distracted parents.

We all had our work cut out for us, and I remember my daily routine was so tightly packed that even the minutes taken in going from one part of the Ashram to another were written down. That is to say, Bapu told me to work out my program in every detail to show him, and when I sat down to write it on paper, I found that I had to make these minute calculations in order to be sure of keeping to time throughout the day, which began and ended with the absolutely punctual Common Prayer. Besides the study of carding, spinning and Hindi, and the sweeping of the latrines, I now had the additional tasks of teaching English to the Chinese student, Shanti, and attendance on a chronic invalid who needed

78

about one hour's treatment daily. Then there was my own cooking, cleaning, bathing, and clothes-washing to be done, not to mention time for eating what one had cooked. It was a tightly packed program.

Never having lived in an institution and having, as I have said, a dread of schools and colleges, this communal life was a tough job for me, but because of my devotion to Bapu I suppressed my aversion. In fact I so completely disciplined myself that I actually believed that I liked it. One's own nature cannot, however, be forced against itself without suffering even though the suffering may not be apparent for the time being.

It was the same with the climate. I was determined not to mind it, yet as the weather began to heat up in March, the body tried to object. However, I refused to take any notice. Bapu was anxious, as he guessed I would feel the tropical heat, but when he saw me carrying on quite happily he was naturally glad, as he wanted everyone to stick to the work in hand and not need the luxury of visits to the mountains in summer. The knowledge of Bapu's gladness added to my enthusiasm, but of course the subconscious strain was there.

During this period I lived the whole time in the Ashram except for an occasional visit to Ahmedabad, where I used now and then to spend a few hours with Anusuyaben, the sister of Seth Ambalal Sarabhai, the wealthy mill owner. It was she who, in all loving affection for her brother, led the strike of mill hands against him in 1918, when Bapu guided and upheld them, with the ultimate result that they won their battle and founded the Textile Labour Association, which Bapu drew up on model lines. Those visits to her house, and on rare occasions to her brother's beautiful and palatial home, were the only glimpses I got of life outside the Ashram. I enjoyed them, but I was always anxious to get back to the Ashram and Bapu's presence without too much delay. At the same time I had the feeling that Bapu was watching me closely to see whether I might not get attracted away from the simple Ashram life. Particularly was he concerned about the food, knowing that the rich and highly spiced Indian dishes would be very bad for my health, both physical and mental. But Anusuyaben always made a point of having some unspiced dishes whenever I came.

I was still wearing my white khadi dresses that had been made in England before I set out, and Bapu seemed rather against my taking to Indian clothes. At any rate he wanted me not to be in a hurry. But I was getting impatient, and began to feel I could not wait much longer. Then one day Anusuyaben showed me how to wear a sari, and as we were both rather pleased with the effect, she then and there gave me one of her own khadi saris (white with a narrow blue border), and sent me back to the Ashram wearing it. I came before Bapu with considerable misgiving. He was definitely displeased, but he restrained the expression of his feelings and said I could wear a sari if I was very anxious to do so, but it should certainly be a white one and not one with a colored border like that. So white saris were procured from the khadi department and I began wearing them. My overanxiety to get out of the European dresses had led me into a hasty step in Bapu's eyes, and the pleasure I would otherwise have felt was marred.

Then the next urges that took possession of me were to have my hair cut off and to take a vow of celibacy. This was a very much more serious matter and Bapu held me back for some time, even though these two things were greatly to his own liking. However, my earnest longing, and the joy he saw I found in the ascetic atmosphere of the Ashram, finally led him to agree. Nevertheless he said he must first tell the other women in the Ashram and let them express their reactions. They were practically all against the cutting of the hair and put forward a variety of reasons, some of which were certainly not without weight, such as the plea that with a closely cropped head I should become conspicuously different from other women and find it a bar to natural association. But I was in no mood to listen, and they gave over reasoning with me. Finally Bapu decided to let me have my way, and told me first to write down the resolve I proposed to make in order that he might see whether I had fully grasped the depth and breadth of his own conception of Brahmacharya, which encompassed not only celibacy but all forms of self-discipline and restraint. This I did and Bapu approved. There was no ceremony or solemn taking of a vow.

८०

Bapu quite simply cut off my hair with his own hands, and gave me a loving slap on the back when I bowed down at his feet for blessings.

After this I did not wish to go on wearing the sari, but to change to the full skirt called a *ghagra* and the short half-sari for passing over the head, more or less in the style of the village women. This Bapu readily agreed to, and the change gave me much more freedom of movement in work.

It was about this time that I first met C. F. Andrews, who, though a devout English Christian, had associated himself whole-heartedly with Bapu's battle for human rights from the early days of South Africa. Watching them together I immediately realized that a very deep and touching comradeship existed between them.

It appeared that Bapu had for some time past been pressing Charlie Andrews to learn to spin, but without success. Now he hit on the idea of getting me to teach him.

"You go along to her every day and have lessons," Bapu said laughing.

"Must I?" was the reply.

Yet he did come, and tried very hard for a few days, but it was just no good. He had become rather stout, and sitting on the floor was not practical. Also the weather was very hot and he was perspiring profusely, which made the cotton fibers stick to his fingers. His gentle bearded face and blue eyes looked quite pathetic as he strove in vain to catch the knack. We had to give it up. We went together to tell Bapu, who scolded him, and they both had a hearty laugh.

Before long Bapu promoted me to one of the two small rooms on the high riverbank quite close to his own quarters. These two little rooms, with a common veranda, had been built for bath-rooms and were very small. However, I fitted myself in with a stove in one corner for cooking, and rejoiced in the situation for two reasons: it was near Bapu, and it was on the riverbank with no other buildings close by.

The occupant of the other room, Chhotelalji, was such a re-cluse, and so completely wrapped up in his work, that one hardly knew he was there. He was one of the most remarkable workers in the Ashram. Before being drawn to Bapu he had been a revolutionary. Now he was devoted to Bapu with a silent, passionate zeal. Slight of build, wiry and strong, he never gave himself a moment's rest, throwing himself heart and soul into whatever work he took up. Surendraji was one of his few friends, and he tolerated me in spite of my being a woman.

Dietetic experiments were a thing in which Bapu took a keen interest. His investigations were twofold: one was the discovery of nutritious and cheap items of diet which could be used by the masses; the other was the betterment of himself and others who sought physical purity and spiritual advance, at the same time keeping the body healthy and strong for service. Another thing Bapu was always seeking was ways and means of reducing the amount of time which had to be devoted to the ordinary methods of cooking.

Bapu's unceasing desire to find a substitute for milk was a personal urge. In the early days of his return to India he had heard of certain malpractices of dairymen for increasing the milk yield of their cattle, which so disgusted and distressed him that he then and there took a vow never again to touch the milk of cows or buffaloes. Then in 1918, when he was thought to be succumbing to a protracted attack of dysentery, the doctors said that curdled milk was the one thing that could save him and build up his strength. He refused it because of the vow. Ba then suggested goat's milk curds. Bapu hesitated. He felt that in taking goat's milk he would be keeping only the letter of the vow and not the spirit, but the desire to live for the service of humanity overcame his scruples. He took the goat's milk curds and recovered, but the longing somehow in some way to find a substitute for milk and thus return to the spirit of his vow remained with him to the end.

Knowing how strongly Bapu felt about food, we realized that he would like to see an end of the various types of kitchens then functioning in the Ashram—each family household with its own kitchen, and the rest of us in small groups or even solitary—but that he doubted the possibility of our all managing to pull together, or of our being able to run as big a kitchen as would be needed for about two hundred people. We of the ascetic group became very active advocates for the common-kitchen ideal. We felt Bapu's doubts were a challenge, and we set going a hot and strong propaganda movement. In our enthusiasm we were not always very tactful and, as I can see now, not very kindly toward the family members, who up to then were still eating spices, fried foods and other things in which Bapu did not believe. We canvassed the whole Ashram including the family quarters, and naturally stirred up opposition. Bapu checked us sternly, and said we should be more understanding and charitable in our approach. In fact he practically called off our activities. We chewed the cud in silence, yet I am afraid we did not stop criticizing in our hearts those who did not see eye to eye with us. But before long we noticed that Bapu had begun taking up the cudgels for the common-kitchen ideal himself, not fanatically as we had done, but patiently, affectionately and humorously, especially with the women members of the family quarters, whose aversion to a common kitchen was naturally the strongest.

I don't remember how long it took, but it must have been some weeks during which time Bapu gently worked toward the objective, sometimes before everybody at the after-Prayer talk, and sometimes in conversation with individuals. There was very strong opposition from some people, and prophecies of certain failure if the common kitchen were ever started. But even the firmest resisters gradually melted under Bapu's treatment, and the stage was reached when the details began to be seriously discussed. A large and suitable building was chosen, and those ready to shoulder the burden of running the kitchen were selected and coached by Bapu. By this time there were plenty of volunteers, but two people remain imprinted on my memory as having been staunch supporters of the idea from the beginning, and who proved to be the backbone of the project once it got started. One was a middle-aged widow, Ganga ben, a very fine person, strong, sensible, quiet, and devoted to Bapu. And the other was no other than my neighbor, Chhotelalji, who took up the work with intense vigor.

83

Stores, cooking vessels, firewood, all was got ready, and at last the day came when the whole Ashram sat down together for food in one big hall.

The idea of having raw food instead of cooked had always attracted Bapu, and the daily demonstration of what cooked food meant in terms of labor and other problems which the common kitchen raised accentuated his desire to try out an experiment. For a time the subject was confined to discussions with members of the Ashram, and friends who came and went. Gradually the idea began to take definite shape, and a dietary was worked out. Bread was to be replaced by sprouted wheat, and milk by ground coconut, while all vegetables were to be eaten raw.

Bapu was, of course, to be the leading and guiding experimentalist, and all others who wished to join were enlisted after a thorough sounding-out by Bapu as to the genuineness of their interest and their realization of what it would mean to carry the experiment through to a point when definite conclusions could be reached. A number of common-kitchen members joined, and as far as I remember I was the only woman among them. Bapu put the preparation of the food in my charge, for which I was relieved of some of my other duties. I can remember having thick damp cloths spread out on grass mats in the storeroom, with wheat grain laid between the folds. This sprouted in about twenty-four hours. Then there was coconut to be grated and vegetables to be cleaned. The sprouted wheat was soon found to be rather difficult to masticate in sufficient quantities to satisfy normal hunger, and for Bapu, because of his lack of teeth, I had to grind it with a stone roller and slab. Before long there was a general demand from the experimenters for ground-sprouted wheat. Now to grind dry, unsprouted grain in a handmill is one matter, but to grind sticky sprouted wheat on a stone slab is quite another matter, and I began to think that raw food was going to prove decidedly more troublesome to prepare than cooked food.

I do not remember exactly the length of time, but I think it was not more than a week or two when people's health began to be adversely affected. I was the first to go down, and my illness took the form of complete constipation. I did not want to give in and

Bapu prescribed various combinations of raw foods for me, but to no avail. So he said I must return to cooked food without any further delay. The moment I did so I began to improve. Next it was Bapu who showed signs of trouble. He was not digesting the food properly, and as dysentery was an old enemy of his, we were all very anxious. But he laughed away our protests. However, his digestion got steadily worse, and I made one more pressing effort to persuade him that disaster was at hand. He only smiled, but I felt he had begun to think over the matter.

Unfortunately it was too late, for the very next morning Bapu was stricken with a severe attack of dysentery. Reluctantly he agreed to take goat's milk curds. Even so, it was some days before the attack subsided. After this he did not return to the milkless raw-food diet, but the hankering after a solution of that kind to the food problem remained with him always.

Now one by one the rest of the experimenters began to suffer. I think there were two or three with tough digestions who could have pulled on a bit longer, but after Bapu's collapse the zest for the experiment faded. Moreover, to have the complication in the common kitchen of a few people requiring raw food was not good enough. So the whole thing was given up.

The next experiment was of a different kind. Bapu, still oppressed with the amount of time that human beings give to the cooking of food, wanted to find a quicker way of making bread than the rolling and heating of *rotis*. So he decided that an oven must be constructed in which all the bread could be baked at the same time. Several difficulties had to be faced. Nobody knew how to construct an oven, or how to use it. Chhotelalji offered to tackle the problem, and Bapu, knowing his tenacity and that he would never give in once he had undertaken a job, agreed to send him to a bakery to learn everything. On his return he constructed an oven and turned out quite good bread.

While all these activities were going on, the outer world was never absent from Bapu's mind. Sardar Vallabhbhai Patel, who lived in Ahmedabad, looked in frequently, and the other Congress leaders from far and wide kept coming and going.

CHAPTER XXI

JUST about a year after coming to Bapu I received news that Father was seriously ill, and within a few days came a cable from Mother saying he had passed away. I restrained my feelings, but Bapu was not quite satisfied about the amount of suppressed emotion which he noticed in me. He reasoned with me gently yet firmly, but at the same time he told me that if I felt a strong urge to go to England and be with Mother for a while, he would not wish to dissuade me. In spite of my grief, such an idea had not entered my head. I had come to India through an inspiration that meant no going back at such a time, and I said so to Bapu.

Rhona, who was then living in the Madras Presidency, where her husband, Harold Vernon, was a Collector, telegraphed to tell me that she was going home to see Mother and hoped I could come to Bombay to meet her while she was passing through. I took leave from Bapu and went.

An incident connected with this trip has always remained in my mind. Rhona was putting up at the Taj Mahal Hotel. This was the first time I had been near such a place since coming to Bapu. I was wearing my usual dress of *ghaghra*, short sari and sandals. I entered the hotel and inquired at the reception office for "Mrs. Vernon." The man on the other side of the counter told me the number in an offhand manner—after all, the Taj was the white man's preserve in those days and what right had a woman in a *ghaghra* to be there? Feeling much amused I went toward the front stairs when the man shouted after me in Hindi: "Where are you going? Get into the lift." I got the idea. The lift was empty and that was a good way of getting me upstairs without risk of any hotel guests running into me. So I obliged his hurt feelings and went up in the lift, but on the way along the passage to my sister's room I did run into a white lady, and she drew in her skirts as she passed me as if fearing contamination.

When on my return to the Ashram I told Bapu this story, he laughed heartily and said, "That was a fine experience for you."

One more job now came my way once a week. It was not lengthy but most interesting. Bapu had begun his autobiography *Experiments with Truth*. He wrote it in Gujerati week by week for *Navajivan,* Bapu's Gujerati weekly, and Mahadev translated it into English for simultaneous appearance in *Young India.* Before going to press it used to come to me for any corrections in English. No matter what other work I might be doing, I had to put it aside when the manuscript came into my hands each week, as there was usually no margin of time left.

This work also brought me into closer touch with Bapu's secretarial staff, foremost of whom was Mahadev Desai, a Gujerati. He was tall, good-looking, with a mustache, and thinning hair on an intellectual head. By nature he was delicately sensitive, which showed particularly in his finely shaped hands. He had an extraordinarily quick and intelligent grasp of the complicated and ever-varying situations in which he was Bapu's right hand, noting, discussing, drafting and writing, always in that swift and exquisitely clear hand. But the most striking thing of all about him was his intense devotion to Bapu. And in this was our strongest bond.

The other permanent member of the secretarial staff was Pyarelal, a Punjabi. He was of lesser stature, clean-shaved and thick-set, but with an equally intellectual head though of another type. He was younger than Mahadev, and at that time was passing through a period of inner development which made him dreamy and often forgetful of his surroundings. He would put in a prodigious amount of work at one time and then, at another, become lost in his dreams. But Bapu knew his value, and, though he was as a rule strict with him, he watched Pyarelal's evolution with affectionate indulgence in many ways.

Other members of the staff came and went in the course of years. There was always a typist, usually South-Indian or Bengali, and often a young woman to help in the Gujerati and Hindi correspondence, all of which had to be done by hand in those days.

All through this first year I struggled with Hindustani but felt very dissatisfied with my progress, and I could see that Bapu was dissatisfied also. This weighed heavily on my mind, because I knew that without the ability to understand and speak Hindustani with comparative ease I could never become any use to Bapu in the way he wished. The great difficulty for me in the Ashram was that the inmates practically all talked Gujerati among themselves, and many of them knew English, so, except at my lessons, I hardly came in touch with Hindustani.

Now that Bapu was, in any case, going out on tour, and was evidently not going to take me with him, I thought the time was ripe for suggesting to him that I should go to North India and live among people who spoke the language I was trying to learn. I felt too in my heart that the separation from Bapu would be less hard if I went out into new surroundings rather than stay on in the Ashram without him.

He agreed to the suggestion and decided to send me to the Kanya Gurukul, then at Daryagunj, Delhi. This, being the leading girls' educational center of the Arya Samaj, which is a reformist sect, was again an institution and likely to be much more humdrum than Sabarmati. I felt serious misgivings, but I saw that it was not easy for Bapu to think of a suitable place to send me, and since he had fixed on this center and had expressed the hope that I should be able to do some teaching of carding and spinning among the inmates, I made no objection.

When I look back on that time I can see how I was progressively crushing my natural independence of nature and putting myself wholly under another's will, a thing I had never done in my life. It was the intense reverential love that I felt for Bapu which made me discipline myself in this way, but it increased the tension which was already there.

The Kanya Gurukul was a big institution filled with girls of all ages. The Principal and teachers greeted me most kindly and gave me a room to myself. One of the teachers was assigned to give me lessons in Hindustani, and a number of girls were selected for me to instruct in spinning. I do not remember many details. It goes without saying that most things jarred on me. It was not anyone's fault—it was just the inevitable pain that I felt in surroundings so antipathetic to my nature and so markedly devoid of the aesthetic sense.

After a few days Vidyavati Devi, the Principal, took me to see the famous head of the Arya Samaj, Swami Shraddhanand. I was greatly struck with his appearance—tall, massive, and attired in the saffron robes of a *sanyasi*. He inquired after Bapu and questioned me kindly as to whether I was comfortable at the Kanya Gurukul.

Only two or three days after this visit came the staggering news that the Swami had been assassinated by a Moslem. The Gurukul was thrown into terrible agitation and grief, and Delhi braced itself for possible Hindu-Moslem riots. Mercifully they were averted. Vidyavati Devi was wonderfully brave throughout. The grief she felt must have been intense, but the strong and quiet way she controlled the Gurukul was remarkable. Naturally she and the teachers had a strong desire to pay homage to their departed leader's remains, but the question was whether it would be safe to go to his house. Finally they decided to risk it, and they took me with them. There was a wildly excited crowd outside the house, but a mounted policeman made way for us to go in.

There lay the body of Swami Shraddhanand, looking even more massive in death—and his chest had been bared, showing the stab wounds. It was deeply impressive, and terrible in the warning it carried.

In the Kanya Gurukul the atmosphere grew very painful. The Arya Samajists had always been hard in their attitude toward Moslems. They had departed from the age-old Hindu custom of tolerance and natural absorption and turned to militant proselytization, which clashed head on with the activities of both Moslems and Christians. Now they naturally were worked up to a fever pitch. Even the young girls were talking wildly. This was all diametrically opposed to Bapu's ideals, but what could one do?

The girls would not, could not, listen to reason. I wrote to Bapu describing the situation, and in his reply dated January 3rd, he said:

I see what you are passing through, and I am glad of it. You have to love humanity in spite of itself.

CHAPTER XXII

WHILE in the Kanya Gurukul I heard quite a lot about the Gurukul Kangri, which was the chief center of the Arya Samaj, a big educational institution for boys. I was told how Swami Shraddhanand, wishing to revert to the ancient ideal of "Forest Universities," had himself chosen the site for this Gurukul opposite Hardwar, on the other side of the Ganga (Ganges), and that it was situated right on the edge of the forested foothills of the Himalayas. Only a year or two previously the place had been seriously damaged by a severe flood, but the professors and students were carrying on nevertheless. The location, so near the mountains, sounded to me most attractive, and I thought too there should be a more peaceful and studious atmosphere there than at this city Gurukul full of girls. So I wrote and asked Bapu if I might shift. He wrote to the authorities and they agreed, but it was evidently a special concession on their part, as I learned afterwards, because no women were supposed to stay there.

I set out for Gurukul Kangri with high hopes of seeing the Himalayas, at least from a distance, and of at last reaching rural surroundings. Even Sabarmati, though situated on the bank of the river and with some fields around, did not have a country atmosphere. One looked across the river at a forest of factory chimneys whose smoke often polluted the air, and as for walks, they consisted in trudging along an uninteresting road from the Ashram

90

gate to the jail gate and back. Though I would not let myself think about it, the longing for the woods and fields had always haunted me at Sabarmati.

When I reached Hardwar station I was met by one of the Gurukul professors with a bullock cart, as that was the only kind of conveyance which could manipulate the boulders and deep sands of Ganga's broad riverbed. I breathed in with joy the fresh air and gazed at the vast forests, but I was a little disappointed to find the snow mountains so very far away. I had not realized the size and extent of the Himalayan foothills.

I was put up in a small guesthouse which stood apart with a little enclosure of its own. Everyone was most kind; provisions, vessels and firewood for cooking were provided, and arrangements were made for my Hindustani lessons.

All this time Bapu was touring in Bihar, spreading the message of self-reliance and at the same time making collections for the newly formed All-India Spinners' Association. Though my new surroundings gave me a sense of relaxation, the separation from Bapu gnawed at my heart. However, I began to make better progress with my Hindustani, and I also started going to a nearby village to teach carding to the inhabitants. This was my first contact with Indian villagers. At the same time the path to and fro passed through a part of the real jungle, with a small stream to ford at one place. Here were trees to make friends with and birds to greet. It was good.

I had reached the Gurukul Kangri in January, and Bapu's program was to bring him there in March for the Jubilee celebrations to which other leaders were also coming, including Pandit Madan Mohan Malaviya, the veteran national leader and the founder of the Benares Hindu University. By the beginning of March great preparations were afoot. A regular camp was erected for the expected visitors, and special quarters were prepared for the leaders. To my joy I learned that Bapu was to put up in the guesthouse which I was occupying. As the time approached, everybody became so busy that my lessons were suspended, and now the guesthouse had to be washed and cleaned and put in perfect order for receiving Bapu and his party of three or four persons. I can't remember exactly, but they must have been Mahadev, Pyarelal and one or two others.

The thought of setting eyes on Bapu again after so long possessed me the whole time. When he finally arrived, I managed to remain outwardly calm, but that evening, after the Prayer, my emotions suddenly got the better of me and I fled into the garden and burst into tears. All my pent-up and suppressed feelings rushed forth. I tried to hide myself behind a tree, but the garden was small, and someone noticing me came out in alarm to see what was the trouble. How could I explain? Such things are not explainable. The matter was reported to Bapu and he was much disturbed. When the Prayer congregation had dispersed he called me and said, "What is this?" Gently but firmly he reasoned with me and reproved me, and it was evident that the incident was making him still more convinced that I must accustom myself to separation.

I had been hoping against hope that Bapu might take me with him when he left, but he now began to talk of sending me to a place which he thought would be better than the Gurukul, where I was more or less segregated from the rest of the inmates. I soon realized that there was no chance of accompanying him except to the station, where our ways would divide and I should have to change trains. When the day came, I was heartbroken but tried not to show it. This time I was to go to Bhagwadbhakti Ashram, Rewari, a place recommended by Seth Jamnalal Bajaj.

Here was entirely new country—Rajasthan. The scenery, the local customs of the peasantry, the cattle, all were different and quite attractive. I missed the glorious forests of the Himalayan foothills, but the open country had a real charm about it, and there were patches of scrub and jungle where one might meet herds of black buck grazing quietly. Certainly it was a pleasing place, but it was a hot climate and summer was coming on.

Though my surroundings were new and interesting, I could not keep my mind off the thought that Bapu had again gone on a strenuous tour though his health was anything but satisfactory, and the pain of our parting would not leave me.

The next day there came a letter from Bapu:

The parting today was sad, because I saw that I pained you. And yet it was inevitable. I want you to be a perfect woman. I want you to shed all angularities. All unnecessary reserve must go. . . .

Do throw off the nervousness. You must not cling to me as in this body. The spirit without the body is ever with you. And that is more than the feeble embodied imprisoned spirit with all the limitations that flesh is heir to. The spirit without the flesh is perfect, and that is all we need. This can be felt only when we practice detachment. This you must now try to achieve.

This is how I would grow if I were you. But you should grow along your own lines. You will, therefore, reject all I have said in this, that does not appeal to your heart or head. You must retain your individuality at all cost. Resist me when you must. For I may judge you wrongly in spite of all my love for you. I do not want you to impute infallibility to me.

22-3-27.

In these few words Bapu had expressed the crux of the struggle which was to face me—to face us both—throughout the years to come. Bapu wanted me to be "perfect" and yet to be myself. The two things just did not fit. "You must retain your individuality at all cost." Bapu sensed that I was crushing my natural self, but if I did not restrain myself in every way I kept on displeasing Bapu. As I cogitated over this letter I could reach no solution. One moment I would feel a sense of lightheartedness at the idea of letting myself be myself, and the next would I realize that I must at all cost strive to overcome my shortcomings. How to achieve that "detachment" needed? And all the time I was trembling in my heart for Bapu's safety, as a presentiment of approaching bad news was weighing on me.

Suddenly, on the fifth day, came a telegram from Mahadev saying Bapu had narrowly escaped an attack of apoplexy, that his blood pressure was still running high and the doctors had ordered complete rest. All my thoughts of composed detachment went to the winds, and I telegraphed and sent anxious letters to Mahadev for more news. After a few days a letter came from Bapu himself telling me he was better, that I must not worry and must submerge myself in my work. I did my best, but the confidence I had tried to have in Bapu's not allowing himself to be overstrained was lost for good. I could not help feeling that two things appeared obvious: first, that the people who organized Bapu's tours had little sense of proportion and arranged the most preposterous programs; and secondly, that Bapu, for the sake of the masses, would go beyond his strength in trying to satisfy everyone.

Bapu wished to take the rest which had been prescribed at Sabarmati, but the doctors would not hear of such a thing and said he must stay at a cool place. So it was arranged for him to go to Nandi Hills in Mysore state, and later to Bangalore. Our correspondence went on regularly, and in one of the letters I wrote to Bapu at that time I quoted some passages from Romain Rolland's *Life of Beethoven*. In his reply, dated April 13, 1927, Bapu said:

> I must write on this fasting day to acknowledge your letter containing extracts from Beethoven. They are good spiritual food. I don't want you to forget your music or your taste for it. It would be cruel to forget that to which you owe so much, and which has really brought you to me.

Virtually all alone, and without any means of hearing Beethoven's music, I buried it within myself. In fact I soon reached the stage where I tried not to think of anything but the life I had now entered. Evidently Bapu did not wish this, but it seemed to be an inevitable part of the *tapasya** which had come to me in answer to my prayers, and neither I nor Bapu could prevent it.

The Bhagwadbhakti Ashram was quite a free and easy place, with none of the segregation rules of the Gurukul. Its head was an old Swami known as Maharajji, and he was looked up to as Guru by the inmates—men, women and children of all ages. There was nothing stiff about the layout of the Ashram, the buildings being dotted about over a large area, with beautiful neem trees everywhere.

* Ascetic penance.

94

Unfortunately there was a snag in the Ashram which neither Bapu nor Jamnalalji seemed to have been aware of, and that was the drinking of bhang, an intoxicant made from hemp. I was still new to so many things, and I had not yet come in touch with the typical Sadhu world, where bhang is looked upon as a matter of course. I was, therefore, rather taken aback when I found some Ashramites lying about in a state of blissful oblivion. I expressed my surprise to the inmates, but they just laughed at me. I evidently had not realized the normality of the thing. When I told Bapu about this in my letters he was perturbed, and he asked Jamnalalji to visit the Ashram. Ultimately the bhangy atmosphere wore off.

My Hindi progressed fairly well, but not as quickly as I wanted. All through this period Bapu's letters referred to the importance of my completing my task of learning Hindi, and his desire that I should not join him anywhere until this was accomplished. "Hindi first, everything else after." It became a sort of nightmare.

By the time the rains set in, Bapu descended from Nandi Hills to Bangalore, and I finally decided that, rather than force myself any further, I would go to see him without trying to "finish" my Hindi. After all, how to say when it was finished? There were no examinations to go through, and if "finishing" meant fluent proficiency, then it would be a matter of years if ever. Let me, therefore, break through the nightmare and go.

I do not remember much about the trip beyond the fact that Bapu did not appear to me anything like so well in reality as he sounded in his letters. My conscience did not allow me to stay long. But I did not return all the way to Bhagwadbhakti Ashram, for Bapu had decided I had better go to Vinoba's Ashram at Wardha for the remaining two months' Hindi now considered to be sufficient. Not that I was anything like proficient.

CHAPTER XXIII

WARDHA ASHRAM suited me the best of all. The atmosphere was congenial, there was open country around, and I had an excellent and patient instructor in Jajuji, a very worthy old man and one of Bapu's best organizers in the khadi-production work.

Before long I suffered a severe attack of malaria, in which my temperature reached 105 degrees. I can't remember whether it was my first, but it was certainly the first bad attack, and from then on I got malaria practically every year for over twenty-five years. That attack was a long one, and when I came out of it I was extremely weak. Bapu arranged for me to go to Poona for rest and change of air.

Bapu had by now finished his convalescence at Bangalore and had started on a tour of South India. News in the papers and even Bapu's own letters showed that he was again on the brink of breakdown owing to the terrible rush. On September 9th, he wrote:

> They leave me just enough time to attend to the program before me. I have been pouring my soul out to the various audiences. That leaves me little energy for anything else. . . . If God wants this tour to be finished, He will keep those who must be, from harm. You are, therefore, not to worry about me.

But how could I be at ease after Bapu's previous breakdown? My own nerves had not been improved by my recent attack of malaria, and the news from South India continued to be most disturbing. So, as I was already halfway to the south at Poona, I could not resist going once to see Bapu before returning to my work. But I had made a big mistake this time. I received a severe scolding and was soon packed off to Sabarmati.

96

Though Bapu could treat one so severely, yet he felt pain in doing so:

I have never been so anxious as this time to hear from you, for I sent you away too quickly after a serious operation. But the sending you away was a part of the operation. Poor Anna! He too tells me that you were gloomy and wants me to soothe you. Jamnalalji says I should have kept you with me. Well, you are going to belie their fears and keep quite well and cheerful. You haunted me in my sleep last night and were reported by friends to whom you had been sent, to be delirious, but without any danger. They said, "You need not be anxious. We are doing all that is humanly possible." And with this I woke up troubled in mind and prayed that you may be free from all harm. And your letter gave me great joy.

I felt terribly repentant for having caused Bapu so much anxiety, and threw myself into my work with a grim determination not to disturb him.

From South India, Bapu was called for an interview by the viceroy, Lord Irwin. "There is no warrant to hope much from the interview," wrote Bapu while traveling in the train to Delhi, "but I could not reject the advance on that ground."

The purport of the interview turned out to be nothing more than the Secretary of State's announcement regarding the Simon Commission. A bitter disappointment.

From Delhi, Bapu went to Ceylon for a short visit and collected funds for the Khadi movement in India, after which he returned to Sabarmati.

I had been in the Ashram all this time, improving my carding, teaching children *takli* spinning, and also doing some work in the dairy, where I milked one of the cows regularly.

During this period the political tension in the country was steadily rising. The "Simon go back" boycott was getting under way, and Bapu, who had again entered into active politics, had to go out every now and then to important meetings and conferences. However, the Ashram continued to receive his detailed attention.

Indeed, the very fact that an intense national struggle seemed to be looming ahead made Bapu all the more anxious to train and discipline the inmates for the ordeal to come.

Ahmedabad, and in fact Gujerat as a whole, is the stronghold of Vaishnava Hinduism, which is the most nonviolent of the Hindu cults. The presence of large numbers of Jains in that part of India has also had its influence. Sabarmati was, therefore, in the midst of orthodox nonviolence, and Bapu himself, coming of a strict Vaishnava family, was expected to be a champion of the accepted ideals. The test now came.

Ahmedabad was infested with stray dogs that, in the hot climate, were all infected with mange, some of them being completely hairless. They spent their lives slinking about the bazaars and back lanes, picking up what they could find, and every now and then sitting down to scratch, scratch, scratch the intolerable itch which was slowly killing them. Because of the orthodoxy of the population, nobody could dare destroy these poor wretches and thus put them out of their suffering. But as the city went on growing—and it was growing fast because of the cotton mills—the stray-dog problem developed into a veritable menace, for added to their distressing condition, the dogs were also developing rabies.

The Municipality at last dared meet the idea of shooting those dogs. There was public indignation, and it seemed that nothing could be done. Then a group of leading citizens, among whom Seth Ambalal Sarabhai played a prominent part, decided to go to Bapu and seek his approval. They came to the Ashram and there was an earnest discussion. Bapu gave his opinion in favor of the shooting, and it was carried out. Indignant protests poured in and Bapu dealt with them in his own quiet way.

But now came a much more severe test. One of the heifers in the Ashram cowsheds had fallen sick and become quite helpless. She lay on her side with all four legs stretched out, and yet she couldn't die. Bapu heard about it and went to see her. A veterinary doctor was called and he said she was past all hope of recovery. Bapu felt his Ahimsa was again on trial, and this time the sanctity of the cow was involved. The heifer was quite big, and it was impossible to lift her about as one could a human being so as to prevent bed sores. She refused nourishment, flies were tormenting her, and in every way her life was a torture.

Bapu decided in his own mind that true Ahimsa required him to put the heifer out of her misery by having her killed in as painless a way as possible, but he did not wish to take the step without trying to convince the Ashramites of its correctness. Intense discussions took place, and most of the inmates accepted Bapu's reasoning. But there were one or two who most vehemently opposed it, and Ba was on their side as was Kishi ben, Ba's bosom companion. So Bapu told them to go out and nurse the heifer, and if they found they could save her from suffering, all very well and good. Accordingly they went and sat down in the straw by the poor creature, whisked away the flies and tried to persuade her to take nourishment, but when they found that they could neither feed her nor ease her pain, they sorrowfully returned to Bapu and said they would no longer oppose him.

Bapu knew that Seth Ambalal Sarabhai would be with him in this interpretation of nonviolence, so he sent him a message asking him to arrange for an injection which would be as quick and painless as possible in its effect. Promptly Seth Ambalal arrived, accompanied by his family doctor armed with a big syringe and necessary poison. Bapu led them to the cowshed, with only the dairyman and myself following. Everyone was silent. We entered the room where the heifer was lying, and the doctor prepared the syringe. Then Bapu stooped down and gently held for a moment one of the heifer's front legs, the syringe was applied, there was a spasm and the heifer was dead. No one spoke. Bapu took a cloth and spread it over the heifer's face, and then walked silently back to his room.

Bapu now wrote a long article for *Young India* entitled "The Fiery Ordeal," describing the incident and giving his reasoning for the step he had taken. He reinforced his argument with two poetic quotations most characteristic of his attitude toward life:

> The pathway of love is the ordeal of fire,
> The shrinkers turn away from it.

> The way of the Lord is meant for heroes,
> Not for cowards.

A perfect bombardment of angry protests followed. "Some of them," wrote Bapu in *Young India*, "seem to have made the violence of their invective against me a measure of their solicitude for Ahimsa."

But Bapu turned it all to the best account, and writing to me a little while afterwards, he remarked, "It has done much good in that it has set people thinking."

CHAPTER XXIV

THE time had now come for me to go forth and work among the rural masses. I had become fairly expert in the carding and spinning of cotton, and my Hindi was tolerable. Bapu asked me which part of India I should like to go to, and I chose Bihar. In those days all the Provinces had their national leaders, men who had burned their boats and thrown in their lot with Bapu for the achievement of independence through nonviolence—Rajaji (Sri Rajagopalachar) first Indian Governor-General, in Madras; Vallabhbai (Sardar Patel) in Gujerat; Rajendra Babu (Dr. Rajendra Prasad) first President of the Republic of India, in Bihar, and so on. I was, therefore, to go under Rajendra Babu's jurisdiction.

As my job was to assist the khadi workers in the introduction of improved methods of carding and spinning, it was decided I should first go to the All-India Spinner's Association center at Madhubani in North Bihar, and from there, with the help and advice of the local workers, select a suitable village in the area.

A village called Chhatwan was decided upon, as it was in an area where there were spinners in practically every house. Then too, a depot had previously been set up there for distribution of cotton and the collection of yarn. The surrounding country was one vast cultivated plain, dotted over with little villages nestling alongside their groves of mango and bamboo.

Such villages as I had seen so far in Gujerat and Rajasthan had been fairly well-to-do. Now for the first time I saw the rural masses in all their poverty and suffering, and the meaning of the fire that burned unceasingly in Bapu's heart was brought home to me.

We selected one of the few brick buildings in the village—it could not be called a house as it consisted of a single small hall with pillared arches on one side opening onto a veranda with the village street in front. There was one tiny room at the side in which I kept my belongings, and a bamboo-and-thatch hut in the yard at the back which served as a kitchen.

Bihar had a splendid team of constructive workers headed by Babu Lakshmi Narayan, who is Secretary of the Bihar branch of the All-India Spinners' Association, and he gave one of his best men, Ramdev Babu, to work along with me in the village. It had also been arranged that we should have two or three young boys from Rajendra Babu's Ashram at Muzaffarpur, thus making a kind of little Ashram of our own.

In order to demonstrate the improved method of carding I decided to sit and card cotton in the Yarn Depot, where dozens of village women came and went daily to exchange their yarn for cotton or money. This very soon caught their attention, and they would stop and watch me. They were obviously very skeptical, but in spite of their doubts they could not help being interested in what I was doing. In order to convince them of the efficacy of the new method I would roll slivers then and there from freshly carded cotton and hand them out, saying, "You take these home and spin with them. If you find them good, then why not learn to use this kind of bow?"

They would examine the slivers with keen interest, turning them this way and that, and passing them around from one to another for inspection, but not one of the women would come forward to try her hand. They would giggle and nudge one another, but retire backwards the moment I held out the bow.

It took some days, but once one or two brave ones had ventured, the difficulty was over. Very soon the problem was how to cope with the demand.

In the past, production of cotton cloth had been a flourishing subsidiary occupation, but since the influx of mill cloth the spinning wheels and looms were one after another becoming idle, and if it had not been for the arrival of the All-India Spinners' Association in their midst, the peasantry would have completely lost that precious little bit of income which had accrued to them from cloth production. Our work was, therefore, very popular among the people, and the enthusiasm I had already felt for the khadi movement grew into conviction confirmed by direct experience.

I used to write of my experiences in detail to Bapu, and despite the fact that he was again touring, first in Sindh and then in Burma, his letters came regularly. He took interest in every detail and often sent practical suggestions.

A veritable epidemic of malaria now engulfed the village. It was of a particularly bad type, and there was hardly a house left which had not one or more patients lying in it prostrate with fever. When I went down the village street I could not get along on account of the distracted women who would rush out and, catching hold of my arm, drag me into their homes. In each case the patient would be sure to be in the darkest corner of the low, windowless room, and for the first moment or two, after leaving the bright outside light, one could see nothing at all, and it would be only the groans coming from the fever-stricken patient that told one where he or she lay.

After a while I began getting fever intermittently myself. Of course in that out-of-the-way place fruit was unprocurable and had to be ordered from some big city like Calcutta. I had, therefore, been trying to do with as little as possible. In a letter, Bapu remonstrated:

> The immediate thing is for you to get well. To spend lavishly on fruit is real economy. You cannot keep good health without fresh fruit. . . . Your primary concern is not to discover a cheap diet, but it is to be able to live in villages without needing a yearly exodus to the hills.

8-4-29.

102

But the fever returned worse than ever, and finally Rajendra Babu came to take me away to his ancestral home in the village of Zeradai. Such was Rajendra Babu's simplicity of dress and manner that he looked just like his khadi workers. He arrived at Chhatwan with nothing but a small roll of bedding tied up with a piece of rope, and stayed in our little Ashram, where at night he slept on a hard wooden bench on the veranda as a matter of course. When the villagers came to see him, he talked to them in their own sweet Bihari dialect and made them feel perfectly at home.

At Zeradai I picked up in health, but it was decided I should not go back to the highly malarious villages of North Bihar.

CHAPTER XXV

THAT summer Bapu's khadi touring took him to the Himalayas, and I joined him just before he went to Kausani, that beautiful spot in the Almora district from which one gazes on the Eternal Snows in speechless wonder. Ten precious days Bapu stayed there, and wrote the Introduction to his translation of the Gita.

But Bapu could never remain in one place for long. The call of the millions impelled him to move on and on throughout the country, and after the short halt at Kausani we descended to the plains to continued the unending khadi tour.

Bapu usually had with him a party of three or four persons from the Ashram—Mahadev was invariably there—who looked after his secretarial and personal needs, as well as a small number of people belonging to the Province in which he was touring, who organized the programs and arranged the meetings, transport and lodging. Long-distance journeys were made by train, the whole party, with baggage, baskets, files and what not, packing into a third-class compartment, at one end of which a little extra space would be made for Bapu to have his bedding stretched full length so that he could now and then lie down and rest. But when the program included a visit to a series of villages, we all traveled in cars, Bapu's in front and two or three following packed to overflowing with baggage and people.

During this touring I was for some time in charge of Bapu's personal needs. Though these were very simple, the circumstances under which they had to be attended to were anything but easy. We were continually on the move, with meetings all along the way and two main halts in the twenty-four hours, one at midday for baths, clothes-washing and lunch, and the other in the evening for dinner and the night rest.

Added to this, there were endless crowds everywhere—thirsting, yearning, desperately eager crowds that thronged the railway stations, blocked the motor roads where they passed through villages, and swarmed all around our halting places.

My job was to see that Bapu's personal routine went on smoothly and punctually in the midst of all this rush. While Bapu was attending the full-blown public meeting which awaited him at each main halt, I would dash to the quarters allotted us to see to the arrangements. Information was always sent some time in advance about all the places we were going to visit, giving exact details of Bapu's requirements. However, one never knew what one was going to find. As a rule we were put up in people's private houses, sometimes in school buildings and the like, and occasionally in a camp. The general instructions sent around were for a room for Bapu to be cleared of all furniture, where a *gaddi* should be placed on the floor and covered with khadi, a bathroom nearby with clean appointments, and fresh raw vegetables, fruits and goat's milk.

Sometimes these directions were excellently understood and carried out, but that was not always the case, especially in out-of-the-way rural areas. One was daily faced with unexpected and sometimes desperate difficulties.

The first thing one did on arrival was to see that water was being heated for the bath and that the bathroom was clean, then one inquired for the goat's milk and vegetables, etc., and a stove

104

for cooking. The hosts and hostesses at all places would be over-flowing in their enthusiasm to help, which often made matters more difficult because Bapu's food had to be *just so,* neither too much nor too little, and absolutely on time. Then there was the problem of the *Panch Vastu* vow of eating only five different things during the day, in which each different vegetable and fruit counted as a separate item. This meant that one must be sure not to serve for the midday meal what one could not repeat in the evening. Kind people would keep pressing one to prepare this and that. "These vegetables we have brought specially, and you *must* prepare them." One had to give precious time to explaining that there could not be more than the five things already fixed. Then where was the goat's milk? If possible I liked to milk the goats myself to make sure of the milk being fresh and clean. And just at the last moment when distant sounds of "Mahatma Gandhi *ki jai!*" warned one that the meeting was over and Bapu would be here in a few minutes, I would remember that I had not looked at the gaddi in the sitting room to make sure that it was covered with pure khadi and not mill cloth. I would fly to the room— Yes, it is all right. But once it was not, and I got a scolding.

The sound of voices rises to a roar, and an intense thrill passes through the house. Bapu has arrived, hot, tired, and covered with dust, but quiet and smiling. He goes to his gaddi. The crowds are somehow checked at the gates and only Bapu's own staff and the owners of the house are allowed in.

In a few minutes I tell Bapu that the bath is ready and he goes off to take it, while I prepare to serve the food immediately he comes out. Then while he takes his meal I wash his clothes, bathe, and wash my own. If the clothes do not get dry during the two or three hours' halt, then they have to be taken on damp to the evening halt.

With luck Bapu snatches a little sleep after the meal, and then everything has to be packed up, and off we go again. And so on day after day, with a never-ending variety of experience.

Sometimes I was able to attend a meeting, and then my job would be to help in the collection of money at the close of Bapu's speech. Several of us armed with cloth bags would move among the audience, all sitting closely packed together on the ground. It was not at all easy to reach everybody, but the eager hands, stretching out to give, beckoned to us in all directions.

I was deeply touched to see the way the peasantry parted with their copper and nickel coins, which they kept tied in a corner of their clothes and tucked into their waists. With sunburned, labor-worn hands they hurriedly untied the knots of cloth, and without counting or hesitation would empty all their little treasure into our bags, while the well-to-do would carefully open their purses and hunt among their rupees for an eight-anna piece.

But there were occasions when the rich gave too in an amazing fashion. I especially remember a women's meeting in which Bapu appealed to the audience in a very stirring way for their jewelry. Their hearts were so touched that they began pulling off their rings, earrings, bracelets and anklets. Rich and poor, young and old, vied with one another to shower their jewelry into our bags.

As I was moving around on the outskirts of the audience a young village woman caught hold of me. She had nothing to give but a heavy silver anklet, and it was so thick that she could not open it up and get it off. "Help me," she cried, "pull, pull!" So we sat down on the ground together, she pulling one way, I the other, and we managed to get the anklet open sufficiently for her to remove it from her leg. She was overjoyed, and pushed it into my hands to give to Bapu.

All this overwhelming affection Bapu received with simple, detached gratitude for the sake of the Cause, but he treasured every copper as a sacred trust and insisted on the most careful and exact account being kept of all donations. Every day at the night halt those in charge of the collections would sit down on the floor of their room to count the money. The notes were an easy matter, but the thousands of little copper and nickel coins were a terrific task. When the bags were all emptied onto the ground, there was a huge pile which took hours to count, but counted it had to be, for Bapu would not rest content until every detail was reported to him. When the collections were in jewelry, then every item had to be listed. And all this money and jewelry had to be carried along from village to village till we came within reach of a big town where everything could be deposited at a bank, after which the collections would again begin mounting up.

CHAPTER XXVI

IN the beginning of the winter Bapu sent me away to work on my own, but he called me back before setting out for the Lahore Congress. On the way there he stopped at Delhi for a meeting with the Viceroy, who was at that time trying to persuade him to attend the forthcoming Round Table Conference in London. The interview was a failure, as the terms on which Bapu would be prepared to go were not acceptable to the British Government, and this added greatly to the already tense atmosphere in which the Congress was meeting.

It was Christmastime, and Lahore was having a cold wave with sharp biting frost at night. Added to this, we were all put up in tents. I tried to keep Bapu's tent warm, but it was impossible, as so many people kept coming in and out, bringing a blast of cold air with them each time. We had all been given beds, but we soon found that it was less cold to sleep on the ground with straw under us. Then the bathroom tents were at a little distance, and this meant often having to go back and forth through frost-covered grass, with only open sandals on one's bare feet. Many of the delegates and visitors from Central and South India suffered badly that year.

The tense political atmosphere grew to a fever point when it was decided to draft a resolution proclaiming Complete Independence as the Congress goal. The evening that this resolution was to be put before the Open Session everyone of our party, which was rather larger than usual, wanted to be present in the Pandal, but Bapu, who always objected to his people pressing for seats on such occasions, or going where they had no particular duty to perform, expressed the wish that nobody of his party should go to the meeting except the one or two who were required by him personally for taking notes, etc.

I saw Bapu off from his tent, wrapped in his warm shawls, and then went back inside to await his return, which I presumed would be in two or three hours. But the time went by and the Session still seemed to be in full swing. The Pandal was not very far away, and whenever there was cheering I could hear it. The night got colder and colder, and I kept putting charcoal on the little stove. Then I began to notice that not one member of our party appeared to be anywhere around. Where had they all gone? Surely not to the Pandal! Perhaps they were listening from outside. It was now nearing midnight, and the charcoal was running out. How to keep the tent warm for Bapu's return? The voices and cheers from the Pandal kept rising and falling. Then there was silence. I listened, wondering if the Session had ended, when a sudden roar of cheering rent the air—cheers and cheers and cheers, and then more cheers. At last they subsided, and after a little while Bapu returned.

What had happened?

The Independence Resolution had been passed by an overwhelming majority exactly at midnight, and with it the New Year had been ushered in—a new year, and a new era.

As if symbolic of this new era it was Jawaharlal Nehru who became President of the Congress at this Session. The political leadership had passed into the hands of the younger generation, but the leadership of the masses remained with Bapu; and it was to Bapu to whom all people looked for the move that must now be made to prove to the British Government that the newly passed Independence Resolution was not empty words but had the will of the nation behind it.

We returned to Sabarmati Ashram. January 26th was observed throughout the length and breadth of India as Independence Day, and a sense of approaching crisis spread far and wide.

In the Ashram everyone was keyed up. What was Bapu planning? He divulged nothing to begin with, but there was a peculiar

108

glow in his look and voice, as of one pregnant with inspired inner thought and prayer. Ashram discipline was tightened to military pitch, and each morning and evening after the prayer Bapu spoke at some length.

Gradually it became clear that he was searching in his mind for some sort of all-India Satyagraha* which would rouse the spirit of the masses down to the poorest in the land. Everyone was expecting an obvious choice, such as refusal to pay revenue, boycott of law courts or something of that sort, but Bapu saw snags for the masses in all these things. It must be something that touched every villager, and his mind fixed on salt. Salt was a necessity of life for all, both man and beast, and could be gathered from the sea as well as from so many soils. And yet salt was taxed, and man was forbidden to collect it for himself. The more Bapu thought about it the more convinced he became that to break the salt laws was *the* thing to decide on.

By the middle of February a meeting of the Congress Working Committee was held at the Ashram. All the great leaders came and were put up in the students' quarters, which had been emptied and arranged for them.

Bapu gave me the job of supervising the arrangements for tea and coffee, which were to be served with breakfast in the guests' rooms, and then twice during the day in the Meeting Room while the Committee was in session. Though tea and coffee were taboo for the Ashramites, Bapu would never force this rule on guests. My other job was to guard the Committee Room door while the discussions were in progress. And this was a very delicate undertaking. Formerly the rule about only members being allowed in was not very strictly kept. But Jawaharlal, the young and ardent President, had vehemently expressed the opinion that this rule should be relentlessly enforced. This was all the more embarrassing at that time as one or two of the elder stalwarts were not on the Working Committee and I had to try and make them feel cheery in another room.

When Bapu put forward his proposal for breaking the salt laws, it was met with incredulity by the Working Committee. "Salt!"

* From two Sanskrit words: *satya* (truth) and *agraha* (insistence).

they exclaimed. "Do you expect us all to go out and just make salt?" But Bapu, with his irresistible humor and persuasiveness, gradually won them over, and by the end of the three days' session everyone was on fire.

I remember so well when Jawaharlal and his father, Pandit Motilal Nehru, were leaving, how the old gentleman, as he bade me goodbye, quoted Shakespeare's lines: "When shall we three meet again? In thunder, lightning or in rain?"

CHAPTER XXVII

THE Ashram now entered three weeks of intense preparation. Bapu decided that he would march on foot with a band of followers to the coast, where they would gather sea water, make salt from it, and thus defy the law. But not till Bapu himself had broken the law was anyone else in the country to do so. The long route was carefully planned, and the persons who should join the march were chosen. This was the most difficult part, as everyone wanted to be on the list. Finally a band of seventy-nine men was selected, and the time had now come for Bapu to send his ultimatum to the Viceroy.

There was a young English Quaker, Reginald Reynolds, staying in the Ashram at that time. He had been with us at the Lahore Congress and had thoroughly imbibed the spirit of the times. Bapu decided to make him the bearer of the letter to the Viceroy.

The day came, the letter went, and the whole nation waited in suspense. There was little hope that the British Government would accept Bapu's terms, and sure enough their "No" was received. The mighty Empire again defied the mightier spirit.

Bapu announced that he would set forth on his march to Dandi on the morning of March 12th. Nearly everyone expected that he would be arrested at any moment. On the afternoon of the 11th the inhabitants of Ahmedabad began turning up in force. Crowds and crowds of men, women and children forded the river, and by the time of the evening Prayer the numbers were so great that the open sandy riverbank was the only place big enough to accommodate the congregation.

The night closed over the heavens, and still no police had come to take Bapu. We were all on tenterhooks, but Bapu was quite calm and carried out his usual routine as if there was nothing exceptional going on. When he lay down on his bed, Ba applied oil to his head and I rubbed his feet with ghee. We kept quiet as he seemed thoughtful, and after a few minutes he was peacefully sleeping.

The crowds that had gathered did not return to their homes, but camping at a respectful distance all around the Ashram, kept vigil till dawn. I think Bapu was the only person who slept that night.

With the coming of daylight more and more eager, thronging crowds collected, but still no police. It seemed as if even the Imperial Power hesitated to snatch Bapu from the midst of such a vast concourse of devotees. So the hour arrived, and he was there with staff in hand. India's soul was awake, and Bapu was the focal point in which it glowed.

The road outside the Ashram gate was cleared of the crowds, and the little group collected in disciplined order, all clad in white khadi and with nothing but a satchel slung over one shoulder—except for the music pundit, who carried his stringed instrument. Here was an army such as had never before been seen, devoid of all physical arms, only eighty strong, and marching off in joyous confidence to overthrow the greatest empire of the world.

As the march began the multitude burst into cries of "Mahatma Gandhi *ki jai!*" and away the little army went, the multitude following.

Those of us who were left behind stood watching and watching till there was nothing left to see but the cloud of dust hanging over the road. We turned to go back to our rooms, and the Ashram seemed silent and empty. Many, of course, were still there, but the spirit had gone forth.

The next day Bapu wrote telling me to send him full Ashram

news while there was yet time, for he was expecting arrest at any moment. But the march continued, and still the Government did nothing.

I kept receiving short and hurried notes from Bapu, which showed that he was bearing the strain extraordinarily well. By April 5th he reached Dandi, and on the morning of the 6th went down to the sea and made his salt. A wave of enthusiasm passed through the country, and people all over the place began breaking the salt law. A most remarkable characteristic of this movement was the way the women came out of their seclusion and joined in the Satyagraha. From rich ladies of Bombay making salt out of sea water to poor peasant women scratching salt off the ground near their villages, they everywhere joined in the fray. Wholesale arrests were begun, but still Bapu was left out. It was as if an unseen hand were holding back the Government till Bapu had done his job, and only then, when the country was thoroughly alight, did they arrest him. They came in the dead of night and swept him off to Yaravda Jail before any news could spread. This was on May 5th, and it acted like oil to the fire of revolt.

On May 12th, Bapu wrote saying he was all right and making up for arrears of sleep.

CHAPTER XXVIII

THIS was my first experience of Bapu being in jail. I had been prepared for it for a long time, yet when it came it was a strange feeling, and do what one would, it kept the mind and nerves in a peculiar strain. One longed to court arrest and go to jail too, but Bapu had forbidden my entering the Satyagraha at that time, just as he had prohibited Reginald. So continuous work was the only consolation.

After some days, interviews were allowed on a limited scale, and I got permission to join a party of friends. The interview was held in the Superintendent's office, and Bapu was most particular not to say a word which would infringe the jail rules, or to remain a minute longer than the scheduled time. It was all so stiff and unnatural that one hardly felt as if one had seen Bapu.

A few days later there was a sudden cessation of letters. Anxious weeks went by. Why was the Government holding up correspondence? Was Bapu ill and were they afraid of letting the public know? Yet they would not dare keep that information hidden for long. Then what could be the matter? At last in June, letters again arrived:

> After many weeks I take up the pen to write Ashram letters again. . . . The way now seems to be fairly clear. . . .

As time went on I became rather restless in the Ashram and felt I should go out on an extensive khadi tour; not, of course, to collect funds—that was Bapu's prerogative—but to propagate improved methods of carding and spinning in the villages, and the purchase and wearing of khadi in the cities. Though I might not join in the Salt Satyagraha it was permissible for me to tour and speak for khadi, and the country was in the mood to listen. So I got in touch with the various Provinces and planned a route taking me through Bihar, then down to Madras and up along the east coast to Calcutta.

The only part of the tour which I can recollect clearly is the return journey up the east coast from Madras to Calcutta. By this time the temper of the police had become frayed, and they were following me all along the route.

I was being very careful to keep just on the safe side with my actions and speeches, because my standing instructions from Bapu were not to court arrest deliberately. But the enthusiasm of the public for anyone connected with Bapu lent a color to the tour which exasperated the authorities. Day by day their attentions grew more marked, and the friends with me were expecting my arrest at any moment.

As we were going along in the train toward Rajahmehendri we heard at previous stations that a very tough British police official was in charge there and we might as well expect trouble. Sure enough, a posse of police armed with lathis was lined up on the platform when we arrived, and no member of the public was to be seen. They had all been beaten up. As the train drew to a halt the police formed into two lines between which I had to step from the carriage and walk to the exit, and as soon as I emerged from the station they dashed out into the open yard, where a long row of charming little South Indian bullock carts was standing, and mercilessly beat up the poor bullocks, who fled with their carts here and there. The driver of the car which had been brought to meet me had been severely beaten to the point of being incapacitated, and I forget now how we actually reached the house where I was to stay for the night. On arrival there I noticed that the Provincial Secretary of the All-India Spinners' Association, a meek and mild little man, was not with us, and when I inquired about him, I was told that he had received a severe blow on the chest at the station and was feeling sick.

All meetings had been banned, and as I was not to court arrest, no public functions were held. However, we had a meeting of workers in the night at the house. The rumor went round that the place was going to be raided, and I am afraid my host and other local friends took no sleep. The police surrounded the house all night, but nothing happened.

We had arranged to start out by road very early in the morning, thinking we might get off before the police became active, but they were up and doing before daybreak, and a large lorryload of them, all bristling with lathis, set out ahead of us, while a carful of C.I.D. people followed us. These attentions were kept up till we passed out of their district. No doubt the tough British official felt he had made a fitting show of force.

What with the hot September weather, the restless nights and the hectic days, I had by now acquired a slight fever, but the east coast tour was over and I looked forward to a little respite at Calcutta. I had not taken into account the fact that the Calcutta Commissioner of Police was one of England's "strong men," or that the Bengalis were born revolutionaries who rose instinctively when touched by the "iron hand."

As the train steamed into Howrah station I heard shouts of "Mahatma Gandhi *ki jai!*" I was astonished, as I had not been told of any plans for a reception and was expecting only my host on the platform. I looked out of the window and saw a group of khadi-clad men and women holding garlands. They ran toward me but were held back by the police, and before I knew what was happening an Englishman jumped into the carriage, preventing me from getting out. He said he was the Deputy Commissioner of Police and handed me a notice forbidding me to join the Women's Procession which had come to receive me and take me through the city. "You see what the notice is," he said, "you will therefore kindly not join the procession." I replied that I could say nothing till I had met the organizers of the program, whom he was having held back on the platform, and would he please let them come in? "I warn you a lathi charge has been ordered if you try to join the procession," he replied, and jumped out of the door.

The group on the platform was now allowed to meet me. They rushed into the carriage, and in their excitement all talked at once as they smothered me with garlands. It took a little time to understand the exact situation. It appeared that the Women's Procession had been stopped on the farther side of Howrah Bridge, the boundary of Calcutta proper. The women, however, had not dispersed, and were standing waiting for me to come over. And this was what the Deputy Commissioner had warned me not to do or else there was going to be a lathi charge. It was a challenge, and my blood was roused. I felt sure that Bapu would not wish me to bow to such bullying and dampen the ardor of the people, so I said to the little group clustering around me, "Come on, let's cross the bridge."

"Yes, yes," they replied, "we have got a car waiting for you."

We went to the station yard. An excited crowd had gathered, and there was the car with policemen standing in front of it. Then one of the Bengali friends whispered in my ear that it seemed that the policemen's orders were to stop the car, and very likely if we proceeded on foot they would not obstruct us. So we started off, and the policemen, with their hard and fast instructions, remained firmly standing in front of the car. No sooner had we crossed the center of the bridge than the lathi charge was ordered. I was not struck, but everyone around was hit at. I could see the Women's Procession waiting for me at a little distance, and then right in the midst of all the excitement the Deputy Commissioner came up to me and said, "Where is the house where you are going to stay in Calcutta? You must go there in this taxi."

"Surely you don't expect me to co-operate with you like that!" I replied.

"Then I must take you to the police station. Get into the taxi, please."

I did not budge, so a policeman jerked me forward with a push in the small of the back and shoved me in through the door. The Deputy Commissioner got in beside me, and a policeman sat on the outside seat by the driver.

"Police station," shouted the Deputy Commissioner and off we went, with the policeman on the front seat leaning out and striking with his lathi at anyone within reach who took his fancy.

We arrived, and the Deputy Commissioner put me in a waiting room and went out. After a short while he returned and said, "The Commissioner has sent for you." He took me across the passage and showing me into the Commissioner's office, closed the door and went away. Sir Charles Tegart, who was sitting behind his desk, looked up sternly. I sat down on the chair opposite him.

"What was all this trouble in the city today?" he said.

"There would have been no trouble at all," I replied, "if it had not been for your police."

It was a fairly long talk, and finally Sir Charles said, "I will let you off with a warning this time, but you should not undertake breaking any more orders."

"That," I replied, "I cannot possibly do, as I cannot tell beforehand what circumstances may arise and what I shall feel called on to do."

He did not press the point, and when I got up to go, he rose and shook hands.

The taxi was still waiting when I came out, so I got into it and told the Sikh driver the address of my host. When I asked him the fare on arrival, he flatly refused to take any money. His heart was with the movement.

Having reached the house at last, I became conscious of the fever which had been on me all this time. My hosts took charge of me and made me lie down, but general excitement was seething all around, and people kept coming in with news.

It appeared that immediately after I had been taken away in the taxi, the Women's Procession had started out through the streets of Calcutta with the police surrounding them on all sides, and when they were passing by the University, some students had looked out of the windows and shouted remarks at the police, who were being rough with the women, with the result that the police rushed into the University building, up through the passages and into the common room, mercilessly beating any students they found. General excitement prevailed in the city and the markets were closed.

The next day the Vice-Chancellor of the University came and took me to see the blood stains on the walls of the passages and common room where the students had been beaten by the police. His indignation was extreme.

The rest of my stay in Calcutta went off comparatively smoothly. The atmosphere was tense, but no more disturbances took place. On completion of the tour I returned to Sabarmati Ashram.

All this time Bapu's letters came regularly from Yaravda Jail. In my own letters I described as much of my experiences as I could without infringing the rules, and to some extent succeeded in giving Bapu a picture of events. On September 9, 1930, he wrote:

I have your Calcutta letter. You are having a variety of experiences. Seekers after Truth turn every one of these to good account.

I had returned to Sabarmati somewhat worn out, but I felt too restless to stay long in the Ashram. I again went out on tour, this time to Sindh.

CHAPTER XXIX

ON January 24th, Bapu was suddenly released. Efforts had been going on all along by those out of jail to effect a compromise, but one could never guess the chances of success in advance.

Bapu went first to Bombay, and from there hurried to Allahabad on receiving alarming news regarding the health of Pandit Motilal Nehru, who had suffered considerably while in jail. As my Sindh tour was practically finished, I went straight there also.

Motilalji was India's outstanding politician and also a renowned lawyer. But not only that. His powerful character and personal charm had won him a unique place in the country's public life, and he was respected by Indians and Englishmen alike. Before throwing his lot in with Bapu he had been the acme of Western style and fashion, even outshining the British governors. But when he joined Bapu's movement in the political field he cast foreign cloth and fashion aside and donned pure khadi in Indian style, making of it something so smart that people's eyes were opened to new possibilities in Indian khadi dress.

Bapu had great respect for Motilalji's political insight and counted on his support in the very difficult period through which the country was now passing, which made the news of his serious condition all the more distressing.

The whole Nehru family had gathered at Anand Bhavan, the house which Motilalji had built for Jawaharlal, and Bapu with one or two others had already arrived. Pandit Motilal's health was rapidly deteriorating and within a few days it was decided to take him to Lucknow where deep X-ray treatment could be had. We were all put up in a big mansion there, but before Pandit Motilal could be taken to the hospital for treatment he died. There was no time for sorrowing or reflection as the body had to be cremated that very day, and at Allahabad. So back we went, following the hearse on which Jawaharlal sat—a lone figure.

It was already evening before the arrangements for the cremation could be completed. Then came the question of who should go in the funeral procession. Bapu said it would be best that he come later, as the crowds were already sufficiently unmanageable. At last the procession set forth for the burning ghat by the sacred confluence of the Ganga and Jamuna rivers. The crowds followed and Anand Bhavan became silent. We sat with Bapu in his room, waiting for the call which was to be sent when the procession reached the ghat. We waited and waited, and it was well into the night by the time a car was sent to take Bapu down. When we reached the ghat we found a vast multitude spreading over the sand, but it had been somewhat controlled and a way through was clear. The body had already been laid on the pyre and more wood was being heaped up over it, leaving only the head exposed. When Bapu arrived, sandalwood was handed to him which he gently laid around the face. Then more leaders piled on the sandalwood, till at last everything was covered. Now came showers of ghee and incense, and finally Jawaharlal was handed a burning torch with which to light the pile. Up went the flames into the night sky. Higher and higher they rose, and the multitude cried, "Pandit Motilal Nehru *ki jai!*" The heat of the flames was terrific, and there came a tense moment when the vast crowds, pressing forward, made the little open space by the pyre where we were standing smaller and smaller. It was only for a moment or two—frantic volunteers waved their hands, the crowds, realizing, eased off, and we could step back. Bapu and Pandit Malaviya made short speeches and after that Bapu came away.

But Jawaharlal's functions kept him till much later, and ended in the dead of night with a ceremonial bath in the holy river. Since the early hours of the morning, when his father died, to that midnight dip in the chilly waters, he had been under an unbroken and intense strain, and it was not to be wondered at that the next morning he went all to pieces with cold, fever and exhaustion, both physical and emotional.

Those were not days, however, when anyone could have any

119

rest. The Viceroy had begun putting out peace feelers, and by March 17th Bapu was invited for talks—those Gandhi-Irwin talks which rankled in the hearts of British die-hards, when a viceroy actually parleyed on equal terms with an Indian rebel for the achievement of an honorable truce. This meant that the whole Congress Working Committee had to gather at Delhi so that they could be in continual touch with Bapu. But it was a Working Committee without Motilalji just at the moment when Bapu most deeply felt the absence of his help and advice.

We stayed with Dr. Ansari at his house in Daryagunj looking over the Jamuna River, and it was turned into a veritable caravansary during the twenty days that we were there. But Dr. Ansari, himself a member of the Working Committee, remained calm, courteous, and smiling throughout. I don't think I ever saw him outwardly ruffled. Bapu had a great and affectionate regard for him, both as a Moslem co-fighter for freedom and as a doctor, while Dr. Ansari, on his part, loved Bapu tenderly.

Lord Irwin (later Lord Halifax) had a deep appreciation of Bapu, and that was what had led him to try for a compromise with the hope that it would ultimately enable Bapu to attend the Round Table Conference in London. Bapu himself realized that in Lord Irwin he had quite an unusual kind of viceroy, and so entered on the talks with some degree of expectation. But it was a tremendous strain on Bapu. Every day he would go to Viceroy's House and carry on the long discussions single-handed; then, instead of resting on his return to Daryagunj, he would find the whole Congress Working Committee anxiously waiting to know exactly what had happened, and he would sit down and report everything in detail. The reporting, in fact, was the least part of it. It was the explaining of the why and wherefore regarding every point gained or yielded during the Viceregal discussions that took so much time and nervous energy. Everyone was in a state of tension. Some would think that Bapu was being too hard in his bargaining, and others would think that he should be less bending. Hours of heated discussion would sometimes ensue. How Bapu was able to stand it all was a marvel.

Besides the Working Committee members there were the three

stalwarts of the Constitutional Method who came and went in between whiles—Sir Tej Bahadur Sapru, Pandit Srinivas Shastri and Dr. M. R. Jayaker. They all three had sincere regard for Bapu, but it was outside their nature to go in for direct action. They were, however, extremely anxious to do anything they could to help toward the desired compromise. Bapu appreciated their sincerity of opinion and having, as he did, great respect for their knowledge and experience, he always gave them a patient hearing whenever they came with suggestions or news of some discussion they had themselves had with the Viceroy.

I well remember one evening when Bapu's talks with Lord Irwin were on the point of breaking off. Bapu got to bed very late and fully expected that the morrow would bring the whole thing to a blank end. Though the weather was still cold, he used to sleep on the veranda overlooking the Jamuna, and I would sleep at a little distance with one eye and one ear open, in case anyone should come and disturb him. On that particular night, after Bapu had gone to sleep and I was just dozing off, I suddenly heard cautious footsteps. I jumped up and dimly saw three dark figures wrapped up in overcoats and mufflers. For a moment I thought of C.I.D. officers coming to arrest Bapu, and then I realized that they were the three constitutional stalwarts. I hurried to them, and they whispered to me that they had come direct from a very important talk with the Viceroy and wanted to report to Bapu and get his immediate reactions. This meant Bapu would have to be awakened, so I went and gently spoke to him. He woke up looking puzzled and I explained what had happened, pointing to the three dark figures standing a little way off. Bapu at once sat up in bed and greeted them. Then turning to me he said, "Bring chairs." An earnest discussion ensued, after which the three figures departed through the shadows as they had come, and Bapu in no time went fast asleep again.

The break which had been expected was averted, and the negotiations continued. On one occasion, when the afternoon discussions had been much prolonged, a message came for me to take Bapu's food to him at Viceroy's House. In those days Bapu's diet was chiefly dates and milk, while the vessels in which this food was served were ordinary jail utensils which he had obtained as a memento when he left Yaravda Jail. I hurriedly put these things together in a basket and proceeded to Viceroy's House. An ADC received me at the porch and asked me to wait. He then went to the double door of the Viceroy's study and, cautiously knocking, slipped in to report my arrival. In half a minute he came back and said I was to take in the food. I was discreetly passed through the double doors and found myself in a handsome study, with the Viceroy sitting in an armchair on one side of the fire, Bapu on a sofa facing the fire, and the Home Secretary, Mr. Emerson, with pencil and paper in hand, taking notes. Bapu introduced me, and Lord Irwin, rising, shook hands with perfect friendliness. Then I looked around for some corner where I could prepare the food. The tables were, of course, all exquisitely polished, and there was a magnificent thick-pile carpet on the floor. Luckily it was not fitted right up to the walls, but left a marble edging exposed, and I caught sight of an empty corner where I could safely open up the basket. The jail utensil in which Bapu used to take his milk and dates was a tall kind of tankard minus any handle. Into this I put the dates, poured the hot milk over them, and handed the vessel to Bapu along with a spoon.

The Viceroy was watching with interest, and when Bapu began scooping out the dates with his spoon, Lord Irwin inquired what it was he was eating. "The Prophet's food," said Bapu with a smile, and the Viceroy got up and peeped into the pot to see what he meant. "And this is my jail pot," added Bapu, proudly tapping his tankard with his spoon.

Bapu now suggested that in order to save time they should go on with their talk while he took his meal, and then inquired whether I should leave the room or not. Lord Irwin said there was no objection to my staying, and I sat down at the other end of Bapu's sofa till he had finished his food. The stage had been reached for the drafting of the Pact, and one point after another was being put in writing. Bapu dictated in the same simple way that he used to dictate to Mahadev, while Mr. Emerson took it down. At one point the Viceroy interrupted with a suggestion, and Bapu incorporated it in what he was dictating.

"You are a remarkably good draftsman, Mr. Gandhi," observed Mr. Emerson, scribbling away with his pencil.

"I have that reputation," replied Bapu quietly.

By now the dates and milk were finished, so I took the vessel, packed up the basket, and saying goodbye to the Viceroy, departed.

CHAPTER XXX

WHILE the great political drama was in progress, a quiet and earnest romance was going on behind the scene. Bapu's youngest son, Devadas, and Rajaji's little daughter Lakshmi, were deeply in love with one another, but the two fathers had disapproved of immediate marriage. It was an intercaste attachment between Gujerati Vaishya and Madrasi Brahmin, and it was better to test the constancy of affections and compatibility of temperaments, so the stern parents—Rajaji was there as a member of the Working Committee—had set a probationary period of five years. Ba, with her old-style orthodoxy still strong in her veins, looked with considerable misgivings on the match, but her great devotion to Devadas, and his to her, softened her heart.

The two young people had unhesitatingly decided to face the five-year testing, and Devadas wanted to have one quiet talk with Lakshmi before she left with her father for Madras. As he knew Ba would not approve of their being left alone together, he hit on the plan for them to sit in Bapu's empty veranda while the discussions were on at Viceroy's House, and he asked me to remain nearby in the adjoining room, with the door open. Ba gave her approval to this arrangement, and the young lovers came and sat down facing one another with their backs against the pillars of one of the veranda arches. To this day I can see them, so fresh and earnest. Beyond them were the trees, beyond the trees was the Jamuna River and the infinite blue sky, while beyond them in time

—though we did not know it then—was a life of exquisite family happiness.

At last the discussions with the Viceroy drew to a close, and the Pact was signed on March 4th. Open-air meetings were then held to inform the public, but the crowds were so great, and so wildly excited, that Bapu's voice was drowned in the cries of "Mahatma Gandhi *ki jai—jai!!—jai!!!*" He had to leave the meeting without being able to tell the public what they had wanted to hear. Really it was to see him that they had thirsted most of all, and that they had done. However, Bapu was determined to speak to the masses once, and so another meeting was arranged two days later. This time some degree of silent attention was achieved, and on the 8th Bapu left Delhi. However, we were back again by the 19th on our way to the Karachi Congress.

Just at that juncture feelings in the country were running very high because of the condemnation to death of a revolutionary of the violent school, Sardar Bhagat Singh. During the two or three days in Delhi, Bapu did his utmost to obtain a reprieve, and though the Viceroy could give him no definite assurance, still Bapu hoped and believed the remission would be granted, especially as the execution at such a moment would greatly intensify the anti-British feelings of the public. We had just taken our places in the special train which was to convey the whole Congress party to Karachi when Bapu was brought the news that Bhagat Singh, along with two of his companions, had been hanged that very morning in the Lahore Jail. Bapu felt deeply shocked. As the news spread among the crowd on the platform, indignant and angry words could be heard on all sides. The public had been enthusiastic over the Gandhi-Irwin Pact, and it seemed that they had got it into their heads that if Bapu could bring off a pact like that, it must have been possible for him to prevent these executions too if he had really wanted to. Bapu had patiently to listen to the hostile shouts and angry questions, for no one was in a mood to stop for a reply. Only the departure of the train brought relief. Being a special, it fortunately did not stop at many places, but wherever it did halt there were angry and excited crowds waiting.

The halt I shall never forget was the one at Sukkur. It was in the middle of the night. A big students' demonstration was waiting ready on the platform with a bust of Bhagat Singh. The students rushed up and down looking for the compartment in which Bapu was traveling, and as soon as they discovered it they all ran, carrying with them the bust, which they placed in front of Bapu's window and garlanded with flowers. Then they made a veritable assault on the compartment, doing their best to burst in through the doors. Besides Bapu and Ba, we were a party of about four. The men held the doors, which seemed about to give way any moment, and I was keeping guard at the windows, when suddenly a student, with his hands all bleeding, burst in through the lavatory door. He had smashed the lavatory window glass and squeezed himself through. I dashed into the closet, to find another student with his head already through the hole in the window, and more students waiting outside to follow him. There was no time to stop and think about methods. I seized him by the hair and shoving my thumb into his neck on the windpipe, managed to bring him to a halt. The madness of the assault slightly lessened, and the student inside tried to have his say, which gave the ones outside a feeling that they were being listened to, though of course no one could hear a word that anyone said. Bapu sat motionless and silent throughout, with his hands folded in salutation. We all thanked God when the train moved out of the station.

But the trouble was not over, for when we reached Karachi in the morning, there was a black-flag demonstration, and the demonstrators pushed forward with flowers made of black cloth to give to Bapu. People were nervous lest things might become violent, and wanted to hold back the black procession, but Bapu said, "No, let them come." And he received them so sweetly, smilingly accepting their black flowers and their angry shouts, that their indignation completely subsided and they automatically formed themselves into volunteers helping to protect Bapu from the crush of the general public.

The Congress Camp was a huge affair, and the awakened spirit of the people was very marked. The resolutions took on a still more confident tone and expressed not only the determination to win independence, but put before the world the Congress conception of democratic rights for India. Another important announcement was that Bapu should be the sole Congress representative at the Round Table Conference. Bapu himself took a vow not to live in Sabarmati Ashram again till he had won India's independence, and that made one realize it was now a fight to the finish without respite.

Right in the middle of all this excitement I began to suspect that something was quite wrong with my health. My temperature was rising and there was some itching on the back. I spoke to Mahadev, and he said, "Let's consult Rajaji, he is the most knowledgeable one of us in these matters." And he then and there went off to tell him. Rajaji came and, lifting up his dark glasses to peer at my back, said without hesitation that I was sickening for chickenpox. A doctor was called and he confirmed Rajaji's diagnosis. Of course I had to be segregated without a moment's delay, and with Bapu's approval I was removed to the fever hospital.

CHAPTER XXXI

AS soon as I was out of quarantine I joined Bapu, who was then in Bombay. The Government was not playing its part with regard to the Pact, especially in the Bardoli and Borsad areas of Gujerat, where the local officials seemed to be thirsting to get even with the population for the spirited part it had played in the recent Satyagraha. So Bapu went to stay some time at Bardoli and some time at Borsad in order to give comfort and courage to the people, and at the same time to investigate the charges and countercharges between the Government officials and the public. Meanwhile correspondence was going on with the new Viceroy, Lord Willingdon, regarding the question of Bapu attending the London Round Table Conference. If the Government did not honor the Pact, it would be impossible for him to go. That was the stumbling block.

I do not remember any particular details till our stay in Borsad.

It was by then June, the most trying time climatically of all the year. I felt that Bapu was getting fidgety about my being with him, and that he would like me to go to Sabarmati Ashram. He often got annoyed with me over quite trifling matters, and one day when he was really upset I made up my mind to go even without his telling me to do so. When I made the suggestion he accepted it, and I departed.

A letter from Bapu quickly followed:

> You are on the brain. I look about me, and miss you. I open the *charkha* and miss you. So on and so forth. But what is the use? You have done the right thing. You have left your home, your people and all that people prize most, not to serve me personally but to serve the cause I stand for. All the time you were squandering your love on me personally, I felt guilty of misappropriation. And I exploded on the slightest pretext. Now that you are not with me, my anger turns itself upon me for having given you all those terrible scoldings. But I was on a bed of hot ashes all the while I was accepting your service. You will truly serve me by joyously serving the cause. "Cheer boys, cheer, no more of idle sorrow."

(24-6-31)

Those were hard days at the Ashram without Bapu, and with bad news from England about Mother's health. I had been counting on seeing her when we went to London, as Bapu seemed to be planning to take me with him if he went. But now it was clear that her health was fast failing, and within a few days a cable came saying that she had passed away. I poured out my heart in a letter to Bapu. He replied:

> So Mother is gone. I read your suppressed grief in every line of your letter. After all, we are very human. The ability to suppress is the preliminary to eradication. God give you the strength. . . .

Ever since leaving England I had written to Mother without fail by the weekly P & O mail, and she, until the last days of her illness, had sent me long letters each week. Her death created a void which time alone could fill in.

127

Bapu's tussle with the Government went on and on. Lord Irwin having been replaced by Lord Willingdon made things much more difficult. It was already the middle of July, and if Bapu was to attend the Round Table Conference he should sail by the latest in the middle of August. He was called to Simla for discussions and wrote to me from there that there were "many difficulties and many hitches." Nothing definite was achieved at Simla, and Bapu returned to the trouble spot in Gujerat.

All this time I was at Sabarmati Ashram, living in my little room on the high bank of the river. The place felt very forlorn without Bapu, who would never live there again till independence was achieved. It made one long to be out and doing.

But a little friend came to my room to cheer me up. He was a myna (Indian starling). After he had looked in at my door several times, I persuaded him to come right in and pick up *kishmish* (currants) which I threw on the floor for him. Next I held out the *kishmish* in my fingers, and before long he took them quite bravely. Then one day when he flew into the room he chose to land on my head. I immediately handed him up some *kishmish,* and from that day I insisted that he should sit on my head if he wanted to be fed. He at once caught on to the idea, and several times a day would fly in through the door and perch on my head, where he would bob up and down twittering away until I attended to him. After this had gone on for some time he turned up one morning with another little myna, evidently his wife. He did not fly onto my head but stood in front of me on the floor where I was sitting, and introduced her. She was very shy and stepped back when I offered her *kishmish*. However, she henceforth came every day with her husband, and soon ventured to take the fruit from my fingers. Though he sat on my head as usual each time, she never dared attempt this, though I tried to persuade her. I now noticed that they no longer ate the *kishmish* themselves but, collecting them in their beaks, would fly off across the garden. This went on regularly for some time, and then one morning they appeared with three little youngsters, and all five of them stood around in a semicircle on the floor in front of me demanding *"kishmish, kish-*

mish!" They were still coming regularly to my room when I left the Ashram to rejoin Bapu at Borsad.

It was by now August, and the very last P & O steamer by which Bapu could reach London in time for the Conference was due to sail on the 29th. In a final effort to obtain satisfaction from the Government Bapu went again to Simla on the 24th, accompanied by Mahadev and Devadas, while Pyarelal and I held ourselves in readiness at Borsad for the telegram which Bapu would send if an agreement was reached. Practically no preparations had been made, nor had any passports been got ready. But Bapu had definitely decided who should accompany him, and it was to be Mahadev, Pyarelal, Devadas and myself.

On August 27th the telegram arrived from Simla saying we were to sail from Bombay on the 29th. I caught the first available train, and Pyarelal said he would follow a little later. He seemed to be in one of his dreams. Bombay was in a great state of excitement, and many friends rushed to help me. The passports and tickets were the first vital things. The passport office had already been alerted from Simla, and so made no difficulties, and Bapu had wired for booking of five lowest-class berths to one of the friends who had come to my help. He told me second-class was the lowest obtainable, and took me onto the steamer to see the accommodation, which proved satisfactory.

Now for the clothes, trunks, etc. We rushed around to all sorts of shops, and by closing time we had collected everything, and rather more than everything, as friends insisted on various things being procured which I felt Bapu would not wish for. When we returned with our carload of stuff to Mani Bhuvan, the house where Bapu always stayed in Bombay, I found that during the day a lot of gifts had been brought for Bapu, such as stockings, socks, shawls, mufflers, bags and wallets, while Pyarelal, who had arrived, had, on his own, collected various gifts and loans from friends for Mahadev, Devadas and himself. It seemed we were going to have a good deal of superfluous stuff which Bapu would never tolerate, but what to do? All night I sorted, packed and finally labeled everything, and in the early hours lay down on the

129

boxes and beddings for a short while without sleeping, for a truck was coming soon to take the luggage to the docks.

Now Bapu arrived, having just caught the mail train by being sent in a special car from Simla to Kalka, and the house became filled with excited people. I made the bath ready for Bapu, and then, to my astonishment, I found that Mahadev and Devadas had brought along a lot more things, all packed in smart leather suitcases. Dr. Ansari had handed over to them his whole outfit which he had had last time he went to Europe. How could we leave this behind? And there was no time left for opening up what I had already closed, in order to remove duplicates. So we just labeled everything.

Bapu came out from his bath, and it was time to serve his food. But the room had become so packed with people that I had the greatest difficulty in getting across to where he was sitting.

By the time Bapu was ready and had been able to extricate himself from the crowds in the house it was the sailing hour for the P & O, but they held the ship back for Bapu's arrival. Somehow we got on board, Bapu being almost lifted off his legs by the enthusiastic people helping him up the gangway. Sarojini Naidu and Pandit Malaviya were already on deck, as they were both delegates to the Round Table Conference in various capacities. Quite a number of other important persons were also passengers, and besides all these, the deck was crowded with Congress leaders and others who had come to bid farewell. Sardar Vallabhbhai Patel, the Congress President, had a last-minute consultation with Bapu, for the situation in the country was tricky and it was an anxious job to be left in charge of the national movement. Then came the goodbyes, and most touching and simple was the parting with Ba. She realized that the rush and tear of the trip would have been too much for her, and did not complain about being left behind, but it was hard to think of Bapu going away across the seas.

The P & O authorities had a job to get the decks cleared of the visitors. When they at last succeeded, the ship drew away, and then the crowds on the quay ran waving to the farthest point they could reach, from where they stood and watched her steam out toward the open sea.

CHAPTER XXXII

NOW, what a change! Suddenly the crowds were gone, the headlong rush was over, and we could relax. Many letters and telegrams of good wishes had come to the ship for Bapu, and he sat down on his bunk to read them. One was from the Viceroy. He went through it with a serious face, and then handed it to Mahadev, saying that it read well and appeared friendly enough, but one had to remember this was not Lord Irwin. "If it had been, I should have felt differently about it," he added. This little incident brought home to one the depths of Bapu's misgivings about the London Conference and the precarious truce in India.

In August the Arabian Sea is not at its best, and before long the ship began rolling. Who was, and who was not, a good sailor very soon became apparent. Bapu was out and away the best, Mahadev came next, then Devadas, then myself, and poor Pyarelal last of all. Bapu went around and looked into our various cabins, and in so doing his eye fell on the boxes and suitcases tucked away under every bunk and in every corner. "What's all this?" he asked, and we began explaining and pleading, the haste, the confusion, the difficulty of refusing gifts, and so on. But Bapu would listen to no excuses. "If you want to travel with such luggage you should be with those who live like that, but here you are with me, and I am going to England as representative of a poor country. What do we want with all these things? And then look at these swanky leather suitcases—people would be shocked to see them. It's no good pleading that they are lent, naturally you will return them when we get back, but you should never have brought them." Then his eye fell on a folding camp bed of American make, which some enthusiastic friend had presented for him to use on deck. We explained as best we could, for we had become fairly rattled by then. "Oh," said Bapu with scathing sarcasm, "is that a camp bed? I thought it was a bundle of hockey sticks."

The end of it was that we promised to make out a list of things to be sent back to Bombay from Aden. So seasickness or no seasickness, we four got together first in one cabin and then in another, unpacked *everything,* made a complete list, and then sorted out as much as we hoped we could persuade Bapu to let us keep, and packed the rest in those swanky suitcases and the smartest trunks, to be sent back from Aden—a matter of seven pieces in all. Bapu accepted our list without further questioning, but the shadow of his indignation was still visible.

There was a public meeting at Aden in an atmosphere of great excitement. Then at Suez and Port Said, the Egyptian leaders sent warmest greetings and expressed the hope that Bapu would visit their country on the return voyage.

As we steamed out into the Mediterranean the air became deliciously fresh. Except for Bapu and myself, none of the other members of our party had even seen Europe, and they gazed with delight on the beautiful island of Crete. We were fortunate enough to pass through both the Straits of Messina and the Straits of Bonifacio in daylight, and as the weather was perfect, we had a glorious view. As we had to reach London by the quickest possible route, we were to land at Marseille and travel straight through via Paris to London.

Originally there had been some hope of visiting Romain Rolland on the way to England, but it was now out of the question. My heart and mind were fixed on the thought of that meeting, and this delay filled me with anxiety lest some unforeseen obstacle come in the way on our return journey. When we reached Marseille there was such a headlong rush of European journalists that the friends, known and unknown, who had come to greet Bapu were almost overwhelmed. Nevertheless, the very first person who managed to greet Bapu was Madeleine Rolland, and with her were Professor and Madame Edmond Privat, staunch and enthusiastic devotees of Bapu's ideals. We were told that Romain Rolland himself had planned to come, but that his delicate health had prevented him at the last moment, and one could only be thankful that he had not attempted it, for the noise and crush would have been very bad for his sensitive constitution.

The Paris train was waiting, and there was no time to linger with friends. As we set off northward through France we all began to feel the change in temperature and started putting on warm garments, but Bapu only wrapped himself up in his shawl, for he had made up his mind to make no change whatever in his dress.

At the Paris station there was again a large and excited crowd. Someone came in great agitation to say a beautiful white goat had been brought to supply fresh milk, and the police had refused to allow it on the platform, but again the noise and rush were so great that one could neither hear nor answer anyone properly. I wished the goat could have been brought, but it was no use attempting to do anything about it.

At last came the Channel crossing and the arrival on English soil. We felt at once the power of the "Raj." We were no longer free agents. Rules and taboos were in the air, all very polite and courteous, but *there* all right. Here was the first one: Bapu was to go by car to London, and the rest of us by train. Bapu would have rather gone by train, but no, this was the Government arrangement, and we got the hint from Charlie Andrews, who had come to meet us, that the official world wanted to avoid any public welcome, which they could not in any decency have prevented if Bapu had arrived at a given time by train. So Bapu along with the persons chosen by the Government went off by car, and we four, feeling thoroughly disgruntled, took the train.

Crowds of hopeful people had gathered at Victoria Station in spite of the rain which was pouring down, and it was so horrid to have to explain that Bapu had come by road. I cannot remember the exact sequence of events, but I think there was first a reception at Friends' House, the Quaker center, and then the drive to the East End, where Muriel Lester was waiting to receive us with open arms at her Kingsley Hall. She had been Bapu's guest at Sabarmati Ashram previously, and now she was going to be his host at her own center among the poor at Bow.

The official chilly correctness had been cast off by the warmth of the meeting at Friends' House, and here, in the midst of the workingmen, women and children, all formality was forgotten.

A row of tiny little rooms on the roof of Kingsley Hall had been put at our disposal, and this gave us quiet, independent quarters with an open view, over the forest of chimney tops, of the low houses which are so characteristic of East London. Of course, it was smoky, but the consolation of the open sky made it worth while. Next to the room given to Bapu was a tiny pantry with a gas range, where I was able to do his cooking, and next to that was a little bathroom. We settled into our respective cubicles, and mine was at the farther end, at right angles to the rest, which was convenient as I could see along the roof and know when anyone came or went.

Bapu had not a day of rest from the moment he arrived. The Conference, if I remember rightly, was just about to begin or had actually begun, and besides that, there were important discussions to be had individually with all the leading personalities connected with the Conference. As Bow was eight miles from the West End, where everyone else was staying and where the Conference was being held in St. James's Palace, it very soon became evident that Bapu would have to have some quarters in the West End also. He was determined not to give up his contact with Bow, so a compromise was hit on. A house was rented in Knightsbridge where he could meet people in between the Conference sittings, and where he could take his midday and evening meals. As a matter of fact, the midday meal often had to be taken in a basket to St. James's Palace, where he used to slip out from the Conference into a small side office room to snatch some food. But for sleeping at night he always returned to Kingsley Hall.

The Knightsbridge house quickly turned into a full-blown establishment. Mahadev, Pyarelal and Devadas all took up residence there, and two friends came daily to assist in the rush of work. And it was a rush! Piles of letters poured in by every post, the telephone rang without ceasing, and visitors of all sorts kept coming and going.

Agatha Harrison also did everything she could to help, for she had become a sort of nonofficial ambassador in London for na-

134

tionalist India's interests. Tall, with a thin pale face, she was an Englishwoman of untiring energy, and was at the same time tactful and patient in the way she handled the many behind-the-scenes contacts that were given her to deal with. Practically every day she came to the Knightsbridge house.

This double establishment made my job decidedly complicated. I had to heat Bapu's bath water and provide his breakfast at Kingsley Hall, then see Bapu off promptly at 8 o'clock, when the Government car arrived each morning to fetch him. After that, I swept the rooms and roof, made up a bundle of clothes for washing, fetched provisions from the neighboring market, cooked Bapu's midday meal, packed it up and hurried off to Knightsbridge by the underground railway with the bundle of clothes in one hand and the food basket in the other. The very first job on arrival at the house was to wash the clothes so that they might get dry by evening. If Bapu came back from the Conference, I would serve him the meal there, otherwise hand the basket over to Pyarelal or Devadas, who would take it along to St. James's Palace. The evening meal I used to prepare at Knightsbridge, and the last thing, often eight or nine o'clock, I would return by underground to Bow and await Bapu's return, which was usually between eleven and twelve o'clock, and sometimes after midnight on account of the long political conferences that used to take place in the evenings.

Not long after our arrival in England the official "summertime" came to an end, and all the clocks and watches in the United Kingdom were readjusted. But not so Bapu's watch. He flatly refused to change it, saying it was not good for watches to keep changing them. We all pleaded with him.

"How can you keep your engagements properly?" said Mahadev. "You may sometimes forget that your watch is one hour ahead."

"No fear," replied Bapu, "I shall manage my timing all right."

"But Bapu," I pleaded, "this will mean that if the morning Prayer is to take place according to your watch, it will be at 3 A.M.!"

135

"What does that matter?" Bapu answered, quite unmoved. "I can go to sleep again afterwards."

It was hopeless, and we had to give it up. The others were not really affected by the change as they all slept at Knightsbridge, but for me it meant a real ordeal. Now it was going to be a case of getting up and down all night.

Here is a picture of a typical night after the new timing had started. Bapu arrives tired out at 11 :30 P.M. I receive the spinning wheel and case of papers from the detective who accompanies him to the top of the stairs, and as soon as Bapu lies down I rub his feet hard to try to bring some warmth into them. He falls asleep within a few minutes and I go off to my room, where I carefully set my alarm clock for 2 :50 A.M. At 3 A.M. sharp I awaken Bapu and by 3 :15 we sit together for the morning Prayer. By a quarter to four he lies down to sleep again, and returning to my room I set my alarm clock this time for 4 :45, when I get up again and prepare Bapu's drink of hot water, honey and lemon, after taking which he goes for a walk along the dimly lighted streets of Bow. We are accompanied by Muriel Lester and one or two members of the Kingsley Hall staff. By the time we return, the dawn is showing in the sky.

There was never a better night than that, and some were decidedly worse, like the one when Bapu came home at 2 A.M. after a visit to Lloyd George at his country home. That night I put my alarm clock against my ear when I lay down. Otherwise there was no hope of getting up at 2 :50 A.M. In the daytime, of course, there was never any time to sleep, and the result was that if I happened to sit down to listen to a discussion or attend a meeting, I had the greatest possible difficulty keeping awake.

CHAPTER XXXIII

THE Conference did not convene on Saturday afternoons and Sundays, so this breathing space was utilized for visits to Oxford, Cambridge, Eton, the Quaker center at Birmingham, Canterbury, Chichester and Lancashire. The train journeys were a perfect boon for Bapu and also for me, as we both used to sleep deeply from the moment we left London until we arrived at our destination. Another time when Bapu used to snatch sleep was while going back and forth in the official car between Bow and the West End. It was an understood thing that he should sleep during those drives, and if those naps had been denied him, it is doubtful if he could have pulled through.

Besides the visits to the Provinces, there were a number of social engagements in London, such as a lunch given by the Vegetarian Society at which Bapu actually drank cider on being told that it was pure apple juice with a negligible alcoholic content, and the Pressmen's lunch, for which they procured mangoes for Bapu, a very rare fruit in England in those days. The biggest social function was, of course, the Garden Party at Buckingham Palace, to which all the Round Table Conference delegates were invited. The kinds of dress in which people could appear before the King and Queen had always been strictly regulated, and Bapu's bare legs and sandal-shod feet did not come within the scope of any permissible attire. This was a problem for the controllers of court etiquette. Tentative feelers were put out, but when it was fully realized that Bapu would not change his style of clothes for any king on earth, and that insistence would result in Bapu's refusal to attend the Garden Party, the question was dropped just as quietly and discreetly as it had been mooted.

Along with Bapu were to go Sarojini Naidu and Mahadev. The

former donned for the occasion an exquisitely embroidered white silk sari, and the latter, spotless white khadi in Indian style. They foregathered in the drawing room at Knightsbridge, where we all admired them with much laughter and joking. But it was almost time to start, and Bapu was still in the bathroom. We looked at one another anxiously. Surely Bapu was not going to be late on such an occasion! Just at that moment he walked in at the door with a broad smile on his face.

Bapu had only one big white double pashmina shawl which, being in continual use, I had not had a chance to wash, and I was anxious at least to turn it in order that the clean side should be outermost. So the moment he entered the room I said, "Bapu, let me turn your shawl."

"Oh, I have already done it," said Bapu proudly, showing off the clean soft folds of his pashmina, and joining in the general laughter.

It was exactly time to start, and off they went, punctual to the minute.

No one could have guessed the pain Bapu had felt at having to decide to accept this regulation invitation in which there was no heart, only artificial outward show. He looked upon it as a moral duty in his position of guest of the British Government, and once having decided to go he could be perfectly merry about the little details.

In spite of all the social functions and group meetings, Bapu was not getting in touch with the masses, and I felt very badly about it. Mahadev was feeling it too, and we talked the matter over.

I said to him, "Why don't we hire the Albert Hall and have a huge public meeting? I have done it with the Queen's Hall for concerts in the past, and I know the ropes."

"Yes, that would be splendid," he replied.

Yet the moment we began to talk about it to others, we found there was hidden but relentless opposition. English friends who were in touch with the authorities hinted to Bapu that he was a guest of the British Government and it would be thought unbecoming to do anything which might embarrass them. As this argument directly touched Bapu's sense of honor, the idea had to be dropped. There is not the shadow of a doubt that, had Bapu been able to hold public meetings, he would have aroused tremendous interest and sympathy among the working classes. The visit to Lancashire made this abundantly clear.

Even the idea of the Lancashire visit was not particularly popular with the Government, and suggestions were thrown out that it might be hardly safe for Bapu to go there, seeing that his boycott of foreign cloth had so seriously affected the mills. As a matter of fact, I think the Government was genuinely alarmed, and elaborate security measures were ordered. They realized full well that if anything should happen to Bapu while he was in England, the reactions in India would be disastrous.

It was for this very reason that wherever Bapu went he was accompanied by two of England's top detectives—burly fellows with charming manners and dressed in smart plain clothes which undoubtedly contained revolvers in the pockets. Probably they had never before protected any celebrity who kept such hours, home at midnight and off again every morning punctually at 8 A.M. But they were always on time and always smiling.

When we started out for Lancashire they were very much on the alert. As usual on our train journeys the second-class compartments were reserved for the party. Into one of these the detectives ushered Bapu and myself, pulled down the blinds, closed the doors and kept guard outside, knowing that sleep was the one thing we both needed. No sooner had Bapu stretched himself out on one of the long seats than he was asleep, and it did not take me long to follow suit. As the train drew into the first Lancashire station I heard noise and excitement on the platform, and drawing up the blinds saw crowds of people looking up and down the train. Mahadev and the others came in from their adjoining compartment and Bapu sat up. The people outside caught sight of him.

"There 'e is, look, look! There 'e is, Mr. Gandeye!" And they rushed to the window.

" 'Ow d'you do, Mr. Gandeye?"

" 'Ow are you, Mr. Gandeye? Glad to see you."

And so on, all very friendly. Bapu smiled at them affectionately through the window, but it was a short halt, and on we went. Now

139

everywhere it was the same thing, and at the station where we alighted there was much excitement. Then as we drove along in cars we found crowds of people collected at crossroads and turnings, and especially in village streets. Men waved their caps and women their handkerchiefs.

"What is this!" exclaimed one of the detectives, next to whom I was sitting in the front seat. "I haven't seen the people turn out here like this even for royalty."

The program was for Bapu to visit several places and have talks with various groups of workers and employers, and, of course, there were to be no public meetings. But restrictions or no, practically mass contact was made with the crowds who poured out everywhere. Then at the group meetings there was a lot of heart-to-heart exchange of ideas.

The burning question in everyone's mind naturally was the Indian boycott of English cloth. Bapu's answer was:

"As a nation we are pledged to boycott all foreign cloth, but in case of an honorable settlement between England and India, i.e., in case of a permanent peace, I should not hesitate to give preference to Lancashire cloth to all other foreign cloth, to the extent that we may need to supplement our cloth and on agreed terms. But how much relief that can give you, I do not know. . . . I am pained," he added, "at the unemployment here. But here is no starvation or semistarvation. In India we have both. . . . I wish well to you, but do not think of prospering on the tombs of the poor millions of India. I do not want for India an isolated life at all, but I do not want to depend on any country for my food and clothing."

These talks went straight to the hearts of his listeners, and afterwards one could hear people remarking:

"We understand each other now. It is a privilege to have seen Mr. Gandhi."

"I am one of the unemployed, but if I was in India I would say the same thing that Mr. Gandhi is saying."

One of the most remarkable episodes was at a mill where Bapu was shown around by the manager, who, at the end of the inspec-

140

tion, asked Bapu if he might have the leave bell rung so that the mill hands, mostly women, might come out and meet Bapu.

"Of course, by all means," Bapu said, and the bell was rung.

Immediately the machinery stopped and the building was filled with the sound of running feet. Across the rooms, along the passages, down the stairs they went, patter patter patter, and by the time we ourselves got outside, there was a large crowd of workers waiting. Bapu said a few words, then two of the women workers suddenly hooked him by the arms, one on each side, and throwing up their unengaged arms shouted, "Three cheers for Mr. Gandeye, hip, hip—"

"Hurrah!" shouted the whole crowd, and then again, and once more, for the third and loudest time.

Outside the friends' little house where we put up for the night there were elaborate security precautions, and there seemed to be a policeman behind every bush, unsuccessfully trying to hide his sturdy form. Friendly people kept coming and going, and a number of women brought their babies and pushed them into Bapu's arms.

In Lancashire, owing to the continual contact with the populace, I was able to keep awake and follow what was going on around me. But when it came to learned discussions at Oxford and Cambridge and meetings with church dignitaries, I found myself dozing off whenever I had the opportunity to listen, and soon gave up the attempt. A few pictures, however, remain in my mind. Bapu walking with the Bishop of Chichester in the Palace gardens —it would have been a perfect subject for an artist. Bapu attending an afternoon service in Canterbury Cathedral, and in the evening of the same day Bapu sitting spinning on the hearthrug in the Deanery drawing room with the Dean, Hewlett Johnson, down on the ground watching closely.

On one of the motor drives we took to various places, I can't remember which, we went through Dorking, and past the entrance to Milton Heath. I longed to peep in, if only for half an hour, and show the place of my childhood to Bapu, but there was no time. As we flashed by the front gate I could just catch a glimpse of the drive, the fields where the Jersey cows used to graze, and the old elm trees with the rookery, and then it was all gone again, like a dream. Like a dream—indeed it was all exactly like a dream. In the six years that had passed since leaving England everything had completely changed. Mother and Father had both passed away, and Rhona was again in India with her husband. But a new home had come into being, for Alec had married and was living not far from Oxford in an Elizabethan manor house. Here Bapu did go, and he was much pleased with the quiet atmosphere, the beauty of the old gray stone manor, and especially the little chapel in the garden.

Lucy and Bertha came to Kingsley Hall to see Bapu, and Mona came to Knightsbridge, but I was so busy and so much absorbed in the work that we had no time for more than fleeting talks.

CHAPTER XXXIV

INSIDE the Conference Hall Bapu's battle was from the beginning tough and relentless. The atmosphere was unsympathetic if not hostile, and the composition of the Indian delegation was artificial.

"The causes of failure," said Bapu, addressing the Conference, "were inherent in the composition of the Indian delegation. We are almost all not elected representatives of the parties or groups whom we are presumed to represent. We are here by nomination of the Government. Nor are those whose presence was absolutely necessary for an agreed solution to be found here."

At the outset Bapu was asked to state the position of the Indian National Congress, about which most people were both critical and ignorant. Bapu gave a full account, in which he said, "The Congress is, if I am not mistaken, the oldest political organization we have in India. It has had nearly fifty years of life, during which period it has, without any interruption, held its annual session. It is what it means—national. It represents no particular community, no particular class, no particular interest. It claims to represent all Indian interests and all classes. . . .

In stating his case, Bapu always made it clear that he did not *want* to break with England, only the connection must be on honorable and equal terms. Speaking at a meeting outside the Conference Hall, he said:

"The object of our nonviolent movement is complete independence for India—not in any mystic sense but in the English sense of the term—without any mental reservation. I feel that every country is entitled to it without any question of its fitness or otherwise. As every country is fit to eat, to drink and to breathe, even so is every nation fit to manage its own affairs, no matter how badly. Just as a man with bad lungs will breathe with difficulty, even so India, because of her ailments, may make a thousand mistakes. The doctrine of fitness to govern is a mere eyewash. Independence means nothing more or less than getting out of alien control."

Of the safeguards which Britain was demanding, he spoke in the strongest terms:

"If all those safeguards are to be granted and all the talk here takes concrete shape and we are told that we are to get responsible government, it will be almost on a par with the responsible government that prisoners have in their jails. They too have complete independence immediately the jail door is locked and the jailer goes away. The prisoners inside that cell, about ten feet square, or seven feet by three feet, have complete independence. I do not ask for that kind of complete independence, with the jailers safeguarding comfortably their own rights."

The British statesmen did not at all like this direct and outspoken approach, and took refuge in playing with words and delaying tactics. But when it was Bapu they had to deal with, they could not escape the truth:

"How can there be any compromise when we each one of us has a different definition for the same words that we may be using? It is impossible. Mr. Prime Minister, I want to suggest to you, in all humility, that it is utterly impossible then to find a meeting ground, to find a ground where you can apply the spirit of compromise. And I am very grieved to have to say up to now I have not been able to discover a common definition for the terms that we have been exchanging during all these weary weeks.

"We have never really come to grips. We have never got down to brass tacks, as you put it, and I am anxious—I have been pining—to come to real grips and to get down to brass tacks all these days and all these nights, and I have felt, Why are we not coming nearer and nearer together, and why are we wasting our time in eloquence, in oratory, in debating, and in scoring points? Heaven knows I have no desire to hear my own voice. Heaven knows I have no desire to take part in any debating. I know that liberty is made of sterner stuff, and I know that the freedom of India is made of much sterner stuff."

But time was running out, and still no settlement was in sight, so at last Bapu struck the note of warning:

"Whilst there is yet a little sand left in the glass, I want you to understand what this Congress stands for. My life is at your disposal. The lives of all the members of the Working Committee, the All-India Congress Committee, are at your disposal. But remember that you have at your disposal the lives of all those dumb millions. I do not want to sacrifice those lives if I can possibly help it."

He would do everything possible for attaining an honorable settlement, but if that could not be, then they should realize what it would mean. At the very last meeting, again the note rang out:

"This is perhaps the last time that I shall be sitting with you at negotiations. It is not that I want that. I want to sit at the same table with you in your closets, and to negotiate and to

144

plead with you, and to go down on bended knees before I take the final leap and final plunge."

Then when it was given to him to move the vote of thanks to the Prime Minister, Bapu said very reluctantly, but in so many words, that as far as he was concerned, it appeared to him that they had come to the parting of the ways.

So now there was nothing left to do but to pack up.

CHAPTER XXXV

THE anxiety that had been weighing on me about the meeting with Romain Rolland had been relieved, because Bapu had agreed to return by way of Switzerland, then on to Brindisi to catch an Italian Lloyd Triestano steamer. He wanted to get back to India as quickly as possible because he knew trouble would be brewing there, but he felt he could not leave Europe without seeing Romain Rolland and allowing time to have long talks with him. He even agreed to a halt of one night in Paris with a public meeting there, and another halt in Rome.

The British statesmen and officials were courteous and correct up to the last, in spite of the fact—as we learned afterwards—that they had already decided on a policy of wholesale repression.

As for ourselves, once we had left their realm we felt a wonderful sense of relief, a sense of being able to breathe, and think and speak naturally. It was the law of imperialism which created that atmosphere—individually Bapu had made many friendships among all kinds of people. One of the most unexpected and touching attachments was that of the two sturdy detectives. They had become so devoted to Bapu that when the time for parting approached they begged to be allowed to accompany him as far as Brindisi. This was a delicate question, as it meant their going outside their Government's jurisdiction. So Bapu wrote a letter to

Sir Samuel Hoare, pleading warmly for their wish to be granted, and it was. They accompanied us right through to the South of Italy.

The Paris meeting was the first public meeting in Europe, and the hall was packed to suffocation, with such crowds left outside on the pavement that mounted police had to be called in to control them. When Bapu finished speaking, questions of all sorts, political, moral, spiritual, and, if I remember rightly, even dietetic, poured in. People scribbled them down on little scraps of paper and passed them along to the platform. The excitement was intense, and everyone was in a fever to get his or her particular question answered. As a matter of fact, it was utterly impossible for Bapu to answer them all, and those of us who kept receiving the little paper slips as they were handed up had to pick out the leading and most varied ones.

That night Bapu slept at a tiny little flat in the Latin Quarter as guest of Madame Guieysse, that wonderful little old lady with limitless devotion to Bapu's cause who had formed an Association of the Friends of Gandhi. The next day we departed for Villeneuve.

Of course what we had hoped for was a quiet time with Roman Rolland, but instead of that his peaceful little home overlooking the Lake of Geneva was bombarded by excited people of every description. Even before Bapu's arrival, visitors, the press, letters and telephone calls had flooded in on poor Romain Rolland, who was already suffering from a bad cold on the chest and was, in any case, a victim of insomnia.

In addition to all this excitement at Villeneuve, two public meetings were arranged, one in Lausanne and one in Geneva.

When I look back now on those precious days, I find it very difficult to recall anything in detail. I must have been thoroughly exhausted by the strain of the London visit, and another, and more fundamental, thing was the strange feeling which had been affecting me unconsciously in England also—a feeling of coming back to the scenes of my former free and independent life, but now under conditions of strictest discipline. In order to maintain that discipline I had, without realizing it, shut myself up in a self-imposed inner prison. It was when I met Romain Rolland again, and felt the influence of his penetrating blue eyes, that I vaguely knew something was wrong—wrong in the sense that I was not my full self. My spirit silently longed to reach out to him, but I could not emerge from that inner prison. It seemed to be part of the *tapasya* which Fate had ordained for me, in answer to those prayers of long ago. So the days passed in a haze of inner sadness which I could not, at that time, explain to myself.

As this has left me unable to recapitulate, with any accuracy, the events of those five days, I turn to a delightful account which Romain Rolland himself wrote to a friend in America shortly after we had left.

> How I should have liked to have you here during the visit of the Indians! They stayed five days—from the 5th to the 11th of December—at the Villa Vionette. The little man, bespectacled and toothless, was wrapped in his white burnoose, but his legs, thin as a heron's stilts, were bare. His shaven head with its few coarse hairs was uncovered and wet with rain. He came to me with a dry laugh, his mouth open like a good dog panting, and flinging an arm round me leaned his cheek against my shoulder. I felt his grizzled head against my cheek. It was, I amuse myself thinking, the kiss of Saint Dominic and Saint Francis.
>
> Then came Mira (Miss Slade), proud of figure and with the stately bearing of a Demeter, and finally three Indians, one a young son of Gandhi, Devadas, with a round and happy face. He is gentle, and but little aware of the grandeur of his name. The others were secretaries—disciples—two young men of rare qualities of heart and mind: Mahadev Desai and Pyarelal.
>
> As I had contrived shortly beforehand to get a severe cold on my chest, it was to my house and to the chamber on the second floor where I sleep at Villa Olga—you will remember it—that Gandhi came each morning for long conversations. My sister interpreted, with the assistance of Mira, and I had also a Russian friend and secretary, Miss Kondacheff, who took notes on our discussions. Some good photographs by Schlemmer, our neighbor from Montreux, recorded the aspect of our interviews.
>
> Evenings, at seven o'clock, prayers were held in the first floor salon. With lights lowered, the Indian seated on the carpet, and

147

the little assembly of the faithful grouped about, there was a suite of three beautiful chants—the first an extract from the *Gita,* the second an ancient hymn of the Sanskrit texts which Gandhi had translated, and the third a canticle of Rama and Sita, intoned by the warm, grave voice of Mira.

Gandhi held other prayers at three o'clock in the morning, for which, in London, he used to wake his harassed staff, although he had not retired until one. This little man, so frail in appearance, is tireless, and fatigue is a word which does not exist in his vocabulary. He could calmly answer for hours the heckling of a crowd, as he did at Lausanne and Geneva, without a muscle of his face twitching. Seated on a table, motionless, his voice always clear and calm, he replied to his adversaries open or masked—and they were not lacking at Geneva—giving them rude truths which left them silenced and suffocated.

The Roman bourgeoisie, and nationalists, who had first received him with crafty looks, quivered with rage when he left. I believe that if his stay had lasted any longer the public meetings would have been forbidden. He pronounced himself as unequivocally as possible on the double questions of nationalist armaments and the conflict between capital and labor. I was largely responsible for steering him on this latter course.

His mind proceeds through successive experiments into action and he follows a straight line, but he never stops, and one would risk error in attempting to judge him by what he said ten years ago, because his thought is in constant evolution. I will give you a little example of it that is characteristic.

God Is Truth

He was asked at Lausanne to define what he understood by God. He explained how, among the noblest attributes which the Hindu scriptures ascribed to God, he had in his youth chosen the word "truth" as most truly defining the essential element. He had then said, "God is Truth." "But," he added, "two years ago I advanced another step. I now say "Truth is God." For even the atheists do not doubt the necessity for the power of truth. In their passion for discovering the truth, the atheists have not hesitated to deny the existence of God, and, from their point of view, they are right." You will understand from this single trait the boldness and independence of this religious spirit from the Orient. I noted in him traits similar to Vivekananda.

148

And yet not a single political ruse catches him unprepared. And his own politics are to say everything that he thinks to everybody, not concealing a thing.

On the last evening, after the prayers, Gandhi asked me to play him a little of Beethoven. He does not know Beethoven but he knows that Beethoven has been the intermediary between Mira and me, and consequently between Mira and himself, and that, in the final count, it is to Beethoven that the gratitude of us all must go. I played him the *Andante* of the Fifth Symphony. To that I added *Les Champs Elysées* of Gluck—the page for the orchestra and the air for the flute.

He is very sensitive to the religious chants of his country, which somewhat resemble the most beautiful of our Gregorian melodies, and he has worked to assemble them. We also exchanged our ideas on art, from which he does not separate his conception of truth, nor from his conception of truth that of joy, which he thinks truth should bring. But it follows of itself that for this heroic nature joy does not come without effort, nor even life itself without hardship. "The seeker after truth hath a heart tender as a lotus, and hard as granite."

Here, my dear friend, are a few hints of those days of ours together on which I have taken much more detailed notes. What I do not dwell on to you is the hurricane of intruders, loiterers, and half-wits which this visit loosed on our two villas. No, the telephone never ceased ringing; photographers in ambuscades let fly their fusillades from behind every bush. The milkmen's syndicate at Leman informed me that during all the time of this sojourn with me of the "King of India" they intended to assume complete responsibility for his "victualing." We received letters from "Sons of God." Some Italians wrote to the Mahatma beseeching him to indicate for them the ten lucky numbers for the next drawing of the weekly national lottery!

My sister, having survived, has gone to take ten days' rest at a cure in Zurich. She returns shortly. For my part, I have entirely lost the gift of sleep. If you find it, send it to me by registered mail!

Among those who stayed in Villeneuve, and came out for early morning walks with Bapu, were Professor and Madame Privat and that remarkable pacifist, Pierre Ceresole. The timing was not quite so early as in London; that is to say, we waited for daylight, as here it was a matter of walking in unlighted country lanes, and also the December cold was getting severe. In fact, just before we left, snow fell on the mountains surrounding the Lake.

M. and Mme. Privat had never been to India, nor had they dreamt of ever being able to go, but Bapu, who was much pleased not only by their sincere understanding of his cause but also by their perfect devotion to one another, made the idea so attractive, and indeed so possible, that they decided then and there to rush off, get passports and clothes, and join us at Brindisi. Bapu, to his great satisfaction, had managed to get deck passages arranged for himself and party on board the Italian liner, so they could travel deck with us at very little expense, and once they reached India there would be many friends ready to receive them with open arms. Pierre Ceresole would have dearly liked to come along too, but his relief work at that time, which was going on in Wales, made it impossible for him to get away.

CHAPTER XXXVI

WHEN we reached Rome, there was beautiful warm sunshine but still a very cold wind blowing from the Alps. Friends had arranged for a meeting between Bapu and Mussolini, but the meeting with the Pope, which Bapu would greatly have liked, unfortunately fell through owing to some kind of mishandling.

Romain Rolland had arranged for Bapu to stay with his friend General Moris, who had a beautiful and spacious villa outside the city, but as usual there was no time to enjoy one's surroundings.

Bapu had a packed schedule. There are only two things I remember clearly—the visit to the Vatican and the visit to Mussolini. In the Vatican, Bapu's eye fell on a very striking life-size crucifix. He immediately went up to it and stood there in deep contemplation. Then he moved a little this way and that way, so as to see it from various angles, and finally went around behind it and the wall, where there was hardly room to go, and looked up at it from the back. He remained perfectly silent, and it was only when we left that he spoke, and then as if still in contemplation— "That was a very wonderful crucifix"—and again silence. So deep an impression did that scene make on me that it stands out all alone in my mind, and I remember nothing else of the visit to the Vatican.

General Moris accompanied Bapu on his visit to Mussolini, and of our own party, Mahadev and myself. We arrived a few minutes early, so were asked to wait in an anteroom which was, at the same time, a medieval armory. Bapu sat down on a seat, flanked on both sides by massive coats of mail. I was still contemplating the fascinating study in contrasts when a bell rang and an attendant jumped up to usher us into the "presence."

As the door opened, we saw a large room as big as a ballroom, completely empty except for one big writing table which stood across the faraway left corner, and behind it Mussolini, who rose as soon as Bapu entered and advanced across the bare floor, meeting us exactly in the middle of the room. He conducted us to his table, and indicating the only two chairs in front to Bapu and me, took his seat opposite. This left the General and Mahadev standing, which made me feel very uncomfortable, but as Mussolini seemed to take it as a matter of course, there was nothing to be done. He addressed Bapu in quite good English, and asked a number of questions about India. Then, inquiring as to what Bapu had seen in Rome so far, he turned toward the General and told him to arrange for Bapu to be shown everything, including the maternity and children's welfare centers, and also to have a display of the Balilla—little boys trained to military exercises and drill. When about ten minutes had passed, he rose from his seat as an indication that the interview was over, and accompanied us right up to the door at the far end of the room. The General told us afterwards that this was quite unusual behavior for Mussolini, who did not rise from his chair as a rule, and indeed would often not even raise his eyes when callers entered the room.

The rest of our two or three days in Rome were now more tightly packed than ever, and by the time we reached Brindisi we were all eagerly looking forward to the relaxation of the voyage. Excellent arrangements had been made for us, insofar as "deck" could be made excellent. The closed top of a hold and its immediate surroundings were reserved for our party, and the convenience had been allowed us of the use of second-class bathrooms. I am afraid Bapu felt this to be an excess of luxury, and there was even fear he might refuse it, but he did not, and we thanked our good fortune!

The last thing I remember as the ship drew out to sea is the picture of the two sturdy detectives standing on the quay and waving, waving.

The voyage luckily was excellent, and Bapu was able to relax and rest, in spite of, or perhaps just because of, the fact that he knew that Herculean struggle was ahead of him when he reached India. The evening Prayer, by special request of the passengers, was held regularly on an upper deck and attended by a large number of people, among whom I particularly remember Sir Akbar Hydari. During the day Bapu would lie down every now and then, between his reading, writing and spinning, and go fast to sleep for half an hour or so, and in this way gradually began to make up for the months of scrappy nights in London.

When we reached Port Said there was mysterious tension and excitement. The Egyptian friends had come with a whole fleet of cars to take Bapu and his party to Cairo and on down to Suez by road to pick up the steamer again there. Bapu was all ready to go, but he was given to understand by officials that the ship was not going to call at Suez and if he landed he would be left behind—a thing he could not possibly afford to do at that juncture. So the whole plan fell through, much to our sorrow and the intense indignation of the Egyptians. When we reached Suez, the ship *did* stop, and there would have been quite enough time for Bapu to be brought alongside in a launch.

As we approached the shores of India, news began to reach us of the repression which the Viceroy had thought fit to launch before Bapu's arrival. Jawaharlal had been arrested, and there had been firings in the North-West Frontier followed by the arrest of Abdul Gaffar Khan. The country was in a state of feverish excitement. The Government might have liked to prevent any public reception to Bapu, but it was beyond even their power to control the millions of Bombay who turned out en masse to greet him. The streets were lined with wildly excited crowds, from every window and balcony women and children waved and threw flowers, little national flags fluttered everywhere, and banners and arches adorned the whole of the long route.

Whom to arrest, where to lathi-charge, it was a hopeless job so the Government kept quiet. But at the quay, where they could control things, they had arranged with their faithful ally, Dr. Ambedkar, for a Harijan black-flag demonstration. The show was petty enough in itself, but it was a significant indication of the way Government was prepared to use the divide-and-rule method in every possible way.

Bapu encamped himself on the roof of Mani Bhuvan, and the Working Committee members, and other important Congress leaders still out of jail, all gathered round him. The Working Committee sat in almost continuous session, and sometimes their discussions lasted till 2 or 3 o'clock in the morning. Bapu got into telegraphic communication with the Viceroy and pleaded for an interview, but Lord Willingdon doggedly refused. Finally, on December 31st, the Congress Working Committee passed a resolution reviving the Satyagraha, which had been suspended at the time of the Gandhi-Irwin Pact.

Now we knew Bapu's arrest must come, but the Government held its hand for four days, and then on January 4th, when the excitement of expectation had died down a little, they came at 3 o'clock in the morning to take Bapu away to Yaravda Jail. Everyone in the house got up and gathered around Bapu. The English Commissioner of Police, handing him the warrant, said, "It is my duty to arrest you." It was Bapu's Silence Day; he intimated that he would like half an hour in which to get ready, which was granted. I hurriedly rolled up Bapu's bedding and fastened the other things which since December 31st I had packed up each night and kept in readiness for the expected arrest. Bapu

153

scribbled down on paper a message to the nation in which he said:

> Infinite is God's mercy, never swerve from truth and non-violence, never turn your back, and sacrifice your lives and all to win Swaraj [Self-rule].

Then we all sat around while Bapu's favorite hymn was sung, the police standing considerately at a little distance. After this Bapu rose, everyone bent down to touch his feet, and away he went surrounded by the police.

The next day Bapu sent me a "business" letter from jail, asking for a larger-sized thermos. "It will be useful for keeping hot water, saving the labour of warders early morning." There was something about a check, and the note ended, "We are both well," thus enabling us to know that Vallabhbhai, who had also been arrested, must have been placed along with Bapu, which was a great relief, because we knew with what care he would watch over Bapu, and at the same time keep him amused with his mischievous humor.

CHAPTER XXXVII

I RETURNED to Sabarmati for the time being. The repression went ahead. The Working Committee was declared illegal, and all the members were arrested. News of police excesses and the heroic behavior of the people kept coming in. By this time Mahadev and Pyarelal were also arrested, so I felt something must be done about systematic collection of news from all over the country and its distribution abroad, as there was no chance of the full truth coming out through the Indian press, which was heavily censored. I therefore decided to go back to Bombay, where a brave friend was ready to put me up. It needed courage in those days, for unless you were very rich and influential, which he was not, you ran the risk of being arrested and fined if you harbored undesirables.

154

I wrote my next letter to Bapu from Bombay and felt much consoled when he replied, on the 21st of January:

Of course, you were right in going to Bombay. You should be the sole judge finally as to where you would stay and what you would do.

No sooner did I start work in Bombay, and people got to know what I was trying to do, than help began coming in from all quarters. Some people came to me in their usual garb, and others, who expected arrest, dressed in various styles. Rich and poor, all helped behind the scenes. I was given a typist, along with a typewriter and cyclostyle. Such Congress workers as were still out of jail organized very successful collection of authentic news by sending messengers to obtain firsthand information from various parts of the country, and news poured in. Some of it was firsthand, some secondhand, and some rumor. Out of all this I sorted, sifted, and finally selected only that which I felt to be thoroughly reliable, prepared a Weekly Report which I sent to friends in England, France and America. In order to escape the censor, I used to send the typist with the envelopes to the main post office just at the air mail closing hour. There he would hurriedly pay the late-letter fee and get the envelopes popped into the bag at the moment it was being closed. It was remarkable how well it worked. Everything got through.

Before many days had passed, I noticed a suspicious-looking man sitting on the garden wall near the gate. He turned up again the next day and the next, and it became clear that he was a C.I.D. man who had been put on duty. So the typist used to turn the other way when taking the post, and vary his timing, his bag, and so on. These simple devices appeared to be quite enough to put this very lazy C.I.D. fellow off the track, as his idea of his duty seemed to consist of sitting on the wall.

Bapu, in one of his letters, now gave the disquieting news that he had again started on a dietetic experiment: "I have just commenced almond paste instead of milk."

With Bapu's arrest the movement had gathered further momentum, and the repression had grown in proportion. From far and wide I was getting reports of shocking happenings. Wholesale arrests, destruction of property, lathi charges and beatings were of course there, but there was a darker, loathsome side—the indecent humiliations and punishments which the police were inflicting. They thought of the most fiendish things to disgrace and shame proud country folk in front of their own women. Not even the Pathans of the North-West Frontier were spared, and disgusting tortures were inflicted on them.

Naturally, when this kind of information began to get around, even behind the scenes, in England, the Government was much annoyed, and after one or two really shocking news items were actually published by someone, Sir Samuel Hoare made an angry reference in the House of Commons. He did not mention my name, but it was clear that he was referring to my reports, and within a few days I was served with a notice to quit Bombay. Of course I did not do so, and was consequently arrested.

I was taken to the court for the mock trial—our practice was not to defend ourselves—and sentenced to three months simple imprisonment, A-class. When the police deposited me at Arthur Road Prison, the jail authorities were flustered. They did not know what to do with me. Owing to the very large number of women political prisoners, the ordinary women's jail had long since overflowed, and the debtors' jail had been converted into a jail for female politicals. But here there was no accommodation for A-class prisoners. Also, they were not at all anxious for me to join the B- and C-class prisoners who were crowded together in one big barrack, thereby enabling them to get all the latest news. I was told to sit in a small side room near the office while consultations took place between the Superintendent, Jailer and Matron. Finally the Matron, accompanied by a wardress, came and took me away to the debtors' jail. She explained that they were going to make A-class arrangements, but that for the present I should remain with the other political prisoners in the big barrack.

It was by now evening, and the prisoners had already been locked up. The barrack was packed with Gujerati and Marathi women, many of whom were my friends and acquaintances. As

156

soon as we were left alone and the gates were locked on the outside we all sat down on the floor to talk. Every scrap of news I could give, especially about Bapu, was eagerly devoured.

Here were some of the leading ladies of Bombay. Practically all of the prisoners were used to good standards of living, and certainly higher than Ashram standards, but they had nearly all been given C-class and of course were dressed in jail clothes. But their spirits were high, and their enthusiasm unbounded. They had mostly been arrested for picketing, which the women everywhere were carrying on with undaunted zeal. The way Bapu's call to action had moved the women of India was one of the most astounding and baffling things with which the Government found itself faced.

The barrack was situated in a cemented yard, with bathrooms at one end and a row of small kitchens at one side. These kitchens had been closed up, as the B- and C-class prisoners were not allowed to cook for themselves. On the third day one of these kitchens was opened up, and I was told that I must make this my quarters and not mix with other prisoners. This latter injunction was, of course, absurd, as we all shared the same yard. So the authorities had to be satisfied with my not going *into* the big barrack.

My new quarters consisted of one tiny room which was almost entirely filled by a large row of cooking stoves. The great advantage of this was that there was no space to sleep inside, and the authorities had to agree to my being left free in the yard at night. So I could sleep under the open sky, which was such a blessing in that climate.

This contact with the open heavens helped me to bear the otherwise complete loss of association with Nature, which this cemented jail meant. There was not a green blade of grass anywhere, and the walls were so high that no trees could be seen over them, except from one extreme corner where I used regularly to go to have a sight of the top of one green tree. When a cabbage or other green vegetable was brought to me for cooking, I used to grudge having to eat it and thus lose the sight of its refreshing color.

CHAPTER XXXVIII

IN my first letter to Bapu from jail I consulted him about books to read, because now was my chance. During the seven years since I had come to India, I had had no time at all for reading. In his reply the chief books he recommended were the Ramayana and the Mahabharata, the two greatest epics of the Hindus. At the same time he reported that the almond-paste experiment was still going on.

Some hitch now came in the correspondence and there was no letter for a month. When at last one came, Bapu reported that "Mahadev has now joined us, and we have become a merry company." I was extremely glad to get this news, because I knew how useful Mahadev would be to Bapu, and also the joy it would give Mahadev, who felt any separation from Bapu acutely. The letter ended with further recommendations for reading, which included the eleven principal Upanishads.

The Ashram discipline stood me in good stead now. I made out a regular daily program of work and exercise, which I stuck to strictly. So much time for reading, so much for Hindi, so much for spinning, so much for cooking, eating and clothes-washing, and so much for walking up and down the yard for exercise.

Before long the socialist leader Kamala Devi Chattopadhyaya, looking the picture of artistic beauty, was brought to our jail. But she also was locked up at night as a B-class prisoner and put into jail clothes. The Bombay Government was particularly harsh in its classification of women politicals. Though large numbers of them were educated women with high standards of living, only Ba, Sarojini Devi and myself were put in A-class when arrested.

Kamala Devi and I began interesting ourselves in the well-being of C-class prisoners, and voiced to the Superintendent some of

158

The author and Mahatma Gandhi on board the Rajputana
taking them to London for the 1931 Roundtable Conference.

Madeleine Slade, when she was about two years old.

Madeleine Slade, shortly after her return from her first trip to India with her family.

Madeleine Slade's father, in the uniform of Admiral of the Royal Navy.

Madeleine Slade as a
young woman.

Madeleine Slade with members of her family, including her mother,
left, and father; her sister Rhona, far right, and Rhona's sons,
John and Edward; and the family maid, Bertha.

*A favorite draw-
ing of Beethoven.*

Mahatma Gandhi.

Romain Rolland.

*Miss Slade, now known as Mira behn, and Mahatma Gandhi in
London at the time of the 1931 Roundtable Conference.*

Mira behn and Gandhi before leaving India for London. (Original caption of this newspaper photograph read HINDU LEADER'S RETINUE INCLUDES ADMIRAL'S DAUGH-TER.)

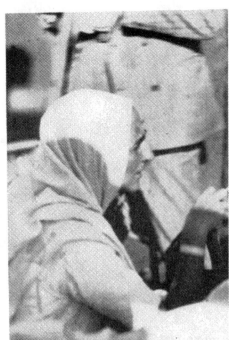

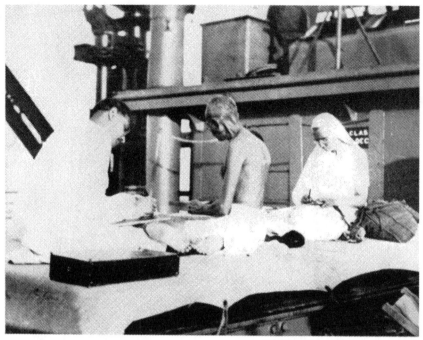

Gandhi, Mira behn, and one of Gandhi's secretaries on board the Rajputana *en route to England in 1931.*

Gandhi discusses a point with Mira behn en route to London.

Mira behn as she looks today.

their grievances. We were told we should keep quiet, but we did not, and as a result we were removed from the debtors' jail and transferred to the regular women's jail where there was a small A-class barrack which had a common veranda with two C-class barracks filled with ordinary prisoners.

Here there was actually a small tree and some flowers. What a joy! But there were troubles also. The open space was very cramped, and most of it was overlooked by another building.

When the evening came we were locked up in our small barrack. We pleaded to be allowed to sleep under the open sky, but were told that now there was room to sleep inside the A-class accommodation there would be no question of being allowed to stay in the open.

The next morning Kamala Devi happened to pick a red flower and put it in her black hair. In the evening when the Matron, a nice woman, came to lock us up, she said with a smile to Kamala Devi, "You must not pick flowers and deck your hair with them."

Then, after washing our clothes, we hung them out in the sun to dry. Again in the evening the Matron warned us: "It is not liked that you should hang your clothes out to dry like that."

"But," we said, "surely we are expected to keep clean, and clothes have to be dried after washing!"

Then the Matron explained: "You can hang them out round the corner where they will not be in sight of the windows up there."

"What windows are they?" we asked.

"That's the Superintendent's flat, and Mrs. —— keeps a sharp eye on the women prisoners."

This was more than we had bargained for.

Another thing which began to trouble us was the endless variety of evil smells. In the debtors' jail there had been a washermen's drying field and a dumping ground for city refuse just outside the walls, which was bad enough, but here we found ourselves in the extreme corner of the main jail wall, with Arthur Road in front and mill laborers' quarters on the left. Along the road, almost daily, stinking carcasses of animals which had died in Bombay were taken in bullock carts to a station for transport to the suburbs, and on the left there were laborers' latrines, the ventilators of which aired themselves over the top of our wall. But perhaps worst of all was the fact that the water drainage was defective, owing to the very low situation of the area, which resulted in the sewer gas coming back up the drains every high tide. As each barrack had a latrine at the back without any doors, in accordance with jail regulations, there was no escape from this gas, especially at night when we were locked inside.

Then, to add a final touch to the situation, the fever hospital was exactly opposite on the other side of Arthur Road, and was full of smallpox patients, with funerals starting out several times a day, the wailing and chanting of which we could hear over the wall.

However, these were not days for being depressed, and we kept ourselves busy and well with our studies and our daily exercise, to which latter Kamala Devi added skipping—out of sight of those windows, of course! We sat together in the morning and evening Prayer, and that was also objected to. However, we did not stop, just made our singing rather softer.

A charming little cat joined us, particularly at meals. He behaved very well to begin with, only taking what he was given, but when he noticed that we closed our eyes while repeating the grace, he started helping himself at that moment. After this I kept my eyes slightly open watching him, and as a result he sat perfectly still looking as if butter would not melt in his mouth.

Kamala Devi was now transferred and I was alone, except, of course, for the ordinary prisoners, or criminals as they were called, in the adjoining barracks. One or two had been convicted for murder, and the rest for prostitution and thieving. I learned quite a lot from the Matron about these people, how many of them came to jail regularly in inclement seasons or hard times, and how some were kept by men for the purpose of stealing, and so on. One particular case I recollect of a woman who, the Matron said, was one of three wives that a man kept, one for looking after him, and two for alternately stealing and going to jail. The plan apparently worked excellently.

I was not alone in my barrack for long. The Superintendent

160

looked in one morning in a rather flustered state, and said, "Mrs. Naidu will shortly be coming as an A-class prisoner." This was a piece of luck for me. I could not resist adding a little to the Superintendent's agitation by remarking that of course Mrs. Naidu was a veritable Maharani, that she was an intimate friend of the biggest princes in the land, and so on and so forth.

I had not been aware of the fact that, as an A-class prisoner, I was entitled to all sorts of conveniences, but now the A-class outfit began arriving in my barrack for Sarojini Devi. A bed, a dressing table with brush and comb, a washstand, a bathtub, etc., and even curtains. The Matron was quite excited. Then the next day came Sarojini Devi, overflowing with vivacity and wit. She was, of course, exhausted with all the rush and excitement she had been going through outside, but neither her age nor her aches and pains ever daunted her. Now it was my turn to hear all the latest news, and there was plenty of it! One was only given the *Times of India Weekly* in jail, and even that sometimes had news items cut out. So the three or four days we had together were hardly enough in which to hear all the news, stories and anecdotes.

Then Sarojini Devi was taken off to Yaravda Prison at Poona, and I was again left alone. The Matron pressed me to keep the A-class amenities, but I explained to her that Ashram life resembled much more the C-class standard, besides which any other prisoners who might be put with me would be sure to be B- or C-class.

In one of Bapu's letters I learned that he also had feline companions, as he referred to them in connection with the value of example in anything one wishes others to do:

> The ideal of voluntary poverty is most attractive. We have made progress, but my utter inability to realise it fully in my own life has made it difficult at the Ashram for the others to do much. They have the will but no finished object-lesson. We have two delightful kittens. They learn their lessons from the mute contact of their mother, who never has them out of her sight. Practice is the thing. And just now I fail so hopelessly in so many things. But it is no use mourning over the inevitable.

(6.5.32)

At the end of this letter Bapu wrote: "Perhaps we shall meet soon." So I knew from this that I could go for an interview with a clear conscience as soon as I was released.

During these last days I began to get the impression that there was something wrong outside; no definite news leaked through, but it seemed that Hindu-Moslem riots had started, and when the day came and I was taken out of the yard to the Superintendent's office, I was told things were so bad that in the area lying between the jail and Malabar Hill, where I was due to go, it was doubtful whether anyone would dare to come and fetch me. But Damodardas, my good host, did turn up in a car, and he dashed me off to his Malabar Hill home.

CHAPTER XXXIX

I IMMEDIATELY set to work on my old job. The riots were in full swing, and news of stabbings, looting and arson kept coming in. It was well known that Bombay had an underworld of bad characters who were always ready to do anything for money, and there was little doubt that these had been put into action. The behavior of the police alone was enough to show it. But not even these methods could crush the spirit of the people.

I took the first opportunity of going to visit Bapu by joining the next party which was due for an interview. But what was my disappointment when, on reaching the jail, I was informed that the Government had given instructions not to allow me to see him. So I had to sit at the jail gate while the others went up to the Superintendent's office.

In the next letter I received from Bapu he said he had asked the Government to reconsider their decision not to permit my coming for interviews, and had hinted that if they refused he would stop seeing anyone. And this was what finally came about.

162

The milkless experiment had been going on all this time, and evidently Bapu had tried to improve on it by taking peanuts instead of almonds, as they were much cheaper, but his companions could not tolerate it. On May 13th he wrote: "Ground nuts are gone. Vallabhbhai and Mahadev frightened me and I have allowed myself to be frightened."

Though Bapu's weight kept fairly steady, there was something wrong with his condition, and almost every letter referred to trouble he was having with pain in the left elbow and right hand, making spinning and even writing difficult. Then Bapu took to practicing writing with his left hand, and recommended that we should all do likewise so as to be well armed.

But everyone was getting concerned over these pains. After all, writing with the left hand was no cure for the right hand. Finally the Inspector-General of Prisons, Major Bhandari, insisted that the milkless experiment *must* be given up, and on June 22, 1932, Bapu wrote: "I am defeated. I have taken milk and baker's bread and therefore salt also. Major Bhandari will not let me make experiments that might endanger health."

The reference to salt was in connection with a saltless experiment which I had been trying in Arthur Road prison. As a result of my own experience, I had thought that perhaps elimination of salt might possibly help to relieve the pain in Bapu's elbow and hand, and he, always ready for such things, had added saltlessness to his milklessness.

The news that the milkless diet had been terminated was a very great relief, and of course Bapu's general condition began to improve.

In the meantime my work outside was going on with ever-increasing tempo. It was obvious that before long I should again be arrested or told to quit, and the chances of my host being victimized were serious. Friends therefore decided that I should move to the house of a very rich and influential mill owner who was quite ready to put me up in his guesthouse. His connections were such that the Government would be most unlikely to disturb him. Accordingly, I moved to his palatial quarters which were on another part of Malabar Hill.

Up to the beginning of July I was still free and decided to go to see Rajendra Babu, who had recently been released from jail and was at his home in Chapra, Bihar. Just as I was gathering up my things ready for leaving, I was served with a notice to quit Bombay. The police evidently did not know of my plans. I decided not to change them and, giving an explanatory statement for the press, I set out as arranged.

In Chapra I found Rajendra Babu stricken with a very bad case of malaria. Bihar's mosquitoes were hard at work day and night, and there was no escaping them. Shortly after my arrival, I was served with a notice. I was in any case due to leave for Benares the next day to see Pandit Malaviya and others. I consulted Rajendra Babu. He said there was very little chance of the police arresting me that evening as there was no women's jail anywhere in the neighborhood, so I stayed over. The police sat opposite the house on the road all night, and followed me to the station the next morning. They were probably glad enough to get out of the bother of dealing with me, and so winked at the fact that I had overstayed their quit notice by several hours.

I was to stay at the home of Shivprasad Gupta, a well-known citizen of Benares, and friend of Pandit Malaviya and other Congress leaders. No sooner had I arrived than I contracted malaria myself. In his anxiety to do everything possible for me, my host sent for a nurse from the hospital. She looked after me very attentively for two days, and was most chatty. Then suddenly she stopped coming. Shivprasad Babu explained to me that they had seen her entering the police station, and as they were convinced she was being used as a spy, they had terminated her services. In any case my fever was now under control, and before long I was all right except for some weakness.

A few of the Congress leaders were, like Rajendra Babu, again out of jail, and so a Working Committee meeting was planned to take place at Shivprasad Babu's house. This was a bit of good fortune for me which I had not anticipated.

As soon as my health was good enough, I set out for Bombay via Ahmedabad. In order to make one hundred per cent sure of me, the Government served me with another order, forbidding me ever

164

to enter Bombay. It was handed to me by a police official while I was walking along a street in Ahmedabad.

"That's all right," I said to the man, "I am leaving for Bombay by the evening train, and you'd better come along too, as you will be needed at the trial."

The next morning, when I stepped out of the train at Victoria Terminus, there were two plain-clothes English police officials waiting for me. They behaved with such discreetness that Seth Ambalal Sarabhai and his daughter Mridula, who had traveled in another part of the same train, came up to me on the platform and said, "Hullo! You've not been arrested?"

"Oh yes, I have," I replied, pointing to the two gentlemen having my luggage removed from the compartment.

I was taken off in a taxi to the police station. They did not put me in a lock-up, but gave me a bench to sit on and even brought me some refreshment. After a time, I was taken to the court and brought before the Magistrate. He heard the particulars of the case and then announced that there was not enough evidence, as the official who had served the notice on me in Ahmedabad was not present, and the trial must be put off till he arrived in Bombay. I remarked that I had asked the man to come along by the same train, and then added that since I was in any case going to plead guilty, what was the need of this police official's evidence? However, the Magistrate insisted that he must be there, and told the police in charge of me to take me away and keep me as an under-trial prisoner.

So I was returned to my old quarters at Arthur Road, which were just then empty. I had started a bad cold in the morning and by now my fever was running high. It took two or three days before I was good for anything. After a whole week I was taken to the court. It was packed with visitors, and I caught sight of quite a number of friends. The usual formalities of a trial were carried through, the man who had served me the notice in Ahmedabad duly playing his part, and finally the judge pronounced a sentence of one year's simple imprisonment, A-class. That got me out of the way for a fairly long period.

When Bapu received the news he wrote to me on August 19th:

165

So you are again in your den. I hope you will regain your lost strength and vitality. And you will be anxious about nothing. Simply concentrate on your spinning and such studies as you can easily undertake. We are all doing well. Love from us all. God be with you.

According to jail rules, if I wished to write to Bapu every week I could not have any interviews, so I went without seeing people and had instead my weekly exchange of letters.

CHAPTER XL

I THOUGHT I was now going to settle down to a comparatively peaceful time with plenty of reading. Bapu, referring to the Vedas, Upanishads, Mahabharata and Ramayana, had written on August 7th:

> This course will certainly give you an insight into Hindu thought that would be valuable . . . I would balance this reading by a reading of the *Koran* and Amir Ali's *Spirit of Islam*.

I had also a nice quiet companion in a young B-class prisoner, Kisan as she was affectionately called. We got busy with our studies, but hardly a month had gone by when the news came that Bapu had decided to go on a fast in order to combat the Communal Award of the British Prime Minister, Ramsay MacDonald, which granted separate electorates to the Scheduled Castes* (Untouchables). Bapu had been firmly against divide-and-rule move policy from the beginning, knowing as he did its sinister potentialities, which would legally and permanently separate the Harijans

---

* Various castes and tribes which were treated by orthodox Hindus as unfit to touch, owing, no doubt, originally to their different customs and habits especially in matter of cleanliness, and in some cases their practice of unclean occupations such as curing of hides, sanitary work, etc.

from the rest of the electorate and make them the tool of designing politicians—especially those who wanted to weaken nationalist India by internal strife. Now that Bapu was in jail, apparently the Government thought it could get away with this trump card, and, of course, Dr. Ambedkar was supporting them. Knowing this background, we had no illusions about the deadlines of the struggle which would ensue. The wording of Bapu's vow also left no room for doubt: "A fast unto death without food of any kind, save water, with or without salt and soda."

I wrote to Bapu, and his reply came on September 20th:

As I wrote that first letter conveying my vow I thought of you and Ba. And for a time I became giddy. How would you two bear the thing! But the voice within said, 'If you will enter in, you must give up thought of all attachment.' And the letter went. No anguish will be too terrible to wash out the sin of Untouchability. You must therefore rejoice in this suffering, and bear it bravely. I know how difficult all this is to do. Yet that is exactly what you have to try to do. Just think and realise that there is no meaning in having the last look. The spirit which you love is always with you. The body through which you learned to love the spirit is no longer necessary for sustaining that love.

We could not tell what was going on outside, but apparently a thrill of indignation and anxiety passed through the country and thousands upon thousands fasted and prayed on the day Bapu commenced his fast.

The Government allowed Ba, Sarojini Devi, Pyarelal and some others to visit Bapu daily. And of course Tagore, who had hastened all the way from Bengal, was allowed. To me they at least showed the consideration of allowing Bapu's messages to come through as often as he sent them.

Owing no doubt to the milkless experiment that Bapu had been carrying on for so long, his body was ill fit for a fast, and added to that, Dr. Ambedkar, orthodox Hindu leaders and others were allowed to come and argue with him for hours on end. The result was that his strength began to give out very quickly, and by the seventh day the doctors became alarmed. On that very day the

167

Government reply came from London accepting the Pact which Bapu had drawn up with his adversaries, and the fast was broken. Bapu telegraphed September 26th:

NO LETTER SENT TODAY. THANK GOD FAST BROKEN
5.15 PRESENCE GURUDEV OTHER LOVING FRIENDS.

After such an experience it took a little time for the mind and nerves to quiet down. Then, when we were getting into our studies again, Kisan was released or transferred, I forget which, and I was again alone in my little barrack.

This was by no means the first time that I had been locked up by myself at night, but unfortunately the Superintendant suddenly remembered a rule in the Jail Manual about women not being left alone. He did not come himself, but he sent the Jailer to inform me that as I was now by myself, and the rules specified that women must not be locked up alone at night, he had ordered that two of the criminals should be locked up with me that evening. I said it was perfectly unnecessary as I had been used all my life to times of solitude which I not only did not fear, but enjoyed. But the Jailer said it was the rule, and the Superintendent had given orders that it must be followed. In vain I reminded him that I had already had many solitary nights in this very barrack in between the coming and going of other prisoners.

"I am afraid we have to follow the rule. You see," he added, "women sometimes faint or have fits."

I assured him that I was not in the habit of fainting and never in my life had had a fit. But to no avail.

"Then whom do you propose putting with me?" I inquired.

He mentioned two of the women in the next barrack.

"That's fine!" I said. "So you propose to lock me up with two murderesses! But why two? One is surely enough."

"The rule is," he explained, "that there should be two, so that if one attacks you the other is there to protect you."

I burst out laughing.

"Certainly this would be the best way to give one fits," I said.

The two women he was proposing to put with me, though in for murder, were as a matter of fact neither of them dangerous

168

characters. But one was terribly dirty. She had been arrested on the charge of killing her newborn baby, and as she was an undertrial, she had not yet been given jail clothes and was still wearing the heavily blood-stained sari in which she had been caught. I told the Jailer firmly that I would not have her locked up with me, and that the other, who had been convicted of murdering her husband, but was clean and quiet, was quite enough. He seemed to sense trouble in my eyes, and finally agreed to this compromise.

My new companion was a nice little country girl of about twenty, and from all she told me, and from what the Matron had related, it seemed she had been wrongly convicted. I tried afterwards to help in getting her case reconsidered, and I believe that ultimately her long term was reduced.

The sight of all these women who lived in the two adjoining barracks was most deplorable. There seemed to be no attempt to rehabilitate them, and no attempt to separate the physically diseased and mentally depraved prostitutes from those who had been convicted for other offenses, and who were often newcomers to jail, as yet innocent of the black underworld of Bombay. I used to discuss this matter with the Matron, and she felt very badly about it but was helpless, as there was no room to segregate the two kinds of prisoners, and both barracks were always overcrowded. I remember there was only one water tap for us all. Here the prisoners washed their dirty clothes and here one also had to draw one's drinking water.

There was no women's hospital attached to Arthur Road Prison, and this was one of the Matron's nightmares, because many of the women were pregnant, and she had to rush them off to the civil hospital in a taxi when they were about to be delivered. As the women did not usually tell her in advance when their pains began, it was a most difficult job.

One case I particularly remember. A woman in the next barrack suddenly gave birth to twins before the Matron could get her away. The jail doctor and his attendants were called. I looked into the barrack before he left to ask him how things had gone. I saw the twins lying on the cement floor.

"Are they dead?" I asked.

"Oh yes," said the doctor, "the woman is hopelessly syphilitic, and no child she has can possibly live."

The Matron was told to take the unfortunate woman and the two dead babies away to the hospital, and they were packed off then and there. Orders were then given to the other prisoners to clean up the floor, which was in a shocking mess, and the doctor and others went out. The women began washing down the floor of their barrack, but it seemed to me that they had no disinfectant, so I asked them.

"Disinfectant?" they exclaimed. "We haven't anything of that sort!"

Luckily I had some carbolic with me, so I poured it into their buckets of water, making a really strong solution.

CHAPTER XLI

I HAD by now got well into my reading. The effect on me of the Upanishads, the Ramayana and the Mahabharata was profound, for here I discovered things that seemed to be part of my inmost self, part of something I had known long before and since lost. Here there was no nightmare of the unanswerable, but instead a vast illumination of the Unknown making its contemplation not a horror, but an infinite inspiration. While reading the Upanishads, and a few extracts from the Vedas, I heard the same note as in the music of Beethoven, and my heart stirred, and then hushed again as if waiting for a later time.

In the Ramayana, and in the tale of Nala and Damayanti in the Mahadharata, I was deeply moved by the conception of woman's devotion to her beloved. My idea of marriage had always been something very sacred which I had silently cherished in my heart, an ideal of utter dedication, and self-expression through oneness with the beloved. And now in Sita and Damayanti I found wonderful pictures of that very ideal.

The next reading I took up was the Koran and I wrote my impressions to Bapu. On October 26th he replied: "You will find many more gems in the Koran, some of them are penetrating."

Bapu never failed to report about his four-footed companions. For instance, in a letter dated December 22, 1932:

> Our cats have suffered disgrace. The mother has been found helping herself to foods without permission and during night dirtying our carpets and papers. Vallabhbhai has therefore cut off the food supply. Thus interdining has stopped. What other ordinances Vallabhbhai will promulgate I do not know. Ordinance rule is the order of the day even for poor kitty!

I, at my end, was having a very interesting time with the ants, whose extraordinary intelligence and industry I had plenty of opportunity and leisure to study.

I was doing my best to keep fit, but gradually the evil smells and gases began to undermine my health, and after a time I mentioned it to Bapu. He wrote back asking me to send details. This I did, and Bapu replied saying he had requested the Government to transfer me to Yaravda and also to arrange for an examination by specialists.

A few days after I had received this letter the Matron came and told me to pack up, as I was going to be transferred. To where she could not say, as it was against the rules. However, as Bapu had asked for me to be sent to Yaravda, and the Civil Surgeon who had examined me had told me he would advise my being sent to a cooler climate, I had high hopes of being transferred to Poona.

After passing through the necessary formalities, I was handed over to an English police sergeant who packed me and my luggage into a police van. We drove off. I could not see out, and so did not know which way we were going, but when we stopped, and I was taken out, I found we were at a small station on the Ahmedabad line, and that we were catching the night train. So I was being transferred to Sabarmati Jail and not to Yaravda.

The sergeant kept me at the extreme end of the platform where nobody was likely to see me, and when the train arrived he hurriedly popped me into a reserved second-class compartment, got in himself, locked the doors, and pulled down the blinds. So there we were. And I thought of the night I had made the same journey by the same train seven years before.

I had begun to realize that the one thing Government was not going to allow was for me to see or even be near Bapu. So I accepted the disappointment of not going to Yaravda as an inevitable consequence of this attitude. The next morning when I reached the Sabarmati Jail I found myself in a spacious yard with several neem trees in it. Even though the temperature was as hot or hotter than Bombay, the purity of the air was a great relief. Then what was my delight when I found that Ba was in the jail, also the good Ganga ben of those common kitchen days, as well as many other Ashram sisters.

Ba and I being the only two A-class prisoners, the jail authorities put us in a barrack to ourselves, but we were able to mix with the others in the yard which had been reserved for the politicals.

On February 12th I received a letter from Bapu in which he wrote: "It is a great joy to me that you have Ba with you."

Ba and I were not locked up at night, so I was once more able to sleep under the stars.

Not three months had passed when suddenly one day we were given the news that Bapu had decided to go on a fast of twenty-one days which he described as a "heart prayer for purification of myself and my associates for greater vigilance and watchfulness in connection with the Harijan cause." I was gradually learning to stand such blows with some degree of composure, otherwise the thought of those twenty-one days would have been quite unbearable.

The Government apparently thought that this fast would be fatal, and they decided to release Bapu. He agreed to be removed to Parna Kuti, the beautiful residence of Lady Thakursay, which was situated on the highest point in Poona and had a fine view and fresh air. Her husband had died even before the house had been completed, and ever since then, the widow had devoted herself to social and welfare work among women. The place, besides

172

its natural peace and beauty, had a pious atmosphere about it, and Bapu used to feel somewhat at ease there in spite of the palatial proportions of the building.

Bapu's messages came regularly. As the days went by they got shorter and shorter, but Mahadev used to write fully. Poor Ba was very brave, but she suffered terribly. Usually so neat and clean, she now became quite dilapidated, with her hair disheveled and her sari carelessly thrown about her. We did our best to comfort her, but there was no hiding the fact that the risk to Bapu's life was this time much greater. Mercifully, within a week the Government decided to release her. The moment Ba heard the news she became a changed person. In no time she tidied herself, we helped her pack, and off she went by the first train available for Poona.

Bapu's next little message was dated May 14th and said:

> So you have no Ba to look after or to keep company. God is trying you through and through. He will give you strength.

At last the twenty-one days were completed and we all gave thanks to God. In a few days came Bapu's little note written with his own hand in large though not very shaky letters:

> I have just broken the fast. The next task commences. He will find the ways and means.

(5-29-33)

Sabarmati Jail had quite a different atmosphere to the Bombay one. The Superintendent, Jailer, and Doctor, all Indians, were sympathetic in their hearts, and the Matron was a simple Moslem woman who treated us quite nicely. Many of the Ashram sisters came and went, and Mridula Sarabhai was also in from Ahmedabad. Most of them had not very long sentences, so it was an ever-changing population.

A characteristic of this jail was its big troop of langurs, large gray monkeys with black faces and long tails. Every day they went the rounds of the top of the jail walls, looking out for anything worth carrying off. There were mothers with babies riding on their backs or clinging on underneath, youngsters of all sizes, and one chieftain, a tremendous fellow, his black face encircled

173

with a big white ring of hair, long, forbidding teeth and a massive body. Everyone in the jail respected him. It was said that on one occasion a man had hit him with a stick. The old fellow did not retaliate then and there, but he bided his time, and some days later fell on the man unexpectedly and nearly killed him. Sometimes he used to come down into our yard, when everyone would give him a wide berth. He had a particular liking for the front door of the little hospital for women, which was just opposite our barrack. Here he would seat himself in the middle of the doorway for half an hour or more, at which times nobody could go in or out. If anyone should be so foolish as to hint that he might move, he would look daggers, bare his long teeth and remain firmly sitting where he was. Nobody ever made the suggestion a second time.

Monkeys were not the only creatures in that jail, and there was an incident which has left a vivid recollection. The sanitary arrangements were of the ordinary "dry" kind, and sweeper women used to come daily. One morning I had gone to one of these latrines, and was just about to come out again, when a sweeper woman coming outside at the back pulled out the tin tray. As she did so, she shrieked "Snake!" Right there in front of me, where the tin had been, a big cobra rose up on his coils, spread his hood and began swaying to and fro as he looked at me. There cannot have been more than two feet between us, and in order to open the door, the chain of which was very stiff, I had to turn my back on the cobra. But it was the only hope, so I turned, wrenched open the door and dashing outside looked around. There was the cobra with his hood expanded still swaying to and fro, all ready to strike. I retired backwards to a safe distance. The Matron, on hearing the news, immediately sent word to the office, and a batch of four or five jail policemen came with long lathis. And that was the end of the poor cobra. In the jail one could not expect Ashram methods.

What was going on in Bapu's mind about the future program I had no idea, because he could not breathe a word in his letters to me. Though he was free, I was a prisoner—quite a new and unexpected situation. From the way Bapu wrote, however, one could sense that he was putting in a prodigious amount of labor on the Harijan uplift, and that he was working up to something. What was it?

In less than a week news reached us in jail that Bapu had come to Ahmedabad and was planning to disband Sabarmati Ashram prior to a new plunge into Civil Disobedience. How this news got through I cannot remember. It must have been brought by a new prisoner.

CHAPTER XLII

THE movement had of late somewhat died down, owing to the imprisonment of practically all the leading Congressmen as well as thousands of rank and file. Another cause was that Government had developed a new technique. Instead of wholesale beatings and arrests they had taken to confiscating the property, including land, not only of the persons who had actually defied the law, but also of parents and nearest relatives. To become a Satyagrahi now meant breaking up the whole family. It was for this reason that Bapu conceived the idea of disbanding Sabarmati Ashram. The Government could have confiscated it, just as they had so many of the other Ashrams devoted to khadi and village development, but up to now they had held their hand. Bapu felt it was not right to expect others to lose everything for the cause, while his "family" retained its Ashram home.

The Sabarmati Jail is situated barely a mile from the Ashram, and I was able to hear from our yard the noise and hooting of motor horns as cars and trucks came and went during the disbandment. I had requested the Government to allow me a "business" interview with Narandas bhai, the Manager of the Ashram, so that I might explain what few books and papers I would like to save from the maelstrom. It was refused, however, and as a result what belongings I had left in the Ashram, including some precious

175

books and a photograph of Romain Rolland on the back of which he had written a line of sacred music, all vanished. Luckily after our return from London, when I saw that jail-going and confiscations were going to be the order of the day, I had packed up all Bapu's and Romain Rolland's letters and deposited them with a very safe friend in Ahmedabad whose house was almost sure not to be searched.

The sounds of the disbandment came floating in on the air for two or three days and as I listened I thought of all the years, and work, and love that Bapu had poured into the Ashram. This sacrifice must mean that Bapu planned stiffer and yet stiffer Satyagraha.

As these thoughts were still passing through my mind, the Jailer came to take me for an interview in the Superintendent's office. With whom? I explained that I did not want any interview which would upset my right to have my weekly letter from Bapu. The Jailer laughed and said, "It is Gandhiji himself who has come." My heart leapt up. I had not set eyes on Bapu for a whole year and a half, and as he was evidently planning something which would send him to jail again before my own release, which was due now in about a month, I had been thinking it might be yet an infinitely long time before I should see him again.

Bapu greeted me with a happy laugh and slap on the back as I bowed to touch his feet. He was very thin and definitely weakened physically by the fasts, but his spirit was radiant. He seemed on the wings of inspiration, but of course he could not tell me what it was. I could only guess that the sacrifice of the Ashram had so lightened his heart, and that there was a coming plunge.

That very night Bapu, Ba and over thirty inmates of the Ashram were arrested to prevent their setting out on a planned Satyagraha march. Ba was brought to our yard, and we learned from her that Bapu was also in our jail. There was general excitement, for the news that Bapu was inside had got around everywhere. I was consoled to hear from Ba that Mahadev had been arrested along with Bapu and was being kept with him. The jail felt a different place with Bapu in it, but it was not for long, as he was almost immediately transferred to Yaravda Prison.

176

No news came through, and it was only afterwards that I learned that the Government had in a day or two released Bapu and Mahadev, put them in a car, and served them with a notice to leave the precincts of Yaravda. They had arrested Bapu this time, as also in January 1932 at Bombay, before he had broken any law, and they didn't want to keep him under detention again, but to get him as a convicted prisoner. This would give them an excuse for being tough about jail rules. Bapu, as was expected, defied the order, so now they were able to convict him. The trial was conducted inside the prison, and Bapu was given one year's simple imprisonment A-class. The facilities which had been granted to Bapu at the time of the Yaravda Pact for doing Harijan work while under detention were now withdrawn. Of course Bapu was not going to endure this, and, as argument proved of no avail, he announced a fast unto death. Ba was released from Sabarmati Prison and thus we came to know that yet another fast had started.

I had just completed a whole year in jail, but that first week at Arthur Road Prison had been undertrial, which meant that I had got to remain seven more days. I appealed to the Superintendent, but he said the rules were such that he could not possibly count that first week. News got through that Bapu was not standing the fast at all well, and people were already becoming alarmed. The next time the Superintendent came on his rounds he told me he would do the most that was within his power, which was to release me a few hours before my year was up and thus enable me to catch the Poona train. Otherwise, I should be delayed another whole day. I thanked him very much.

The morning came. I was packed up ready, and sure enough the Superintendent, true to his word, released me early. I hastened straight to the station and caught the train for Bombay, where I should get a connection for Poona. No sooner had I taken my seat in a third-class compartment than I noticed that people around me were talking about the fast. Everyone seemed to think that Bapu was going to die. Resentment and despair were written on all faces. That journey seemed unending.

When at last I reached Poona I went straight to Parna Kuti.

177

There I found people wringing their hands. They said Charlie Andrews had been striving his utmost to get the Government to yield, but it seemed they were set on letting Bapu die this time. He had been removed to the hospital but still kept a prisoner. Just then Ba came in. She had been to the hospital. "Bapu is dying," she said in a distracted voice. "He has refused to drink any more water, and has distributed his few belongings amongst the hospital attendants. It's all over!" And she became speechless. Though I had no material grounds to go on, I felt a profound conviction that God would not let Bapu die at this juncture. I said so to Ba and others, but what comfort could that be!

That morning Andrews had gone again to the officials in the hope that the intense indignation and resentment of the whole nation might bring about a last-moment agreement. We waited and waited. All hearts were praying. Then a message came that Bapu was being released. Our eyes misty with tears of joy, we gazed out from the terrace, and before long we saw a Red Cross ambulance coming. It wound its way up the steep drive, and stopped at the front door. Charlie Andrews, beaming with delight, was sitting by the driver. Then they jumped down, opened the back door and lifted Bapu out on a stretcher. His spirit was still smiling in his eyes, but those eyes were sunken as I had never seen them before, and the whole body was wasted away. But he laughed as he was carried into the house and, catching sight of me, even put out a skinny arm and gave me a little slap as he passed on the stretcher.

Bapu had broken the fast in the jail with some orange juice before being put into the ambulance, and now we all sat around his bed and had the Prayer.

This unconditional release was so unexpected to Bapu that he felt dazed at finding himself with life ahead. In a statement he released for the press he said:

God's ways are inscrutable. The most unexpected event of my life has just occurred, though I have been used to the most surprising and unlooked-for things happening in the course of a very long public life. What is now in store for me? How shall I make use of this freedom from jail? I do not know. . . .

The rest of the statement was a heart-searching appeal to Caste Hindus to wipe out the practice of untouchability.

The dictating of the statement exhausted Bapu, and the doctors begged him to take complete rest and not to think about anything for a time. But before many days had passed, his mind was busy considering the next move. Seeing that he had been convicted to one year's imprisonment, he felt that he owed it to Government not to use his unexpected freedom for any political work during that period. So he decided to devote the whole year to intensive propaganda for the removal of untouchability. It was as though Fate had checked Bapu in his fight for freedom, and was saying, "No, first this has to be done." Here was the internal revolution which had to be achieved, and without which there could be no lasting strength in the nation.

So Bapu planned to go on an All-India Harijan Tour as soon as ever he regained sufficient energy. Doctors and others begged him to go slow, but in less than two months he began getting restive. The tour was chalked out, and the workers throughout the country were informed that Bapu planned to set forth at the beginning of November. First we returned to Wardha for a while.

During my year's imprisonment there had come two new visitors from the West, and now they joined Bapu at the Ashram. One was an extremely earnest young woman from Germany who had fled the Nazi persecution of the Jews. Bapu told me to instruct her in Indian methods of cooking and clothes-washing, but it was a hard job for her, perhaps because of her overanxiety. The other was a young woman from America, with a Greek background of dancing and poetry, the very opposite of my pupil in cooking and washing. She had come to Bapu previously and had stayed at Sabarmati Ashram just before and during the disbandment of the place, after which she had come on to Wardha for a time. So she was familiar with her surroundings. Bapu told me simply to look after her in a general way. This time the job was hard for me, because Nilla was a sprite, a spirit, dancing and singing her way through life like a bird. Earnest she was too, but it was an earnestness of exaltation, and one fine morning we found that she had flown from the nest, like the bird that she was. When we next heard of her she was at Brindaban, where she had been taken to a missionary hospital with a poisonous thorn in her leg as a result of dancing all alone in the woods of Lord Krishna. Bapu did his best to extricate her from this predicament, but the Missionaries and the British Government combined to send her all the way back to America. Bapu was pained. It was clear to me that, in spite of the extraordinary escapades, he had seen much more in that passing spirit than the rest of us had at the time.

On November 7th we set out by road to Nagpur, the first place on the schedule, which was to take us right down to the southernmost tip of India and then up again as far as Bombay by the following summer.

As in the khadi tours of the past, there was to be no respite except on Monday (Silence Day), when Bapu would devote the whole day to writing for his weekly paper and attending to correspondence. So on and on we went with everywhere crowds, enthusiasm and overflowing affection. This was in itself a tonic to Bapu, who had been so long divided from the masses, and enabled him to bear the unceasing strain. Bapu, in his enthusiasm for the work, now went so far as to suspend the Civil Disobedience movement, and he asked everyone to join him in the Harijan campaign.

I was again in charge of Bapu's personal requirements, and such was the rush, that I remember clearly only a few isolated incidents. The most beautiful recollection I have is that of the sacred pool where Bapu bathed, which was formed by natural rocks jutting out into the sea at the uttermost end of India. The water of the pool was still, and deep in color, and beyond the rocks the blue, blue Indian Ocean stretched away to the horizon, dotted here and there with the white sails of the little fishing boats.

I sat in silent contemplation of the scene, and that inner joy which had for long lain buried away, stirred within me. It was like an oasis, at which something very thirsty in me drank. But only for a moment. Then the coming and going started again and off we went.

180

Bapu's ceaseless attack on untouchability had begun to bear fruit, and the orthodox Hindus of the fanatical type were becoming seriously alarmed. They tried various devices for checking the tide of awakening, and one was to organize a group of Sadhus, in saffron robes, to dog Bapu's steps and endeavor to create disturbances at his meetings. At one place in Orissa our cars were attacked by men with lathis. The organizers of the tour were very disturbed and felt that Bapu should have better protection. But Bapu's mind worked in its own way. He said that if these were the methods the demonstrators were going to employ, then we should no longer go rushing in cars, but should get out and walk on foot and receive the blows on our heads, if they wished to give them.

"You can't do that, Mahatmaji," exclaimed the poor organizers who were, after all, responsible for Bapu's safety. "These demonstrators are terrible fellows, and they may do anything."

But Bapu's mind was fired with this idea, and he insisted that we must finish the rest of the Orissa tour on foot. This, of course, meant readjusting the whole schedule, and it was decided that we should stop at Puri, which we were then approaching, and allow two or three days for sitting in conference and rearranging the program. So it was from the city of the great temple of Jagannath, stronghold of orthodox Hinduism, that Bapu and his little party set out on foot.

It was just as Bapu had anticipated: nobody attacked us, and we marched peacefully along, the only hindrance being the crowds of enthusiastic peasants who collected at the villages we passed through, or came running to the roadside from their work in the fields. Bapu had always believed that walking was the ideal way of moving about the country, and this experience delighted him beyond measure.

At the big meetings, however, the Sadhus with their leader, Swami Lalnath, continued to turn up. One such occasion I particularly remember. The meeting was arranged on the broad sandy banks of a big river. A wooden platform had been raised and the audience was all gathered around waiting when we arrived. Volunteers made a passage for Bapu and the rest of us through the crowd, and we mounted the dais. Just as Bapu was about to address the audience we saw Swami Lalnath and his Sadhus approaching across the sand, bearing flags and shouting. There was a stir of angry indignation in the crowd and it looked as if there might be a scuffle, if nothing worse. Bapu immediately stood up and signed to the excited audience to keep seated and make way for Swami Lalnath to come to the platform. The people obeyed Bapu's wish and did not rise, but angry murmurs could be heard. When the Swami reached the side of the platform, Bapu, smiling sweetly, invited him to come and sit beside him. Then turning to the audience he told them that Swami Lalnath, who felt differently about untouchability, would address the meeting first, and that he should be given a patient hearing. By this time all the swagger had gone out of the Swami, who had been hoping for a disturbance, but he stood up and, putting on a brave face, made a short speech in opposition to the Harijan movement, which was not at all well received, and then sat down, after which Bapu addressed the audience and received a big ovation.

On one accasion Swami Lalnath did manage to create a disturbance after Bapu had left the meeting, with the result that the Sadhus received some blows. They then came to exhibit to Bapu their wounds, some of which were bleeding, as a demonstration of the violence of Bapu's admirers. Bapu called for bandages, etc., and had the Sadhus attended to then and there in front of him.

It was by now the month of June and the damp heat was intense, for the monsoon season was approaching. But on we marched day by day. We used to start in the early morning, before sunrise, and during the middle of the day we usually camped in a mango grove. At every halt the villagers would bring basketfuls of mangoes and green coconuts. Immediately the sound of chopping would begin, as the ends of the coconuts were cut open. We were told that the "milk" should not be poured into glasses but drunk straight from the nut, as otherwise the flavor, and certainly the fun, would be spoiled. This needed a little practice, but we all became adepts, including Bapu.

We managed to complete the walking program just before the

rains began, and then we went to Bombay. The rest of the tour in the north was now to be rushed through in train and car, as it would be the rainy season.

CHAPTER XLIII

MISREPRESENTATION of Bapu and his cause had been going on unabated in the West, and the urge now suddenly came to me to go to England and get in contact with the working classes. I went to Bapu and told him, and he immediately agreed. The clothes I had had for the Round Table Conference visit were still intact, so nothing extra had to be bought. The passport was quickly arranged, and a second-class berth taken on the very next P & O steamer. For funds in London, Bapu spoke to Seth Ambalal Sarabhai, who forthwith wrote to his London agent to supply me with all the money I might need, and within five days of putting the idea before Bapu I was on the ship sailing for Europe.

Within a day or two there came news on the wireless that the fanatical elements in the orthodox Hindu community had tried to throw a bomb onto Bapu's car at Poona but hit the wrong vehicle, injuring seven people. This brought home to me fully the realization that Bapu was now going with his life in his hands, and it was God alone Who could, and would, protect him.

I landed at Marseille and went straight to Romain Rolland and his sister at Villeneuve. Again the longing to be myself, and the fact that I was not, weighed on me just as it had in 1931. Even more so, because this time I seemed more conscious of it. So those happy days were also a little sad.

When I reached London I found that the English friends there who were supporting Bapu's cause were disturbed at my sudden arrival, as they were evidently apprehensive of what I might say and do, and of what the official British reactions might be. I as-

183

sured them that Bapu had given me full advice, and that my first job was to get in contact with Sir Samuel Hoare. This did not seem to lessen their anxiety, but rather to make them more anxious. However, after I was able to report to them that Sir Samuel had not objected to my proposed plan of a lecture tour, they felt relieved and helped me in every way to get in touch with people who could organize meetings throughout the country.

In the first letter I received in England from Bapu, dated June 20th, he said: "You will stay out as long as necessary and return as soon as you can."

After a meeting at the Friends of India Society in London, in rather a stodgy atmosphere, I started out through the Provinces. Wherever I came in direct touch with the working classes I felt immediate contact and sympathy with the audiences. In Lancashire the response was most touching. The little halls were sometimes packed to overflowing, and on one occasion when I arrived at the place of meeting I found the whole audience emerging from the hall, each carrying a chair. "There's no room left here, so we're shifting to a bigger hall," they explained. "Please come along." So we all went together to the larger place. Wherever possible I stayed with the working people. I remember being put up by an unemployed weaver and his wife in one of the Lancashire towns, and at another place by a retired engine driver, and so on. Everywhere was love and sympathy and nowhere did I find resentment against Bapu.

My tour took me right up to Dundee, where I rejoiced to be among the Scottish people. The meeting was very good and quite big too.

Bapu's letters now warned me of another fast which he was going to commence shortly:

> You will understand the coming fast. The incident calls for penance because there was a clear breach of pledge. Nothing on earth is so serious perhaps as breach of pledge of safety.

It was that same Swami Lalnath who had again managed to create trouble and get himself damaged. Bapu's fast passed off with much less suffering, as his health was better, and also he was a free man in his own surroundings at Wardha.

Other things besides the Harijan problem were pressing hard on his thoughts at that time. He wrote on August 7th:

Many changes are taking place in my mind just now. The corruption in Congress is preying on me as it has never before done. I am conferring with friends as to the advisability of leaving the Congress and pursuing its ideals outside it. It is good that the corruption agitates me. I shall take no hasty step, but there it is.
7-8-34

As soon as I got back to London I again felt the stiffness and stickiness of the Imperial City.

There happened to be going on at that time in England interesting gatherings of pacifists in various parts of the country, to which I was invited. And then there was the meeting with the Independent Labour Party, which was very bracing.

Another interesting experience was meeting with Lloyd George. He invited me down to his home at Churt for tea. Vitality, energy and quick intelligence radiated from his rosy face framed by vigorous white hair. He was most friendly, and spoke with warm appreciation of Bapu.

"I had always known he was a saint," he said, "but I had never realized till I met him that he was a statesman."

After we had talked for a time about India he took me to the drawing room for tea. Looking at the sofa by the fireplace, Lloyd George said, "That's where Mr. Gandhi sat." Then he proceeded to relate how a little cat had come to his house a day or two before Bapu's visit. "She seemed to be someone's pet cat," he said, "because she had on a collar, so I tried to persuade her to go away. But she absolutely refused. Then on the evening when Mr. Gandhi arrived, she went straight to him, as he sat down on that sofa, and settled herself in his lap, where she remained till he got up to leave. And what do you think! The next morning she had gone and I have never seen her again."

The episode had touched the Celt in Lloyd George.

I allowed myself hardly any time for anything but the work

in hand, but I did go to stay a night or two with Alec and also Rhona, whose husband had now retired. I did not let myself think about music, and therefore went to no concerts. The *tapasya* was holding me in its grip.

On September 14, 1934, just as I was thinking of returning to India, there came a cable from Bapu saying: STAY IF POSSIBLE TILL ANDREWS ARRIVAL OCTOBER TWENTIETH.

This meant staying on another month. What then to do? People suggested my starting out on another tour of the Provinces, as there were many inquiries for lectures. But the idea came to me that it was to America that I should go. I immediately cabled to Dr. John Haynes Holmes asking him if it would be feasible, and he cabled back that a schedule was being arranged. So I sent a cable to Bapu saying I was leaving for America and his reply came on September 29th: GOD LIGHT YOUR PATH. BLESSINGS. Off I went on the *Majestic,* which was then the biggest ship afloat, but even she shuddered and shook as she plowed her way out into the Atlantic in the face of a fierce equinoctial gale.

As I had never crossed the Atlantic before, I tried to stay on deck to watch the tremendous waves and flying foam swept over at intervals by squalls of driving rain. But giddiness and seasickness soon overcame me, and I hurried to my cabin. The great ship was creaking from end to end, and then came two successive shudders of terrible violence. When the steward looked in to see how I was getting on, he reported that those two shudders had been caused by two gigantic waves which had gone right over the bridge, smashing the thick plate glass and severely wounding the Captain, who had been carried to his cabin. "And the bridge," he added, "is sixty feet above the level of the sea, so they were some waves!"

As a result of such weather the ship was delayed by twenty-four hours. It was only as we were nearing New York that I ventured up on deck again, and before I had time to enjoy the fresh air and collect my thoughts, a whole bevy of reporters came out on the pilot boat and pressed me for an interview. This was my first experience of America, and I found it sufficiently breathless. Next came a troop of cameramen, and then Dr. John Haynes Holmes and other good friends. From the time I had come up on deck, two hours previously, to sniff the fresh air, I had not been able to get back to my cabin.

Now I was told that owing to the ship's late arrival I should have to plunge straight into my schedule, which began that evening with a meeting at the Barbizon-Plaza Hotel. From then on, for a fortnight, the meetings, receptions and other gatherings continued without a break. It was a totally different world to anything I had ever known before, but in spite of its speed and amazing efficency, it had a bighearted, easy swing about it which enabled one to swim in the racing current, albeit somewhat breathlessly.

My headquarters in New York had been arranged at the Henry Street House Settlement, which gave me a glimpse of the poverty which lies in the back parts of that great city. Here too, in the Settlement itself, everything was convenient, spotlessly clean, and even luxurious, compared with Indian standards, though austere for New York. The neighborhood, however, was very drab and out at elbows.

Outside New York I spoke at colleges in Philadelphia, West Chester and Boston, including Harvard University, and at the Church of the Redeemer in Newark. Then there was a welcome meeting with Mrs. Roosevelt at the White House in Washington, where I also visited the Howard University for Negroes.

The gatherings in New York City were of every description. The two biggest were those of Dr. John Haynes Holmes' Community Church, in Town Hall, and Rabbi Wise's Free Synagogue, at Carnegie Hall. Then there was a luncheon at the McAlpin Hotel, given by the Kiwanis Club and attended by businessmen and their wives. I had anticipated rather a stodgy audience, but on the contrary it proved very responsive and gay. The New History Society was another packed meeting, and finally there came the Farewell Dinner by the American League for India's Freedom.

The whole tour mounted up to twenty-two gatherings and five broadcasts, and by the time it was over I was completely exhausted. The meetings were much bigger than in England, and everywhere extraordinary interest was shown in Bapu as a person. Every sort of question was asked about him, while the political aspect, so much to the fore in England, was of secondary importance to these American audiences. Gandhi the man, the Teacher, the Apostle of Truth, was what they sought, and with such thirst and earnestness! It was this deep interest, and the overflowing openheartedness and affection, that kept me going to the end of the fortnight.

After New York, London seemed like a village with its low houses, slow traffic and open parks. A letter from Bapu, dated October 10, 1932, was awaiting me:

> . . . I am looking forward to a recital of your experiences in America. . . .
>
> Things are shaping themselves here. I do not know what is going to happen. My mind is certainly set on going out of the Congress. I feel quite sure that it will do good to the Congress and to me. I shall better influence the Congress by being outside. I shall cease to be the weight that I am just now, and yet I shall be passing my views on to the Congress whenever occasion demands it. . . .

It was now the end of October, and I was anxious to return to India as soon as possible. But news came from Bapu that Khan Abdul Gaffar Khan wanted me to bring along his young daughter, Mehar Taj, a girl of about fourteen years of age, who was at that time staying with Dr. Khan Saheb's English wife, her aunt by marriage. This set in motion a string of complications. In the first place the aunt did not want to let her niece go, and as she was a somewhat excitable woman, this problem looked as if it were going to be insurmountable. Then when it was at last overcome, it was found that the girl's passport was in a trunk which was stored away in some warehouse. Again we were on the rocks. I had booked a deck passage on a Lloyd Triestano steamer from Brindisi, and as I had a meeting in Paris on the way, I could not postpone my departure. So someone had to be found to bring the young girl all across Europe to meet me at Brindisi. It was only thanks to Agatha Harrison's indefatigable help that Mehar Taj did finally get off from England in time to catch the steamer.

188

CHAPTER XLIV

🌿 DURING the last days in London, while all these domestic agitations were going on, I managed to have interviews with the statesmen whom I had not been able to see before going to America. On November 1st I saw Lord Halifax (formerly Lord Irwin), and on November 2nd General Smuts, Sir Samuel Hoare and Winston Churchill. So now there was nothing further left to be done, and I set off for Brindisi via Paris.

Deck passage with Bapu and his party was a very different thing to deck passage on one's own, especially when one was in charge of a pretty young girl on an Italian ship. We were given half a closed hold to live on day and night, but the surrounding little piece of deck, instead of being reserved, was the playground for the stewards and the scullions, who came there every evening and played various games of ball up to midnight. Mehar Taj used to fall fast asleep in spite of the noise, but as the players made a point every now and then of bouncing the ball over her and, if possible, getting it lost somewhere around her bedding, I had to sit up without fail each night until they had finished their games and gone away.

The weather was excellent, and I think it was the first time I had ever made the voyage without once feeling seasick.

On arrival in Bombay, after handing over my pretty charge to her relatives I went straight to Wardha, where Bapu then was. There was lots to tell, but Bapu as usual had very little time to listen, which always made it difficult to express oneself. The Harijan tour was over, but the work for removal of untouchability was still in full swing, and Bapu had just added another big item to his constructive program by forming the All-India Village Industries Association, which had for its object "revival, encouragement and improvement of village industries and moral and physical advancement of the villages of India." So, in spite of the fact that he had suspended Civil Disobedience, and had just recently made his final severance from the Congress, even as a four-anna member, he was as busy as ever.

CHAPTER XLV

THOUGH Bapu had left the Congress officially, yet the Congress had not left him. They wanted to go their own way, but whenever they got into difficulties they wanted Bapu to help them. In a statement written September 17, 1934, about a month before the final severance, Bapu had stated:

> It has appeared to me that there is a growing and vital difference between many Congressmen and myself. I seem to be going in a direction just the opposite of what many of the most intellectual Congressmen would gladly and enthusiastically take if they were not hampered by their unexampled loyalty to me. No leader can expect greater loyalty and devotion than I have received from intellectually minded Congressmen even when they have protested and signified their disapproval of the policies I have laid before the Congress. For me any more to draw upon this loyalty and devotion is to put an undue strain upon them. Their loyalty cannot blind my eyes to what appears to me to be a fundamental difference between the Congress intelligentsia and me.

To have guided the nation his own way would have been for Bapu a straightforward job, though difficult enough. But now it developed into a process of watching, advising from outside and helping when difficulties arose—a much more troublesome task. It was not to be wondered at, then, that I found Bapu under a considerable strain. He was cheerful as usual, but there was a difference. The buoyancy of the Salt Satyagraha days was no longer there. In the whole country the atmosphere was oppressive and the suspended struggle lay there like an indigestion.

At the end of December Bapu went to Delhi to lay the foundation stone of the big Harijan Colony, financed by Sri Ghanshyamdas Birla, at which the inmates would receive both literary education and training in crafts. We stayed a whole month at the Colony site, after which we returned to Wardha.

Seth Jamnalal Bajaj, the leading Marwari businessman of Wardha district, with headquarters in Bombay, was big and expansive both in heart and body and devoted to Bapu and Vinoba. Bapu he looked upon as a parent, and Vinoba as a Guru. It was he who built the Wardha Ashram for Vinoba, and now he donated his large house, with twenty acres of orange orchards, to Bapu in memory of Maganlal Gandhi, Bapu's favorite nephew and the first manager of Sabarmati Ashram, who had died of fever in Bihar some years previously. Bapu immediately turned this into the headquarters of the newly formed Village Industries Association, and named it Maganwadi.

Soon after our return from Delhi, Bapu moved from Vinoba's Ashram to this new center, and we all settled down there, or at least thought we had. Sri J. C. Kumarappa, a South Indian Christian and brilliant economist, who had been completely converted to Bapu's theories, took charge of the Association, which now rapidly developed. He had his offices in one corner of the spacious house and lived quite independently, while Bapu's party of some fifteen to twenty people filled the rest. And what a party it was! A few of the old Sabarmati Ashramites were still there, but a strange medley of various kinds of cranky people had collected around Bapu, and since we were all cheek by jowl in one building, there was no peace and no escape. Even at night the disturbances went on, for one of the inmates was a somnambulist, and when he walked in his sleep another inmate, who had St. Vitus's dance, always got up and tried to catch him, with the result that in the dead of night blood-curdling shrieks would rend the air. In spite of all this Bapu carried on with a prodigious amount of work.

And now on top of everything else Bapu started another dietetic experiment with the inmates. This time it was soya beans.

Just then quite a lot was being written in the press about their wonderful qualities, and how they could be made to replace milk in the daily diet. Here seemed to be the very thing Bapu had been seeking, so he had them cooked in a variety of ways and served at meals. The only difference between them and the ordinary Indian pulses appeared to be that they were less tasty and much less digestible. They were of course said to be richer in proteins, but that very richness seemed to make them indigestible. Anyway they disagreed with everybody, including Bapu, and soon had to be given up. On this occasion I had kept clear of the experiment myself.

As the days went by in this extraordinary atmosphere I felt my nerves getting undermined, and tried to find relief by going for long solitary walks in the early morning. In order to reach the open country I had to pass through a village called Sindi. I was disgusted with the dirty condition of its surroundings, and mentioned it to Bapu.

"If that is so," said Bapu, "we should do something. We have come to Maganwadi for helping to improve the villages morally and physically, and we can't afford to sit here with our neighboring village in that state, and not do anything about it."

I agreed. So Bapu pronounced the method to be adopted. I was to go every morning to clean the Sindi lanes with two or three volunteers whom he would enlist from among the Maganwadi inmates and even visitors. Bapu's enthusiasm for this job was such that one could not hesitate to take it up, and without any delay I started on the work with my party.

Though the lanes were so dirty, the insides of the little houses, no matter how poor the inmates, were clean and neat, especially the kitchens. In this the Harijans' houses were no exception, indeed they were sometimes the cleanest. This fact made one feel the outside cleanliness would surely come sooner or later.

In May Bapu went for a short while to Borsad to investigate on the spot the reports of Government vindictiveness in the surrounding villages. He did not take me with him, as he did not want my Sindi work to be interrupted. On May 25th he wrote:

192

Sindi cleaning must not be omitted even for a day. But at the same time you must have that silent walk up the hill.

And the next day:

I have your two fine descriptive letters. They show how much you need the solitary walks for self-expression. You must have them more frequently if not daily.

Bapu not only noticed this need for an outlet in the country, but also agreed to my having a small cabin made of matting under one of the trees in the garden near the house where I could go for my reading and writing. I knew he would have liked me to be able to remain undisturbed in the midst of all the other people, but such an attempt would have resulted in a breakdown.

By the time Bapu returned from Borsad the heat had become terrific. Wardha district is one of the hottest places in India. The temperature in early March goes up to 100 degrees F. and by May and June it reaches 118 degrees and over. Bapu kept his head perpetually wrapped in a wet cloth, and I did likewise, else I should have been done for. All metal things, even inside the house, were so hot one could not bear to touch them. By the middle of June the sky became somewhat cloudy and the temperature dropped a little, and when the rain came, by the end of June, there was definite relief. But it was relief from heat only to be followed by horrible stuffiness in September and a widespread epidemic of malaria. So this was the climate Fate had led Bapu to settle in! It needed all one's courage to face the prospect.

In spite of the daily packed routine, Bapu found time also for visitors, of whom there was a large number from various parts of the world. At this distance of time I cannot recall many of them, but two clearly remain in my mind: Halide Edib Hanum, the celebrated woman writer of Turkey, and Swami Yoganand, founder of the Self-Realization Fellowship of America.

One not so pleasant visitor was a snake charmer who came and displayed his pet snake in front of Bapu, and then, just to show how tame it was, placed it on Bapu's shoulder. It at once coiled itself round his neck, but Bapu sat motionless with a slightly wry smile, until the man removed it.

CHAPTER XLVI

AS the days went by, we all felt more and more uneasy about Bapu's health. His nerves were becoming severely strained, and one of the things which was weighing on his mind was the problem of the Sindi villagers, who had failed to respond to our efforts at sanitation. Suddenly one day Bapu announced that he would go and live in Sindi all alone, taking what help he required in the way of personal service from the villagers there. Everyone was aghast. And yet how to persuade Bapu not to go, once his mind had become set on the idea? In a desperate effort to save the situation I offered to go and live there myself if he would accept the compromise. Very reluctantly he did, and we all breathed again.

As there was no place where one could live in the village, a small one-roomed brick cottage was prepared for me according to Bapu's instructions, and I moved there within a week or two. Most of the inhabitants were Mahars, who are the equivalents of the Chamars (leather workers) of North India. There were a few houses of other Harijans whom the Mahars considered inferior to themselves, even though these were not sweepers, and one or two caste Hindu houses. Each of these groups had its own well. The very first day I happened to accept some water from a man of the lowest group for washing my hands, and as a result I was not permitted to come near the wells of either the caste Hindus or Mahars. As the well of the lowest group was not very clean, I did not wish to use it for drinking or cooking, so this meant I had to take my buckets to one of the other wells and, placing them at a little distance, request the owners to be good enough to give me some water. Sometimes it so happened that these people were all out in the fields, and then one had to go without. I was now getting direct experience of what it was like to be an untouchable.

Before long an attack of cholera broke out in the area, and in Sindi village a young man of about eighteen was stricken. I hurried to the civil hospital and got a bottle of cholera mixture, but by the time I returned he was on the point of death. The village hut in which he was lying was very small and low. I entered the first room and saw that he was in an inside room without windows. There, in the half-dark, he was stretched out with his head in his mother's lap. As I came in he was giving his last gasps, and the poor distracted mother was wiping the saliva away from the sides of his mouth with her bare hands. In a minute or two it was all over. Everyone began wailing, and the mother, rushing out of the house, plunged her hands into the big vessel of drinking water which stood outside the door, and washed her streaming eyes. I explained to everyone that that water should be thrown away and the vessel disinfected with fire, but no one could listen to or take in anything. I went away feeling sure the whole household would get the fell disease.

I informed the rest of the village that I had brought the medicine, and that if anyone felt the slightest symptoms, they should inform me, no matter what time of night. Mercifully, by immediate administration of the cholera mixture all further cases came under control. What amazed me was that there was not a single new case in the house where the young man had died and the water vessel had been polluted.

In the next village there were twelve deaths, and I cannot remember how many more in the surrounding area. Such epidemics, we were told, were of common occurrence, and no wonder, considering the insanitary state of the villages. After I had reported the outbreak to the civil hospital, a doctor was deputed to go around the affected area with an inoculating and disinfecting squad, and before long the epidemic subsided. But why wait for the epidemics to start? Never had I realized more clearly the meaning of Bapu's insistence on sanitation, and why he always refused to let his workers concentrate on medical relief in preference to other work. He looked upon this as a lazy way of winning popularity. The best medical aid was to overcome insanitation and malnutrition.

As the days went by, the attitude of the villagers gradually softened. Close to the back of my cottage there was a biggish room where the Mahars used to foregather for singing *kirtans,* congregational singing of Hindu religious hymns and chants accompanied by cymbals. One day a young man came and invited me to join them. Here was something new indeed! I followed him to the room. About a dozen men were sitting around in a circle. "Come along, come along!" they said, and made room for me to sit down in the ring. Then the young man who had fetched me handed me a pair of cymbals. The old men in the circle were quite fatherly about showing me how to hold them, and then off they went singing with throbbing rhythm to the clanging of cymbals of all sizes and sounds. It was rather deafening, but certainly exhilarating.

After this they invited me each time they had a special *kirtan* party. Of course everything did not become easy all at once, but slowly, slowly the atmosphere changed and even the scavenging work became lighter.

Though things had improved, I was all the time restless because I felt we were not getting at the problems of the real villages. After all, Sindi was a suburb of Wardha, to which it was practically joined on one side. I suggested to Bapu that if anyone from Maganwadi would be ready to stay in Sindi, I might look around for a typical village. He agreed, and as a young man was prepared to come to Sindi, at least for a time, I began investigating the surrounding villages within a radius of five miles. They were not very promising. It was a hard, dry, rather unresponsive countryside, and the inhabitants were also rather dry in their temperament. In some places the Harijans were positively hostile. It was therefore difficult to find any suitable village. After walking out day after day in all directions, I finally decided that a village called Segaon (the future Sevagram), about five miles to the east of Wardha, would be the best, or rather the least unsatisfactory.

196

Here, at any rate, there was an orchard and farm belonging to Jamnalalji, and the villagers were a little more responsive. I explained the position to Bapu and he spoke to Jamnalalji, with the result that I very soon moved there from Sindi.

To begin with I stayed in an empty bullock shed on Jamnalalji's farm, where I immediately made the acquaintance of cattle ticks that fixed themselves around my waist and under my knees, and were quite difficult to pick off. I began moving about the village looking for a place to build a hut, and chose an open spot between the blacksmith's house and a small temple, with a well close by. The farm manager told his Mahar laborers to construct me a hut according to my directions. I asked them to make it of the same materials that they used for their own houses, and measured out seven feet by five feet with a little side alcove for stores. Within less than a week it was all ready. The materials used were wood and bamboo, the center stems of date palm leaves, mud plaster, and tiles for the roof. While watching the men at work I noticed that the mud plaster could be molded into designs, so I added with my own hand some decoration in low relief, of palm trees, animals and birds.

Before very long there came the news that Bapu had had a sudden breakdown, and that his blood pressure had risen alarmingly. The next news was that he had moved to Vinoba's Ashram, where he could be quiet, as the doctors had ordered that he should take a complete rest. I was told that Jamnalalji had taken charge of the arrangements, and three or four others were in attendance.

The Ashram was on the Segaon side of Wardha and scarcely four miles away, so I walked over, that I might just set eyes on Bapu and sit quietly by his side for a little while before returning to the village. Bapu was staying in the big room on the roof of the main building. When I reached the foot of the steps leading up to the roof, a man standing there barred the way. When I remonstrated, he said he had had orders to stop me. The words hit me like a thunderbolt. I leaned back against the wall and tears ran down my cheeks. I could not take it in. The shock was so great that I did not get over it for years. Of course Bapu knew nothing of what had occurred, and I was warned that if he should happen to hear that I had come from the village, his blood pressure would go up.

I walked back to Segaon and carried on somehow. After a few days Jamnalalji sent me word that I might come and see Bapu for a few minutes. I went across the fields feeling half dead, and when I went up to Bapu's room Jamnalalji accompanied me and sat there like a jail superintendent. I think I was permitted to stay about five or ten minutes. The others who were looking after Bapu were in and out of the room. Again I was told that I must at all cost remain in Segaon, otherwise Bapu's blood pressure would become dangerous. Of course all this was being done out of devotion to, and anxiety for, Bapu, and I tried to appreciate it in that light, but my nerves, which were already under a severe strain, could ill stand this new development.

CHAPTER XLVII

BAPU'S health began to improve, but the blood pressure remained too high, and the doctors advised a change, so he moved to Ahmedabad for a while. I had been permitted a few fleeting interviews during these days, but that was all. It was not so much the shortness of the visits as the strange artificiality which had suddenly been raised between Bapu and me, which haunted me like a nightmare. And all the time that Sword of Damocles was being held over my head, the fear that if I breathed a word Bapu's blood pressure would rise. So I struggled on, but before long I broke down and had to go to Maganwadi.

Now that Bapu was away, I was allowed to write to him, and this brought back some of the nearness and naturalness which had been wholly lacking in those supervised interviews. Bapu must have detected in my letters a certain dread which I felt about

Segaon. It was not a dread of the village as such, but that dread of a thing or place which is connected with some terrible shock. Had it not been from Segaon that I had gone to see Bapu and had found the stairs to his sickroom barred against me, and was it not to Segaon that I had returned to strive in solitude in spite of so deadly a blow? Yes, once I had come away from the scene of that suffering, truly I dreaded to return to it.

On February 13th, Bapu wrote from Ahmedabad: "I see you dread going to Segaon. Don't if you do not have the urge."

Then the next day:

> I do not think you need go to Segaon by way of penance. You should go there only if you cannot be happy otherwise. . . . When I go to Segaon, as I must, if you are not there, nobody of the present company can be with me. I must make new friends and co-workers in Segaon. You can settle in any neighbouring village if you like, so as to be near me. . . . My heart is in the villages. I want an excuse for going there. Of my own volition I lack the courage to go or to combat the arguments of friends. But if you can persuade yourself to leave Segaon, as soon as I return from my convalescence, I would love to go to Segaon, not as any punishment to you, but as a welcome God-given opportunity for going to a village.

After this letter my mind was all in a turmoil. For years my dream had been that Bapu would someday settle in a village and that I might be there to study his way of handling the people and problems. Now this dream was shattered as far as my part in it was concerned. Then too, Segaon in any case was not the place I would have chosen for Bapu. Yet even so, perhaps it would be better for him than Maganwadi, where he would be bound to break down again before long.

I don't think I came to any conclusion beyond that I should return to Segaon at once and work away hard, leaving the outcome in God's hands.

On my return to the village I concentrated on the sanitation problem. Though Segaon was not a village one would ever have selected as a suitable place for a center if one's choice had not been restricted by circumstances, it was, at any rate, a great improvement on Sindi. Thanks to the open land around Segaon, the lanes were in a much better state than at Sindi, but even so there was plenty of room for improvement.

By the beginning of March Bapu's health had so far improved that he was able to begin moving about as in the past. The first place he went to was Savli, a small country town where the newly formed Gandhi Seva Sangh (Gandhi Service Society) was holding its first conference. This society had been the subject of much discussion between Bapu and his co-workers. They wanted to systematize and develop Bapu's ideals, and Bapu maintained that he had no "ism" to be so handled. This resulted in one of the most valuable utterances that Bapu ever made about himself and his work. Addressing the Society on March 28, 1936, he said:

"There is no such thing as Gandhism, and I do not want to leave any sect after me. I do not claim to have originated any new principle or doctrine. I have simply tried, in my own way, to apply the eternal truths to our daily life and problems. There is, therefore, no question of my leaving any code like the Code of Manu [an ancient Hindu lawgiver]. There cannot possibly be any comparison between that Lawgiver and me. The opinions I have formed, and the conclusions I have arrived at, are not, by any means, final. I may change them tomorrow if I find better ones. I have nothing new to teach the world. Truth and nonviolence are as old as the hills. All I have done is to try experiments in both, on as vast a scale and as best as I could. In doing so I have sometimes erred and learnt by my errors. Life and its problems have thus become, to me, a series of experiments in the practice of Truth and Nonviolence. By instinct I have been truthful, but not necessarily nonviolent. As a Jain Muni once rightly said, I was not so much a votary of Ahimsa as I was of Truth, and that I put the latter in the first place, and the former in the second. For, as he phrased it, I was capable of sacrificing nonviolence for the sake of truth. In fact, it was in the course of my pursuit of truth that I discovered nonviolence. Our scriptures have declared that there is no Dharma [law] higher than truth. But

200

nonviolence, they say, is the highest duty. The word Dharma, in my opinion, has a different connotation as used in the two aphorisms.

"Well, my entire philosophy, if it may be called by that pretentious name, is contained in what I have just said. You will not call it Gandhism, for there is no 'ism' about it. And no elaborate literature or propaganda is needed to explain it. The scriptures have been quoted against my postulation, but I have held faster than ever to my firm conviction that truth ought not to be sacrificed for anything whatsoever. Those who believe in the elementary truths I have laid down can propagate them *only* by living them. How am I to convince the world merely through books that my entire constructive program is rooted in, and based on, the practice of nonviolence? Only my life can demonstrate it."

From Savli, Bapu went to Delhi for a short rest at the Harijan Colony at King's Way, and from there proceeded to Lucknow to attend the annual session of the National Congress.

During these journeyings Bapu's letters came regularly, and they showed that his mind was fast turning toward the idea of coming to settle in Segaon himself. On March 14th he wrote: "My heart is there. What my effort will end in I do not know."

I cannot remember any details, but my general recollection is that practically everyone opposed the idea of Bapu going to live in a village, and I was openly criticized as having been the cause. Among those who surrounded Bapu there was hardly a soul who loved the countryside, and suburban Maganwadi was as far as most of them would have cared to go.

Again the hot weather was coming on and I found it difficult to get around everywhere on foot, so I procured a local village horse. He was quite small, no bigger than a pony, but strong, intelligent and affectionate. I looked after him entirely myself, and we became close friends. His name was Sejila.

My tiny hut right in the village became unbearable when the temperature rose to over 100 degrees, and I moved back to Jamnalalji's farm. But this time I camped under the trees in the fruit garden, in order not to get involved again with those ticks. I added a little bamboo matting to the rather thin protection of the trees, but even so the heat was tremendous.

Bapu was growing enthusiastic about the idea of coming to live in Segaon himself, but he would make no final decision without first "converting" Jamnalalji. On April 14th he wrote:

Jamnalalji is half converted.

It is a great joy to me that in Sejila you have found a faithful and intelligent companion. I dread your nightly adventures. I know it is wrong to do so. We are all in His keeping. But I am anxious for you to avoid all mishaps which can be anticipated. I expect to find you hale, hearty and joyful.

My nightly adventures were my rides back to Segaon after dark. I often had to go to Wardha about some matter or other, and as the weather was very hot, I used to set out on Sejila in the early morning and return in the late evening, sometimes after dark. The track between Segaon and Wardha, in those days, was not without its stories of robberies and murders, so Bapu's anxiety was understandable, and I tried to get in before dark in future. But there is a fascination about being out at night all alone with one's horse on a lonely road, which I had been enjoying.

On his return to Maganwadi, Bapu evidently completed the "conversion," and wrote:

Jamnalalji has given full authority to commence building operations. If you come on tomorrow evening or 23rd morning I could explain everything.

(21-4-36)

I rode over to see Bapu, and he explained to me that he would come to stay in my little camp under the trees for a few days so as to be able to look at the village and the site I had provisionally selected for his cottage.

I no longer felt heat, tiredness or any troubles. I made the little camp as neat and nice as I could. The gaddi for Bapu I arranged under the big tree, and tied up a milch goat nearby along with Sejila and my cow. When Bapu came, Jamnalalji organized a meeting in the village, at which Bapu spoke to the villagers. The

202

Kumbi headman, a very charming and aristocratic old man, made a graceful and honest speech in which he welcomed the idea of Bapu coming to live amongst them, but made it quite clear that he personally would not be able to co-operate in Bapu's Harijan program. Bapu appreciated his frankness, and they got on well together from that day.

I had selected for Bapu's cottage one acre of ground in the first open field on the north side of the village toward the high ground. Bapu now went to look at it, and we measured out the foundations of the cottage according to his directions. It was to be one big room thirty feet long and fifteen feet broad, with a good plinth and open verandas. No other details were gone into at that time.

CHAPTER XLVIII

BAPU had not fully recovered from that attack of high blood pressure, and when the doctors insisted that he should go away to a cool climate till the rains began, he went to Nandi Hills, which had suited him well in the past. Before leaving, he arranged that two energetic workers should come out from Maganwadi to help me in collecting and supervising the labor, one was Balwant Singh, thin, wiry, with a little scrubby beard, and the only person in Bapu's group who had a real farmer's background. The other was Munnalal Shah, tall and strong, a lawyer by profession who had thrown up his practice and joined Bapu. We set about our work with the utmost dispatch, for the rains would be coming in a little over a month, and whatever happened everything had to be finished before then. The walls were to be made of solid mud, and if rain came before the roof was on, they would collapse.

Bapu was planning to come straight to Segaon on his return from the south, which left us only one month in which to finish everything. Laborers, both men and women, were called from all the surrounding villages, and about fifty little bullock carts were engaged for bringing stone from the hill for preparing the foundations and plinth of Bapu's cottage. From daybreak to nightfall we were at it. Besides the cottage there was a cowshed to be constructed, as well as a road between the fields of deep black soil up to the negotiable high ground where the soil was hard and even rocky.

When the construction work was at its height I suddenly suffered an attack of malaria. My temperature ran up to 105 degrees, and as the maximum daily temperature of the air was just then 118 degrees, I felt pretty well cooked up. Poor Balwant Singh and Munnalal bhai (meaning "brother") had to nurse me in addition to looking after the building operations, as we could not afford to stop work for a single day. I can remember lying under the trees with a raging temperature, and Balwant Singh rubbing goat's milk on the soles of my feet, which brought definite relief. When news reached Wardha of my condition, I was taken away to Jamnalalji's house. I would much rather have remained in our little camp, where I could keep at least one eye on the construction work in between the attacks of fever, but people insisted.

Luckily the fever came under control quickly, and within a week I was back again at Segaon. June had come, the clouds had begun to make their appearance, and yet the roof of Bapu's cottage was not on. At last the mud walls became dry enough to bear the weight of the timber, and then onto the beams had to be hammered a complete covering of split bamboos for carrying the tiles. When the last tile was in place, we stopped and looked at the cottage with a gasp of relief. But the question still remained as to how to get the room dry. We kept all the doors and windows open, but on account of the damp air, it was a slow process.

On Sunday, June 14th, came a note from Bapu, who had reached Maganwadi, saying he hoped to arrive in Segaon on Tuesday morning at about 7:30 if the weather was fine.

We spent Monday clearing away the rubble and rubbish which always surround a newly constructed building, and started burning charcoal stoves in the room in an effort to dry it up. In the early hours of Tuesday it began pouring with rain. We said to one another: "Bapu wrote that he would come if the weather was good, now in this pouring rain we can't expect him. Let's go on drying off his corner of the room with the charcoal stoves. Perhaps by the time it clears up the room will have become fairly inhabitable."

We were all three squatting on the floor and pushing the charcoal stoves around in the corner where the gaddi was to be placed, when Bapu suddenly walked in, drenched to the skin and laughing heartily.

Bapu's plan, of course, was that he should live alone in Segaon, so as soon as my cottage was ready I moved there with Sejila, for whom I had prepared a little shed. I think it was within a week or ten days of Bapu's arrival. Balwant Singh and Munnalal bhai, however, remained at Segaon, and Lilavati ben, one of the women members from the Sabarmati Ashram days, arrived from Maganwadi. The result was quite a different establishment than Bapu had intended. On July 20th, in answer to some verbal message which I had sent to Segaon about three weeks after moving to my Veroda cottage, Bapu wrote on his silence day:

> No one understands what message the bearer has brought. Lilavati is too careless to understand. I can't speak. Munnalal is half dead. B. threatens to follow suit. In these circumstances, it is better to write out what you want. This has become a confused household instead of a hermitage it was expected to be. Such has been my fate! I must find my hermitage from within.

CHAPTER XLIX

WHEN the plan was made for me to go and live on the lands of Veroda village, I had thought that I should be able to go to Segaon quite often, but Bapu laid down definite restrictions. As far as I remember, I was to go to Segaon only once a week. Living all alone, a good deal of time had to be given to cooking, cleaning, and of course attendance on Sejila. The rest of the time I devoted to investigating conditions in Veroda village. But I had become too run down to be able to carry on in this way, and intermittent fever started. Bapu was worried and sent someone daily to help me with the cooking, etc. But malaria got the upper hand, and I became prostrate. So Bapu came that way for his walk, and brought along a bullock cart into which he had me put. I can remember now lying in the cart and watching Bapu walking along behind, which made me feel very ashamed of myself. After a few days in Segaon I was better and able to get around and help with the general work of the establishment.

Balwant Singh was away, Lilavati ben had returned to Magan-wadi, and there were now no women in the party, but some other men had joined, among whom was Nanavate bhai, a music teacher. Bapu was busy with his incessant writing work, and also preoccupied with Khan Abdul Guffar Khan, affectionately known as Badshah Khan, who was there on a long visit.

In a short time Nanavate bhai came down with fever, and it was diagnosed by the doctors as typhoid. Almost at the same time, Balwant Singh returned in a collapsed condition with malaria. I helped to nurse both patients along with Pyarelal. Even Badshah Khan had been recruited by Bapu for giving fruit juice, etc. Balwant Singh soon improved, but Nanavate bhai's illness was bound to be long.

Then I fell ill with typhoid. Bapu was perhaps a little anxious, but his anxiety took the form of quietly undertaking to nurse me entirely himself. I protested as strongly as I could under the circumstances, but Bapu simply said he enjoyed nursing, and that as he did not wish to call any woman to Segaon at that time, he would look after me himself, and I was not to worry. As I was rapidly becoming helpless, I gave in and allowed myself to reap the infinite blessing of Bapu's gentle, loving care. With perfect regularity he saw to my every need, even to rising each night at one o'clock to come to me. The fever and splitting headache allowed me no sleep, and I used to lie awake too weak to move this way or that, just living for the sight of Bapu, wrapped in his big

206

white shawl, coming along the veranda, where my bed used to be put at night. And he never once failed to come.

During the day we used to be all in the one big room. Bapu and Badshah Khan in one corner, Nanavate bhai opposite them, myself in the farther corner on the same side as Bapu, and the rest of the party fitting in here and there. All day long I lay watching that scene, and it has remained imprinted on my mind. Sometimes Badshah Khan came along and pressed my head with his big hand to try to relieve the headaches. Sometimes doctors came and went, and sometimes visitors. Then Nanavate was given cold-pack treatment when his condition was becoming serious. I watched everything in a half-dazed and yet conscious condition.

Typhoid must run its course of fourteen, twenty-one or twenty-eight days, and in very bad cases, sometimes even thirty-five—if the patient does not die first. Nanavate, who had become ill before I did, was under fever for twenty-one days, and toward the end began to get unconscious. When my fever had run for thirteen days Bapu said to me, smiling, "Tomorrow you have got to come out of the fever." "Shall I?" I replied faintly. "Yes, you ought to," said Bapu. And I actually did!

Very soon after this, Bapu had to go to Benares, Rajkot, and Ahmedabad. By the time he returned, my health was much improved, but he did not press me to go back to Veroda in a hurry, because of the strain of living there alone. In fact I was allowed to build a small cottage for myself in the corner of Bapu's one-acre plot, with a room attached for teaching carding and spinning to the Segaon villagers. I had it constructed on the wattle-and-mud-plaster model, which was much quicker and cheaper than the two-foot solid mud walls.

It was about this time that Bapu himself had an attack of malaria. Jamnalalji became very anxious, and managed to persuade Bapu to go for treatment to Wardha Civil Hospital. I helped with the nursing. Luckily it was a fairly mild attack, and Bapu soon recovered. What has remained in my mind most clearly about the time in the hospital is the visit of another snake charmer. He was an educated modern type of man who had the gift of controlling snakes, and he came to the hospital to see Bapu, bringing his reptiles along with him in boxes. I devoutly hoped that he would not throw any snakes around Bapu's neck as did the man who came to Maganwadi. But he did the next worst thing. He let several snakes loose on Bapu's bed. One of them was a wonderfully beautiful creature of many colors, with sky-blue and orange predominant. As the visitor let it loose he remarked that it was an exceptionally poisonous kind. Bapu, who was sitting up in his bed, quietly watched the graceful, slow dance of the snakes on his blanket, and wisely kept his legs perfectly still. The colored snake was rather more lively than the rest, and kept rising up as if wishing to have a good look at Bapu. The visitor made passes over its head with his hand, and it immediately quieted down. It was no doubt very interesting to watch, but we onlookers felt greatly relieved when the snakes were put back in their boxes.

I thought the performance was all over, when the visitor suddenly let loose two cobras on the floor. They were more active and less controllable than the smaller snakes had been, and I thanked God that at least they had not been put on Bapu's bed. One of the cobras now began making unpleasantly vigorous turns on the floor, and the man quickly said, "Stand back." Everyone stepped backward as far as possible, but I was already with my back against the wall by the head of Bapu's bed, so just had to remain where I was. With a little maneuvering on the part of its owner the lively cobra was persuaded to go back into its box, and the other one followed. After closing them in, the visitor explained that the lively one was rather hot-tempered, and only a few days ago had eaten its mother. It was kind of him to give us that piece of information after the cobras had been shut up!

Bapu was soon able to return to Segaon. He had thrown off the malaria, but the blood pressure, which had remained unsteady ever since the dangerous attack in 1927, was again giving trouble. There was an experienced doctor staying in the Ashram at that time, and he said it was imperative that Bapu should move to some quieter place than his big room, which was by now packed with inmates. The cowshed and my recently built hut were the only other buildings available. The doctor came to me and said, "Can I bring Bapu over here?" I needed no persuading! The

208

question was how to persuade Bapu. I was expecting it to be a
hopeless job, but the doctor succeeded and that very day brought
Bapu across. The only pity was that Bapu refused to use the little
living room at the front and insisted on settling down in the
carding room. But at least it was quiet and he had it to himself.

This arrangement lasted till Bapu left in January for a tour of
South India connected with entry of Harijans into temples. While
he was away I showed Jamnalalji a plan I had thought out for
turning my hut into a proper cottage for Bapu. He liked the idea,
and immediately gave orders for the work to be carried out. It
was all finished before Bapu returned. It looked very nice, and at
the same time was, of course, much more convenient for Bapu.

We had not asked approval by post beforehand, as there would
not have been time, and we were rather apprehensive about how
Bapu would react. Sure enough we got a scolding, but Bapu
gradually reconciled himself to the alteration. This was how the
little cottage came into existence which is now known as Gandhiji's *kutia,* and is yearly visited by thousands of people.

Though I was living in Segaon, yet I could find no happiness.
I knew in my heart of hearts that Bapu would like me to be working somewhere outside, but each time I went out my health broke
down.

So many people had now come to live at Segaon, and Bapu distributed all his work among them. For his personal work there
were Prabhavati ben, wife of the Socialist leader Jaya Prakash
Narayan; Amtus Salam, a devoted Moslem young woman from
an aristocratic family of Patiala; and Lilavati ben, besides Pyarelal's young sister, Sushila, who had just taken her degree as a
medical doctor. Then the Rajkumari Amrit Kaur of the princely
house of Kapurthala, who had recently joined Bapu, assisted in
the secretarial work with exquisite neatness and efficiency. So the
result was that I had nothing whatever to do beyond the teaching
of spinning to two or three village boys.

I did not admit it to myself in those days but in reality khadi
work was not a natural outlet for me, not because I lacked any
faith in the ideal, but because it was an indoor kind of occupation.
Of the various activities going on in Segaon, the one which was

most congenial to me was the animal husbandry, and I discussed cows with Balwant Singh and shared his interest in developing the local breed of Goala cattle. But this was only a side interest. I had no definite work connected with the animal husbandry.

Inner misery and outer aimlessness began to tell severely on my health, and in the summer of 1937 Bapu sent me to Dr. Dharmvir, at Dalhousie, a Himalayan summer resort, of from 6,000 to 8,000 feet altitude. Subhas Chandra Bose, then a young active Congressman, was already at the doctor's house taking treatment and change of air, so we used to go for walks together. I enjoyed his charm as a cultured intellectual, and found that side of him quite different from the one which came out in his public activities. At that time we had no idea of the full length to which his differences would extend. We only knew that he did not see eye to eye with other Congress leaders, and that he was filled with restless overweening ambition. Jawaharlal had been twice President of the Congress, so he must be too. He achieved that office, but even that left him unsatisfied and restless. Then, when the war came, he vanished, turned Nazi, went to Japan, and gathering up elements of the Indian Army in Burma announced that he would help free India from the British in co-operation with the Japanese. A wild ambition to serve his country which ended in a fatal air crash.

The walks with Subhas Babu were not daily, and I more often went for long solitary rambles. Finding myself in those beautiful surroundings, the old urge to do sketching came up again, and I sent my drawings to Bapu. He wrote: "Your drawing is good. Do continue the practice. It would be good recreation for you." (6-29-37)

Bapu sensed the inner need I had for self-expression of that kind. But my normal self was under such restraint in those days that it was only on very rare occasions, such as being face to face with the great Himalayan mountains, that it came to the surface.

CHAPTER L

🌿 THOUGH Bapu had separated from the Congress officially, yet he was getting ever more occupied with the political developments that were going on. In July of the year 1937, just when I returned from Dalhousie, the Congress took office in nine out of the eleven Provinces of India, and this naturally added greatly to the problems and responsibilities to be faced. Whenever the Viceroy had to be approached, which became a more frequent need with the shouldering of governmental responsibility, it was always Bapu who had to do the interviewing, and in spite of his blood pressure, which was giving continual trouble, he had to do a lot of traveling for one thing and another.

In December, however, the doctors called a halt, and Bapu agreed to go to the Birla bungalow by Juhu beach on the outskirts of Bombay.

From there he returned for a little while to Segaon. The place was by now turning into a regular Ashram, and one activity after another was being developed. Khadi and animal husbandry were already there, now the making of *gur*, country-made brown sugar, and sugar making from date palms was taken up. This proved very successful, and greatly pleased Bapu because the juice of the palms, which up to then had been used exclusively for the preparation of *tody*, was now being turned into a nourishing food. The next, and very important, activity to be taken up was Bapu's recently expounded theory of education through craft, which was given the name of Basic Education. A remarkable and highly cultured couple, Aryanayakum and Ashadevi, joined Bapu in this work. He was a handsome Ceylonese, tall and studious, and she a very artistic Bengali, both formerly of Santiniketan. Their coming gave me a new kind of companionship, and I helped them plan out the buildings which were to be constructed for their center. Bapu was very keen on this new branch of his activities, and he thought perhaps I might like to throw myself into it. But an educational center was something I could not face.

In May, Bapu made his first tour of the North-West Frontier Province, from where he went to Delhi for a time. I remained in Segaon, and while he was away I got news of Rhona's sudden death from heart failure. It was a severe shock, as she was not known to have had a weak heart.

Things in India were moving rapidly, and all the time I felt the pull was going against Bapu. The Congress, now that it was in office, was getting more and more conventional in its attitude. Next, a National Planning Committee was set up which went all out for industrialization, not that it had power to implement its programs, but there was no doubt left now as to which way the Congress would go if and when it did get power. It would go the way of all the Western nations.

In Europe a crisis seemed to be rapidly approaching, and everyone was expecting war to break out. The Congress leaders were vigorously discussing what their attitude should be if war were declared, when news came of the Munich Pact. So for the time being the question was shelved.

From Delhi, Bapu again went to the North-West Frontier Province and I continued to remain in Segaon. The European situation was stirring me deeply, and I wrote to Bapu asking him whether he would not broach the subject in his articles. He replied, in a letter dated October 9, 1938:

> I have anticipated you all. For I have plunged into the European waters. You will give me your reactions to the articles. . . .

The longing for nonviolent resistance to be tried out in Czechoslovakia possessed me, and when Bapu returned from the Frontier I asked him whether he would approve of my trying to get there to throw in my lot with the people in an effort to create nonviolent and fearless resistance against Hitler's next move, whatever it might be. Bapu said, "I thought you would be feeling the call. You should certainly go if it can be arranged."

212

I should have been off to Europe without a doubt if it had not been for the fact that just then Bapu found himself in urgent need of someone to send to help Badshah Khan in the Frontier. I saw how anxious Bapu was about this matter, and I offered to go. Bapu agreed, and I reached Peshawar before the end of November.

Badshah Khan met me. At that time his elder brother, Dr. Khan Saheb, was the first Congress Prime Minister of the Province, and I was taken to his house, where I stayed with the family for some days before going on to Badshah Khan's village home at Utmanzai.

I had arrived in the depths of winter, and it was sufficiently cold. This I could have enjoyed thoroughly, only my warm clothes were insufficient, and at Utmanzai, Badshah Khan kept a Spartan establishment in which a fire in the grate was a rarity.

There was not actually very much to do. A few Red Shirts came for lessons, but how could Pathans practice a woman's art? It was only their respect for Bapu and their devoted obedience to Badshah Khan that induced them to take a little instruction.

I felt very restive in the beginning when I discovered that Badshah Khan wished me, as a woman, not to go out alone anywhere, not even out of the gate into the bazaar, let alone for solitary walks in the countryside. "It is not done," he explained. I endured it for a little while, and then one fine day, without asking anyone's permission, I went for a long walk all alone. The villagers looked at me, and greeted me quite nicely. From that day I went for daily solitary walks, and enjoyed them thoroughly. They helped to warm me up, too.

I found the Pathans a most friendly, hospitable people when they had no doubt as to one's connections, and since I was associated with Badshah Khan, I was welcome everywhere. It was only by seeing Badshah Khan among his own people that one could realize the significance of his influence. Everywhere in the villages he was respected, and could be seen walking about, tall and loose-limbed, in his plain gray khadi clothes that matched his gray hair and short beard, and with not even a stick in his hand, whereas all other Khans were armed with rifles.

213

One day Badshah Khan took me with him to a friend's house in a neighboring village. We drove there in his tonga, and as we went along he told me how this was the season for family feuds to be dealt with by sniping at one's enemy from the thick high sugar-cane plantations, quite a number of which we passed, and how this custom of eternal revenge was one of the things he was doing his utmost to eradicate. Just as we were reaching our destination, we heard a rifle shot in the far distance. What was it? Well, we hoped it was nothing serious.

The place we had come to was a large old-fashioned Pathan farmhouse, strong, thick-walled, and with its lands all around. Everyone was delightfully friendly, and the women of the family took me off to see the vegetables they were preparing for me without meat. They could speak only Pushtu, so we communicated with one another by signs intermixed with laughter.

Then I was shown the room where I was to sleep that night. It was high up on the roof, and they explained that it was "the safest place." When the time for the meal came I was taken down to a kind of porchlike room where I found Badshah Khan, our host, and one or two other Khans reclining on beds, with little tables in front of them. I was shown an empty bed on which I took my seat. No other women were present because it was not the custom. I noticed against the walls in the corners two or three rifles and a revolver lying on one of the beds.

A little table was placed in front of me also, and then the food was brought, piles of the best fresh country food imaginable. It seemed to me my bed was rather hard and uncomfortable, and I looked under the mattress. There was another rifle! It was removed and put along with the rest as a matter of course. In usual Pathan style one or two dogs were there on the lookout for bones, and when they got their titbits they crunched them up under the beds.

The next morning as we drove back to Utmanzai, Badshah Khan explained to me how our host had a deadly feud on with someone who had decamped into the tribal area, and might come over any day to try to murder him. Therefore, whenever he went

214

out he always had two men with rifles with him, and kept a revolver permanently in his pocket.

Shortly after we reached Utmanzai a message was brought to Badshah Khan that a friend of his, who lived a little beyond the place where we had spent the night, had been shot dead by someone sniping from the sugar cane. That rifle report which we had heard in the evening had been the fatal bullet. It was not necessary to fire more than one. The Pathans' aim was always sure.

January and February were very wet, which made carding of cotton an impossible job, and even the small spinning class was not practical, so I spent some time at the Prime Minister's house in Peshawar.

Toward the end of February Bapu went to Rajkot, as there was trouble between the ruler and his people, and on the 3rd of March I received a telegram saying he had gone on fast, but mercifully a compromise was reached on the fourth day.

By May the heat in Peshawar and Utmanzai became intense, and since I was having difficulty in maintaining my health I decided to go to the Hazara district, which was at least semi-mountainous, and where I could do some investigation of the area for khadi development. But my health did not improve and finally I returned to Segaon.

In August, the Congress Working Committee met at Wardha under the shadow of approaching World War II. After the declaration of war between England and Germany, Bapu had to go several times to see the Viceroy, but otherwise he stayed in Segaon.

It was about this time that the name of Segaon was changed to Sevagram. The reason for this change was that there was another and larger village some miles away that was also called Segaon, which meant that there was often confusion in the post. Bapu consulted the villagers on the subject, and when there was general approval of the new name, the authorities were asked to register it.

CHAPTER LI

WHILE I had been away in the Northwest Frontier a well-known Punjabi revolutionary, Prithvi Singh, who had been absconding for some time, had come to Bapu. On my return I heard from Mahadev and others how this revolutionary had expressed himself converted to Bapu's ideals and had, on Bapu's advice, surrendered himself to the police. Since then Bapu had been pleading for his unconditional release. I listened with interest, but thought nothing more about it.

Suddenly one day a powerful, fearless-looking man appeared in the doorway of Bapu's hut. Bapu recognized him with delight. It was Prithvi Singh. Bapu's pleading had done the trick, and he had been released. I watched the whole scene with peculiar satisfaction, though I did not then know the complete and remarkable history of this man.

When the story of his adventures, which he had written down, was given to me for polishing up the English, my interest in him greatly increased, and I read through with avidity his account of the Second Lahore Conspiracy Case Trials, the condemnation to death of himself and several companions, the reprieve, the life in the Andamans prison, the transfer to jails in India and then his escape from a running train in spite of the chains with which he was fettered, his later recapture, his re-escape and long, successful absconding, which lasted till, after several years, he came openly to Bapu.

In the beginning he spent most of his time at Sevagram and I saw a good deal of him. I felt at home with him, and rejoiced in his frank and fearless manner. I began to feel, Here at last is someone with whom I could perhaps work outside independently, as Bapu always wanted me to do. This feeling grew so pressing that

I spoke to Bapu about it. Bapu looked at me with unexpected seriousness and said, "If you feel like that it means to my mind that you should marry," and added, as if thinking aloud, "Perhaps marriage has been the unspoken word in your life."

I was taken aback and left speechless. Bapu saw my astonishment and said, "Your former resolve not to marry, to my mind, should not stand in the way. As far as I am concerned, you are absolved from it."

My mind and emotions were in a whirl. Was this the way out of my frustration? Bapu was probably right. Could I be of use at last if I made the plunge? Bapu, in his usual unhesitating way, said, "I shall speak to him." And I accepted the situation without further ado. The whole conversation did not take five minutes. I felt perfectly breathless, and then for a little extraordinarily happy.

After all the pent-up suffering I had been through I could not catch any balance in this completely new orientation, and my emotions ran riot. Fate was tossing me around like a little cork in a rough sea. Prithvi Singh wisely resisted all proposals whether from Bapu or others. He suggested my going to see his best friend and co-prisoner of the Andaman days, Pandit Jagat Ram Bharadwaj, who had recently been released after twenty-one years in jail and was living with his wife in his Punjab home at Hariana near Hoshiarpur in a completely broken state of health. Bapu agreed and I went. I found in Pandit Jagat Ram a most noble and interesting person, small and thin, but with a will of iron. We had long talks which were a great comfort to me, and we became good friends.

From Hariana I went to a small Ashram at Oel in the Sivalik Hills. No town was anywhere near, the Sone River flowed at a little distance, and the countryside was varied and somewhat wild. The people at the Ashram had started constructing a large and ugly red brick building, which they had had to leave unfinished for lack of funds. I suggested that if they had constructed small buildings with the local materials and style employed by the villagers, it would have been much better. Then to demonstrate my meaning I got hold of two or three old villagers, and with their help prepared the solid mud walls of an 8- by 8-foot hut. A car-

217

penter was called to fix the beams for the thatched roof and the front veranda, and the final result was a delightful little hut which had only cost me eighteen rupees plus the few beams of wood, which had been given free. The Ashramites agreed it would have been better if they had done the same thing, instead of being left, as they were, with a white—or rather *red* elephant.

In order to solve the difficulty of getting milk, I went out into the surrounding villages to look for a small cow. After a few days I found a man who had two cows for sale, one white and one red. We sat down on the grass outside the cowshed to discuss the price. The owner brought out a hookah, and after taking a few puffs to get it going, held it out to me. He was quite surprised when I declined the offer, for, as I afterwards learned, any bargaining regarding the purchase of cattle was always done over a good smoke. Anyway, hookah or no hookah, I managed to strike the bargain at seven rupees for the little red cow with her tiny calf.

I brought the two of them back to my hut and tied them under a nearby tree. At night I kept them one at each end of my veranda where I slept, and had a lantern burning because of the danger of leopards, who sometimes prowled around at night looking for dogs, calves, goats and the like. The lantern I was told would keep them off. It did keep off the leopards, but not a local madman.

It was a very hot night, and I was sleeping out under the sky with the cow and calf tied up close by, when I was awakened by the sound of a voice, and, on opening my eyes, saw an almost naked, strong and very hairy man standing by my bed.

"That's my cow!" he shouted at me as I sat up. He was obviously a lunatic, so I reasoned with him gently. I did not like to call for the other Ashramites who were sleeping in the open at a distance, because the man had a big stick and looked as if he might attack me.

"That's my cow and I'm going to milk her."

The more he shouted the better, as the others would then surely wake up. And they did. One of them was a friend of Pandit Jagat Ram, and though not a Lahore Conspiracy Case revolutionary, yet a man of the same caliber. He went straight up to the madman

218

and just told him to clear out in such a way that the fellow decamped without another word.

The next day I was told that the lunatic belonged to a neighboring village, where his relatives usually managed to keep him locked up, but just occasionally he escaped. They had caught him again I was assured, and were making better arrangements this time for his confinement. I felt relieved.

When the weather heated up I went to stay with Lala Kanhaiyalal Butail, who had a big tea estate near Palampur in the Kangra district, at an altitude of about 4,000 feet. Lalaji was one of the kindest and most simplehearted people I have ever come across, a little under middle-age, with a smiling face and loving manners. He was a widower with children, and his mother, younger brother and family all lived together with him in the old joint-family style.

My experience of the Himalayas up to then had been only that of hill stations. Now I found myself on an estate far away from any city and surrounded by little villages, so I wanted to get a closer insight into the life of the people than could be acquired by living in the big family house. Lalaji therefore arranged for me to spend some time in one of the villages on the mountain slopes above his estate. I stayed in a cottage by myself, and watched the life around me. At the same time I introduced a new method of wool carding which took on well with the people.

But this was only outward activity. Inwardly I was painfully restless, not knowing where I was or what was going to happen. When the rains began I returned to Sevagram, but I could find no peace and felt myself useless. A terrible anguish took possession of me, and out of its depths came the decision to take silence and devote myself entirely to meditation and prayer, till God gave me light. I felt I wanted to go and live all alone in some forest where I would read only the Vedas, Upanishads and Puranas, receive no newspaper, and no letters except Bapu's. To sit for long periods in motionless meditation being unnatural to me, I decided I would spin 1,000 yards of yarn daily. I felt that during this spinning the mind would work in a healthy way, and I should run no risk of hallucinations.

I went to Bapu and told him everything. He entirely agreed to my idea and said he thought the best person for me to go to would be Lala Kanhaiyalal, who would no doubt be willing for me to stay in the forests on his estate.

I returned to Palampur in September. Lalaji, in his usual big-hearted way, told me to choose any place I fancied on his estate and he would have a hut put up according to my directions. After walking all around the place and looking at every nook and corner, I chose the end of a wooded ridge, just before it dipped down into a ravine where a stream flowed. Lalaji's house was about half a mile away, and except for the cowshed, which was situated at the upper end of the ridge at a distance of over a furlong, there was no building anywhere around.

The hut was quickly constructed of local materials and thatched with grass. Lalaji said nothing would induce him to live in such a place all alone, for there was known to be a leopard in the area, and there was a story of one having been seen once just where the hut now stood. But the solitude suited me to perfection, and on Bapu's birthday, October 2nd, I went to live there.

To the north, between the trees, there was a fine view of the steep, rocky Dhaula Dhar range, running up to 15,000 and 16,000 feet, to the right below the pine trees was a little glade of rice fields, and around to the south and east the forest dropped down into the ravine. I now took silence and settled down to my spinning and reading. For Lalaji's sake I undertook to speak for half an hour in the evenings if he came that way for his walk.

All this time my correspondence with Bapu had been going on regularly. He now wrote:

I have your long letter. It enables me to follow the struggle that is going on within you. . . . What is essential is the spirit of dedication to God. Whatever your outward activity it must be all for God. . . .

As the days went by, my surroundings began to ease and open my heart. The trees and bushes befriended me, the great boulders of gray rock, covered with lichen, were a perpetual joy, and the sound of the stream in the ravine made sweet and gentle music. As for the birds, they rapidly became companions.

As the season advanced the elements began to remind one of their all-powerful presence, and one night in late December they burst upon the forest in full force. It was the coming of the winter rain and snow. I shut the hut up tight, but even so the air was all astir inside. The wind came in waves. I could hear it coming, coming through the forest. With a roar it would arrive, tearing at the trees and the little hut, and pass on down the ravine, only to be followed by another and another wave. Then came rain, torrents of it, and the thatch began to leak. Soon there was no dry place. I put up the mosquito net and over it my waterproof and umbrella, and under the bed I put all my books. As long as the thatch did not blow off I could feel myself lucky. Now the rain was followed by lashing hail, which beat into the grass of the thatch, and after that the storm subsided. But the thick layer of hailstones went on melting all night and dripping through the roof. However, I finally fell asleep under my improvised tent. At sunrise when I peeped out, I beheld the great Dhaula Dhar range glistening white against a clear, pale blue sky. The winter snows had come.

The reading of the Rig-Veda, which I had begun, harmonized exactly with the glory of the elements with whom I was day and night in silent, solitary and direct contact. It was from this pure and mighty source that strength began to come to me.

CHAPTER LII

IN February I returned to Sevagram, or rather Veroda, and stayed in my little cottage on the ridge, which was at that time empty.

For the journey I had to break my silence, but took it again as soon as I got to my destination, with this difference that, instead of speaking for half an hour daily, I spoke twice a week for about twenty minutes or so, when I went to see Bapu. By April the heat became intense, and Bapu sent me to Charwad in the Junagarh State, where a rich friend had a fruit garden about a mile from the coast of the Arabian Sea. It was a beautiful place of about twenty acres, containing a wonderful variety of fruit. There were mangoes and bananas of all the best kinds, lichis, chikus, and tall coconut palms which waved high above the rest. But more striking even than the fruit were the birds.

I lived in a small mud cottage in the middle of the garden. There was a little veranda on which I used to sit and do my spinning, and the peacocks and peahens used to come walking around on the open space in front to see who this new arrival was. I kept grain which I threw down for them, first on the open ground, then on the veranda, and finally on the spinning wheel itself, from which the bravest of the peacocks used to come and pick it up. To begin with they did not spread their tails, but when they got used to me, they almost always gave a dance performance after eating their grain.

At night I used to sleep out in the open, and was awakened every morning by the birds. Here is a description I wrote to Bapu:

> This seems to be the very height of the season for the birds. The peacocks dance, the koel flash about from tree to tree singing riotously, even the vultures, a pair of whom frequent the palms just opposite, have become amorous, but when they start love-making it sounds more like animals being killed than any birds singing! Week by week the birds have begun to wake up earlier—now the chorus begins at 2:30 A.M. Koel start calling and are forthwith answered by the peacocks who trumpet and shout "*Jaya ho!*" and all this within a few yards of one's bed. Luckily it is a short outburst, not followed by another till about 3:30 or 4. By 5 o'clock it becomes a regular hullabaloo, in which crows, crow-pheasants, parrots, fork-tailed blackbirds, bulbuls and a quantity of smaller birds all join!!

About once a week I would go down to the sea and watch the waves breaking on the solitary rocky coast. Here again, as in the

222

Himalayas, there was the breath of strength. That strength which is also peace.

In those days I knew nothing of what the outer world was doing or thinking beyond what came to me through Bapu. On May 22, 1941, he wrote:

> An inquiry has come from London whether the report is true that you have severed all connection with me and are living away from me!!! How wish is father to thought!

I kept my silence as usual, and was deep in the reading of the Rig-Veda. The translations at my disposal being rather dry and stiff, I began rendering those hymns that specially appealed to me into language which I tried to make nearer to the spirit as I had learned to know it through direct contact with Nature and the elements. These renderings I used to send along to Bapu day by day, and he would return them with a remark or two, scribbled on a slip of paper, such as: "It is very interesting"; "It will be a good selection in the end."

Though the cottage I was in did not have very attractive surroundings, it did not lack interests of other kinds. One evening when I was sitting on the floor spinning, a big toad made his appearance, drawn by the insects who had collected around the light of the lantern. Hop, hop, hop he came right up close, his golden eyes gleaming at the sight of so much food. Having sat himself fair and square in a strategic position, he proceeded to flick out his tongue whenever an unwary insect came within his reach. And the reach of his elastic tongue was something I had never imagined. Having discovered this easy way of dining, he made it a regular habit, turning up without fail every evening.

But where did he go in the daytime? I hunted around and found him squeezed behind a stone in the cemented corner of the kitchen where vessels used to be washed. So I made him a more comfortable abode of two bricks with a stone on top, and every day made a point of pouring some cool water over his house. He accepted these attentions as a matter of course. Next time Bapu came that way I brought the toad out to show off his beautiful

223

golden eyes. This he also accepted quite naturally. Squatting between my two hands, with just his head showing, he gazed calmly at Bapu, who was so pleased with him that, whenever he brought any visitors along on his walks, he would say, "You must bring out your pet toad."

After a while I noticed that there were one or two more toads about, but none so big as my special friend. Then from one or two they increased to four or five, and on and on, until there were forty!

I said to the old toad, "Now really, I'm very sorry, but this is becoming too much of a good thing. It will be better that you should all go and live in some nice hedgerow."

His golden eyes gazed at me quietly, but I hardened my heart and, catching them all, put them into a tin and deposited them at the other end of the neighboring field. When I got up the following morning, there they all were back again! I hardened my heart once more, and deposited them several fields away by a nice little stream. But the next morning the old fellow and several of the bigger ones were again with me.

So I said, "Very well, then we had better all live together."

And we did.

Not so pleasant were the scorpions. Often when I came in of an evening, I would find two or three running around on the floor. Having three times experienced the intense and prolonged pain (at least twelve hours) of a scorpion sting. I was not anxious to keep them as companions, so whenever I found them about I used to catch them with the aid of a twig and a small pair of tongs, put them in an old kerosene tin, and then carry them out the next morning to a distant hedge. They were of all sizes, some big and some quite small, and I noticed that the little ones had a way of disappearing. How did they manage to get out? The problem was solved when one morning I found the previous evening's catch of three reduced to one big scorpion who was sitting with the tail of one of his victims still sticking out of his mouth. After that I took to putting the little ones separately in a bottle. In all I caught fifty-two scorpions during my stay in that cottage.

Two snakes were regular inhabitants of the building, but they

224

kept to themselves. One I sometimes saw with his tail hanging down from the bathroom rafters, and the other seemed to live in a crevice between two stones of the plinth outside.

As the days went by I became more and more devoted to the Vedas. Ever since that time alone in the Himalayan forests, they had been part of me. No learned scholar had expounded their meaning. They entered into my inmost being through the medium of the very elements which had drawn them out of the human heart thousands of years ago. The intellectual approach was, I knew, quite different, and my understanding of the hymns would be counted as of little worth. But what mattered to me was the inspiration and strength that they gave me.

It was now over a year since I had taken my silence. The time seemed to be coming when I must give it up and go back into the everyday world. Asha Devi, who was a very good friend, pressed me hard. I listened, I understood, and could even agree, yet I could not seem to bring myself to do it. At last the moment came. I remember feeling a strange wrench, and then bursting into a flood of tears, after which the silence was over.

My cottage next to Bapu's had, of course, become the office, and was packed to overflowing. So Asha Devi suggested my staying in her home, and I gladly accepted. This also gave me a grand chance of going through with her the Vedic verses which I had selected. Being the daughter of a very learned father, she had known Vedic Sanskrit from her childhood, and I greatly enjoyed the hours we spent together over the hymns.

CHAPTER LIII

THE atmosphere in the country at that time was one of frustration and rapidly growing discontent. As the Japanese advanced through Burma the tension went on increasing, and a crisis seemed inevitable.

Faced with the reality of approaching armed might, the Congress leaders had more than once repudiated Bapu's ideal of non-violent resistance, but in January 1942, at a crucial gathering of the Congress Working Committee followed by the All-India Congress Committee, Bapu was again asked to lead the country. He agreed to take up the burden along his own lines, and straightaway started preparing the public mind through weekly articles in the *Harijan* for the kind of compaign he visualized.

At this stage the British, with the idea of reaching a compromise with the Indian National Congress, sent out a mission headed by Sir Stafford Cripps.

Such was the situation when I came out of my fifteen months silence. It did not take me long to look out for active work, and as Kamla Devi and Mridula were needing help in the organization of a women's camp which they were starting near Navsari, north of Bombay, I went there at the end of March. They were too busy to be there themselves for the preliminary preparations, so I had to lay out the camp and get it constructed. I employed my usual method of using local materials and local craft, and in this way got the place ready just in time. When the camp opened and training began, I took on the job of guidance and inspection of sanitation, clothes-washing, and a little instruction in horseback riding and bicycling.

All the while I was keenly watching the development of events through the newspapers. India was being used as a military base by the Allied forces, and she was being sucked dry for the benefit of their war effort without any definite promise being given her for freedom after victory. And to add insult to injury, foreign troops were now being poured into the country because the British did not trust the Indian soldiers in the present circumstances. Bapu's ceaseless flow of articles, interviews, etc., was awakening the country as never before to a sense of its abject position, but there was a lot of conflicting talk going on even in Congress circles as to what should and could be done, especially in case the Japanese invasion materialized. I became so stirred up that I wrote Bapu a long letter which, as I afterwards learned expressed much the same sentiments Bapu was himself expressing at the time in an article he was writing for *Harijan*. I ended my letter to Bapu with the request that I might go to the meeting of the Congress Working Committee and the All-India Congress Committee, to be held shortly at Allahabad, and plead behind the scenes with the leaders for the organization of nation-wide nonviolent resistance to the approaching Japanese invasion.

Bapu wired in reply:

IF YOU FEEL LIKE THAT COME AT ONCE.

The camp was drawing to a close, and the others readily agreed to my going off immediately. On April 20th, just before starting, I got a short letter from Bapu saying:

> I have your letter. I must let you come here and see what can be done. You are undertaking a job which leaves you no other consideration. I have sent you a wire. I do not know whether it will reach you. Everything has become so uncertain now-a-days.

When I entered Bapu's room at Sevagram, I could feel that something which radiated from Bapu at times of crisis. He was alert and sparing in words. Handing me two sheets of typed paper he said, "Read this. If it appeals to you, you take it to Allahabad by the next train. In the meantime I will give you an hour's talk so as fully to explain to you my state of mind which you must make clear to the members of the Working Committee." And he added, "I am not sending Mahadev or anyone else from here to Allahabad."

There was no time to think over the unexpectedness of all this. I took the two sheets and went and sat down in a corner to read. What was this I was to take posthaste to Allahabad? It was Bapu's original draft of the now-famous "Quit India" Resolution. Of course it appealed to me.

So the next morning I was off by the first train, carrying in my bag three copies of the resolution—two with covering letters from Bapu to Jawaharlal and Maulala Abul Kalam Azad, the then President of the Congress, and one copy for my own reference.

The train was due to arrive in the evening, but it was somewhere around midnight when it drew into the Allahabad station.

227

There were many people on the platform, among them Jawaharlal, as he was expecting some members of the Working Committee to turn up by that train. But no one had come. I saw at once that he was under a great strain and in no mood to be trifled with. I went up to him.

"Hullo, Mira!" he exclaimed, and his voice implied, "What on earth have *you* come here for?"

In the hubbub and bustle of the platform I explained in a few brief words, but held on tight to the letters in my bag.

After giving one more look up and down the platform for any possible Working Committee members, Jawaharlal said, "Come on, we'd better go. I've been meeting every train since the morning, but still some of the members have not turned up."

And then he let off a burst of steam about people's intolerable unpunctuality, etc.

As we drove to Anand Bhavan in the car, he did not say a word, and I kept discreetly silent. When we entered the house he took Bapu's communication, sat down in a chair by an electric standard, opened the envelope and read. Again not a word.

I said, "I've got another copy for Maulana Saheb with a covering letter from Bapu. Shall I give it to him in the morning?"

"Give it to me," he replied. "I'll see to it."

I then mentioned that Bapu had told me to explain his meaning in more detail to the Working Committee.

"Maulana Saheb will decide what to do about that tomorrow morning," he said. "And now you'd better go to bed. The house is packed, but Mridula has, I think, a spare bed in her room." And he pointed me out the door.

The next morning when I entered the dining room I found Maulana Saheb sitting at the table having his breakfast. Sarojini Devi, Asaf Ali and others were also there, and of course Jawaharlal, who said to me, "You'd better tell Maulana Saheb what Bapu said."

After hearing me, the Maulana said I should come to the morning sitting of the Working Committee so that all the members could hear whatever it was Bapu wanted me to explain.

In the adjoining big house, Swaraj Bhavan (Pandit Motilal

228

Nehru's original home, which he had donated to the nation), were staying other members of the Working Committee. They included Dr. Rajendra Prasad, Sardar Vallabhbhai Patel and Professor Kripalani with his fiery tongue and hooked nose, whose revolutionary blood was all astir. As their quarters were quite separate from ours, they had known nothing of my arrival with Bapu's resolution till the morning.

The Working Committee gathered in a big room upstairs. When all had assembled, Maulana Saheb read out Bapu's communication. Such a resolution, at such a moment, and no Bapu! It was a testing of the members' capacity to hold together and reach a definite decision on this most vital question, without having the influence of Bapu's presence. Bapu must have kept away expressly for that purpose.

No sooner had the Maulana finished reading the draft than a sharp division in the members became apparent, and heated remarks and discussion began at once. The first flush of reactions over, they asked me to explain whatever Bapu had told me, and then settled down to a prolonged and tough argument. The division of opinion coincided almost exactly with the two house parties, those staying in Swaraj Bhavan being staunch supporters of Bapu's draft, and those in Anand Bhavan being opposed, some strongly and some mildly. In the first sitting no agreement was reached, and the Committee met again in the afternoon. I was not called this time, but I gathered the news from Rajendra Babu and others. On the second day I was again present. The differences were still there, but there was a growing effort at compromise. The Swaraj Bhavan group did not want to force the situation to the breaking point. They knew that the mood in the country was such that if Bapu's resolution was put before the All-India Congress Committee, there was likelihood of its being accepted; but they knew also that this would lead to an open breach in the Congress, a thing to be avoided if at all possible at such a juncture.

Finally a compromise resolution was agreed upon, put before the All-India Congress Committee and passed. Somehow the Socialist Party had got wind of Bapu's draft and the fact that it had been altered, and severely taunted the members of the Working Committee. Great excitement prevailed, but no new development ensued.

As soon as ever the meetings were over I left for Wardha along with Rajendra Babu, Dr. Praphulla Ghosh of Bengal, and Shankar Rao Dev of Maharashtra. We were very anxious as to whether Bapu would accept the amended resolution.

The journey was terribly hot. However, as we were all keyed up to the tension of the crisis, we endured it cheerily, and Rajendra Babu, I remember, regaled us with one story after another of train robberies and similar dacoities.

On reaching Sevagram we went to Bapu, and Rajendra Babu put the amended resolution into his hands, explaining at the same time what had happened. Bapu read it through. He was not very satisfied, but said that as it gave him enough scope to work, he would manage with it.

CHAPTER LIV

BAPU now gave us all marching orders. Rajendra Babu, Praphulla Ghosh and Shankar Rao Dev were each to go and prepare his own Province for the coming struggle, and to me Bapu said, "I give you the choice of three undertakings: either you go to Madras and plead with Rajaji [who in certain matters was at that time in disagreement with the Congress]; or you go to Delhi and reason with the Viceroy and other high British officials; or you go to Orissa and help to prepare the masses for nonviolent nonco-operative resistance to the expected Japanese invasion of the east coast."

I had no difficulty in deciding, and chose at once to go to Orissa. Bapu wrote a letter to Hare Krishna Mehtab, the Congress Provincial leader (afterwards Chief Minister), and off I went.

Mehtab Babu, a sturdy man of Punjabi ancestry, met me at the

Cuttack station and took me off to the Congress quarters, where we discussed the situation. We immediately planned out a tour program all down the coast, and lost no time in setting off. Nowhere was there any sign of the British forces, and it appeared that they had retired into the wooded hills which lay inland. The whole of the coast and flat rice fields were thus left unprotected.

There was no time to lose. The atmosphere in the towns and cities right down the east coast was particularly panicky. The Madras Government had already had a false alarm and had ordered evacuation of the city, which was partially carried out and then rectified. So we first visited the towns, and then toured the villages. As most of these were unapproachable except by narrow footpaths between the rice fields, we had to be continually on the move. I was given a pony, and the rest of the party went on foot.

After this first survey we returned to Cuttack, the capital of Orissa and seat of Government. The problems facing us were tough and complicated. There was a government in office which was completely under the thumb of the British, who were carrying on a policy which was estranging the population more and more. Such orders as destruction of rice stocks, drying up of canals, destruction of fishing boats and other "scorched earth" policies, in a country where there is a people's government and the masses are ready to sacrifice everything for the sake of defeating the enemy and retaining their own freedom, have meaning; but where the masses are already profoundly discontented and so impoverished that they feel any other rule would be better than the one they are groaning under, the addition of "scorched earth" on top of everything else creates intense bitterness and hatred.

Even unarmed volunteer organizations for self-defense and internal order during crises were objected to by Government unless under their own control. This was preposterous considering it was an open secret that the moment the Japanese approached, all Government officials were to burn their files, blow up the bridges, which had already been laid with dynamite, and decamp to the hills. For the evacuation of the population, or for their protection against air raids, etc., no arrangements had been made.

This was the situation with which we were faced. The thing

231

now was to try to achieve some co-operation from the Government, and I wrote to the Chief Secretary, Mr. Wood, asking for an interview, which he gave for May 25th. Mr. Mansfield, another member of the Government, was also present.

After the interview I wrote a detailed account to Bapu, from which I take a few extracts:

> I started by saying that no doubt they read *Harijan,* and therefore know what Gandhiji's stand is today, namely that for their sake and for ours, for their safety and for ours, the only course left open is for the British Raj to remove itself bag and baggage from India. They said "Yes," quite quietly, and made no comment. "But I think you must also know," I added, "that Gandhiji would like your departure to be friendly and orderly." Again they said "Yes." I then explained how you had sent me here to work, how I had seen and heard many things for myself, and now wanted to discuss with them certain urgent matters in order that we might try to get over these difficulties if possible by agreement and avoid unnecessary friction. They expressed their willingness to approach matters in this spirit. . . .

I then explained to them in detail the situation facing us, what we proposed to do and what kind of co-operation we should like from them. The Note ends:

> Before leaving I said: "I would like you to visualize the situation in a realistic way. Sooner or later, probably sooner, the British Raj will be going. When it goes a vacuum will be created. If we do not fill in that vacuum the Japanese will. Which will be better in the long run for you and the world? A free, peace-loving India, or India in the hands of militant Japan?" They agreed that the former would be the best. "Then," I said, "do not make it impossible for us to prepare ourselves for filling in that vacuum. If you do not want to throw the nation into the hands of the Japanese you should co-operate with us in the present situation, and in the method of your withdrawal." They could not deny the truth of this.
>
> We parted with friendly handshakes . . .
>
> The interview lasted exactly one hour.

232

By the same post I sent Bapu a full description of the situation as we found it on our tour, and asked his advice as to how we should act in the face of the Japanese invasion.

To these communications Bapu replied on May 5, 1942:

> I have your very complete and illuminating letter. The report of the interview is perfect, your answers were straight, unequivocal and courageous. I have no criticism to make. I can only say, "Go on as you are doing." I can quite clearly see that you have gone to the right place at the right time. I therefore need do nothing more than come straight to your questions which are all good and relevant.
>
> . . . Remember that our attitude is that of complete noncooperation with Japanese army, therefore we may not help them in any way, nor may we profit by any dealings with them. Therefore we cannot sell anything to them. If people are not able to face the Japanese army, they will do as armed soldiers do, i.e., retire when they are overwhelmed. And if they do so the question of having any dealings with Japanese does not and should not arise. If, however, the people have not the courage to resist Japanese unto death and not the courage and capacity to evacuate the portion invaded by the Japanese, they will do the best they can in the light of instructions. One thing they should never do—to yield willing submission to the Japanese. That will be a cowardly act, and unworthy of freedom-loving people. They must not escape from one fire only to fall into another and probably more terrible. Their attitude therefore must always be of resistance to the Japanese. No question, therefore, arises of accepting British currency notes or Japanese coins. They will handle nothing from Japanese hands.

Then Bapu added detailed replies to all my specific questions regarding problems which would face us, such as currency, bridge repairs, and attendance on wounded. In every case except for service to the wounded his instructions were for complete non-co-operation.

CHAPTER LV

NOT far from Cuttack a big airdrome was being constructed near a village called Churwad, and for this purpose large numbers of coolies had been brought from far and wide, many of them convicts who had been released for war work. One of the labor camps had been established alongside the village, and many reports began coming to us about the bad behavior of the coolies, and the villagers' fear of disturbances. Mehtab Babu and I went to see the Collector, and while we were sitting talking to him there came an urgent call saying that Churwad was on fire and being looted by the coolies. The Collector rushed off posthaste with the police.

We decided we had better move our camp over to the village so as to try to give some feeling of security to the inhabitants. We should also be in a position then to examine the damage in detail and help obtain Government compensation. So we packed up and moved out to Churwad the next morning.

The village was a tragic sight, about half of it having been burned out and looted. Particularly I remember the Harijan quarters. They were a flattened-out mass of ashes, and on a mound in the middle of the desolation stood a solitary, black he-goat gazing blankly at the wreckage of his world.

We camped in the school building, which had escaped the fire because of being on the outskirts. I quickly got in touch with the military officer in command of the airfield. He was a young Irishman, tall, thin, red-haired, who had arrived in India for the first time only three months previously. He welcomed our arrival and discussed everything in detail. As a military man he keenly appreciated the desirability of keeping the civil population contented, and when I told him of the sullen mood of the surrounding vil-

234

lages he was much concerned, for he had airplanes standing about all over his airfield, without any sheds, and sabotage would have been the easiest thing. He also agreed with me that trenches should be prepared for enabling the civil population around the airdrome to get some protection from raids, and he had them dug. What a refreshing contrast it was to the way the civil authorities functioned, tied up as they were in red tape and generations of the rulers' aloof prestige.

By July the rains had set in properly, and the tension eased off, for there was little likelihood of the Japanese attempting a landing in that season. As there was going to be a Congress Working Committee meeting at Wardha, Mehtab Babu and I decided to go to Sevagram, talk things over with Bapu, and meet the many leaders who would foregather there.

This time the Congress leaders had Bapu in their midst, not the tired and patient Bapu of the long days of frustration, but the inspired and glowing Bapu of pending action, and it brought them together in one solid group, determined for the struggle if the British Government would not yield.

At the completion of the meetings, which reaffirmed the Quit-India Resolution, many press correspondents, including foreign journalists, came for an interview with Bapu at Sevagram, and they received such answers to their questions as made them sit up and think.

This was in the middle of July, and a meeting of the All-India Congress Committee was fixed for August 7th and 8th.

I had been expecting to go back to Orissa, but events were now moving so rapidly that Bapu sent me to Delhi to seek an interview with the Viceroy, Lord Linlithgow, in order to explain to him, in a more personal way, Bapu's meaning behind the resolution.

I went straight to Birla House in New Delhi, where Bapu now often stayed, and which we looked upon as a Delhi home, and wrote a note to the Viceroy. The next day I got a letter from his private secretary, Mr. Laithwaite, saying that His Excellency would have been very glad to see me, but having regard to the main resolution of the Working Committee, and in view of the fact that Mr. Gandhi had been reported to have described in an interview to the press the position vis-à-vis the Government as that of "open rebellion," he felt sure I should appreciate his difficulty in giving an interview to a direct representative of Mr. Gandhi. At the same time, as His Excellency would much regret not to be in possession of any message or information which Mr. Gandhi might desire to convey to him, he hoped I might agree to see Mr. Laithwaite instead.

Accordingly I went to see Mr. Laithwaite at 3 o'clock that afternoon, and immediately afterwards sat down and wrote Bapu a full report:

The first part of the conversation I devoted to impressing upon him the need for mutual understanding and contact. I could see his mind was attuned to the die-hard outlook. "But," I said, "Gandhiji is a unique man and you have got to handle him in a unique fashion. His Excellency must draw on his imagination if he is to save the situation." The next point I dwelt on was the anti-British feeling which was sweeping the country today. I saw that he was skeptical. I said, "You are not in touch with the people, you live in an atmosphere of unreality, and it is impossible for you to know what I know. Let me take you by the hand and lead you to the places where I spend my life. There you will realize." I then related to him some personal experiences and finally said, "If things go on as they are going, the peasants of Orissa will garland the Japanese when they land. . . . The people with whom you associate," I added, "and from whom you hear things, are as out of touch with the masses as you. What do your Knights and Barons of the Viceroy's Council count for? Nothing!" We entered on the question of declaring immediate independence. Laithwaite tried to appreciate what I said, but the die-hard in him was always struggling up. . . . "What I want you to realize," I said, "is that this move of Gandiji is out of the depth of his love for England. He knows that this is the only way to save India from going helplessly into the hands of Japan. If you do not feel you would know how to proceed to hand over freedom to India, you should consult Gandhiji. It is he who can tell you."

Finally, as the clock hand was approaching four, I said, "I have taken much of your time, but I want at the last to put before you the most vital, the most terrible thing of all. Gandhiji is in deadly

236

earnest. This time it will be impossible for you to hold him. No jail will contain him, no crushing will silence him. The more you crush the more his power will spread. You are faced with two alternatives; one to declare India's Independence, and the other to kill Gandhiji, and once you kill him you kill for ever all hope of friendship between India and England. What are you going to do about it? You do not know the latent power lying buried in this coming move. Even we do not know the force of Gandhiji's spirit, but I can sense it, and I tell you that if the rebellion has to burst, this Viceroy will have to face a more terrible situation than any Indian Viceroy has ever had to face before."

Laithwaite looked a bit serious. Then I cheered him up in a friendly way and got up to leave. "I want you to try to realize," I concluded, "that even this rebellion is a *friendly gesture.* Perhaps it is difficult for you to conceive of a rebellion as a friendly gesture, but with Gandhiji such a thing is possible" . . . "After all you have told me," he said, "I am more able to realize it."

At the end of the interview I asked Mr. Laithwaite if the generals would follow the same policy of aloofness, because, if not, I much wanted to talk to them about purely military matters. He said he thought they would be rather differently placed, that General Wavell was away, but that General Hartley, the Deputy Commander in Chief, was there, and that he would get in touch with him at once and let me know by evening. We went down together to the front door, and as we came into the porch a car drove up out of which stepped General Hartley himself. He greeted me warmly, said he had met me in the old days and well remembered my mother and father. When I mentioned my desire to talk to him about affairs in Orissa he said, "Come to lunch at my house tomorrow at 1:30." So there were no difficulties or aloofness there.

The next day I went to lunch. General Hartley, Lady Hartley and one other general made up the party. After lunch General Hartley took me to another room and listened with sympathetic attention to all I had to say about Orissa. He took down some notes and said I should see General Molesworth. I suggested perhaps he could come to tea with me at Birla House. General Hartley said he would find out and let me know.

237

I stayed on at Birla House for some days, and before long received a note from General Hartley to say that General Molesworth would come to tea with me on the 29th. When he came, he was very understanding. We had a long talk, and it left me with the feeling that if I could develop liaison work between the military and the people, I could do much to help the masses.

CHAPTER LVI

I LEFT Delhi in time to reach Bombay for the All-India Congress Committee meeting, and joined Bapu at Birla House.

I learned from Mahadev that Bapu had drafted comprehensive instructions and guidance for the prosecution of the struggle if it became necessary, that the Working Committee had been discussing the draft, and that they were going to meet again on the 9th, when Bapu put before them in detail his view of the negotiations which he was to carry on with the Government in a last effort to reach agreement. The idea was that these negotiations might last about three weeks, and only after that, if all attempt at compromise failed, would the struggle be launched. The draft instructions, which were to guide the movement if it had to be launched, laid stress on the need to avoid violence or even coercion. The beginning was to be a nation-wide hartal (cessation of work) accompanied by prayer and fasting. All Congress members of Provincial Assemblies and Municipalities should resign to join the movement, and all other people whose hearts were with the cause, and who were prepared to employ the nonviolent methods laid down, should throw themselves into the struggle. Refusal to pay land tax by those who had the courage, and independent preparation of salt in villages was advised. But direct embarrassment of the war effort was to be avoided as long as possible.

Such was the draft which was to be discussed and polished up

238

by the Working Committee, and then to be held in abeyance during the period of negotiations.

Public excitement had reached fever pitch. The meetings were packed to overflowing, and it was all the volunteers could do to make room for Bapu and other leaders to get in and out of the huge pandal (marquee).

It was at midnight, on the termination of the second day's session, that the Quit India Resolution was passed by an overwhelming majority amid deafening applause.

Bapu, in his long speech, had referred to his burning desire to avoid a clash, and announced his intention of trying once more to reach a compromise with the new Viceroy, Lord Linlithgow, of whom he spoke as a personal friend.

That night, between 1 and 2 o'clock, when we were gathered around Bapu's bed and he was having oil rubbed on his head, the telephone rang. Mahadev went to answer it, and came back to say that the call was from a friend who had heard rumors that Bapu was going to be arrested within a few hours.

"Never!" said Bapu. "It's impossible after what I have just been saying in the meeting." And he went to sleep quite peacefully and unconcerned.

I went off to the little garden house at the end of the lawn, in which I was staying, and soon fell into a deep sleep. About three hours later I woke up with a start. Someone was calling out to me:

"Good news for you. You are arrested along with Bapu and Mahadev, and you've got to be ready within twenty minutes."

I jumped up and hurriedly packed my things in a new hold-all and kit bag which I had bought the day before, thinking that I should, in the near future, have a lot of traveling to do for this military liaison work.

When I reached the house, the Prayer was already finished, and Bapu was standing surrounded by the whole household. The police officers who were nearby handed me my warrant, and in a few minutes Bapu, Mahadev and I were ushered into a big car standing in readiness at the door. Two police officials got in beside the driver and off we went. The dawn was just breaking as we passed through the empty streets. When we reached Victoria Terminus, the place was strangely quiet. Only police and a few porters could be seen. Evidently the coup had been most carefully arranged. Our car drew up alongside the Poona platform, and we were immediately shown into a first-class saloon special which was standing ready. No sooner had we taken our seats than a broad-backed C.I.D. officer planted himself in the corridor doorway.

Now one car after another came driving up. Here was Jawaharlal, here Vallabhbhai, and so on, with all the members of the Working Committee, but they were placed in other compartments, except for Sarojini Devi, who was brought to ours. Then came more cars with all the leading Congress workers of Bombay. It was clear that the British Government was making a clean sweep regardless of any consequences. Bapu sat watching and hardly spoke. His mind seemed full of the thought of the nation from which he was being divided, and which he knew would rise and struggle with the mighty force oppressing it, while he would be put away powerless to do anything to guide or help.

I was very anxious to pass down the corridor to meet the others, and asked the C.I.D. officer at our door what the plan was. He said after the train had started and passed Kalyan Station, we should be able to move about, and breakfast would also be served in the dining car.

The train was now packed with prisoners, and the signal was given to start. As soon as restriction of movement was lifted, Jawaharlal, Maulana Saheb and others of the Working Committee came to talk to Bapu. It appeared that all telephones had been cut off in Bombay before the arrests, so no one had been able to communicate with anyone else. Seriousness and laughter alternated, and all agreed that the British knew how to do this sort of thing well. Breakfast was announced, and Bapu told me that I might bring him something from the dining saloon, so I trailed along the corridor with the others. We found a first-class breakfast waiting for us with waiters, menus, and all the rest—all the rest except freedom! It was indeed the velvet glove delicately covering the mailed fist.

None of us knew where we were going, but we presumed it was Yaravda, as we were on the Poona line. When we returned to our compartments after breakfast, a plain-clothes police official came around with paper and pencil, making lists of who was to go where. He came into our compartment and very agreeably said to Sarojini Devi and myself, "I think you will like to be with Mr. Gandhi."

"Certainly," we replied, feeling very surprised, for that meant we were not going to a regulation jail, where men and women are kept strictly apart. Mahadev, of course, he listed with Bapu, and then went on to the other compartments.

Before reaching Poona the train stopped at a small station, and all the Bombay Congressmen and women were taken out and put into prison vans. Then we were guided out and put into a closed car. But what of the Working Committee members? We looked anxiously. They had not been taken out. Our car and the prison vans went off, but still they were not to be seen. For a little while the road ran alongside the railway and there came the special, going on to some further destination, and there was Kripalaniji waving to us from their carriage window. We waved back, and wondered what it all meant.

When we reached the turning for Yaravda only the prison vans turned down that way, and our car went on to the outlying area of Poona. Then came in sight a tall barbed-wire fence with armed guards standing around. The car slowed down, the guards opened the wire-protected gates, and we drove through into a garden full of flowers and a big three-storied house standing in the middle. Another velvet glove. But what was this place? We were now told.

"It is the Aga Khan's Poona Palace, which has been arranged as Mr. Gandhi's place of detention."

A tall, kindly Parsee, Mr. Kateley, introduced himself as the Jail Superintendent in charge, and took us up to the ground-floor rooms which were on such a high plinth that they almost seemed like an upper floor. The Palace was constructed in one long line, with big verandas all around. The ground floor with its verandas was for us, and we were asked to select our rooms. Bapu chose a small room next to the bathrooms, and refused to consider any of the larger ones. Then Sarojini Devi chose the big room next but one to Bapu's, leaving in between a small narrow room. Mahadev

241

went to the big room beyond the bathrooms, and I selected the farthest corner of the large dining room, which was otherwise going to be left unused and which came first in the long line, making it a little apart.

"What about goat's milk?" I said to Mr. Kateley anxiously. "Bapu has had hardly anything to eat."

"Goats are kept ready," he replied. And there they were, two or three of them, in the kitchen line on the other side of the garden.

We began to settle down. The flowers in the garden were glorious, and there was also a nice view of distant hills. But we soon discovered that our isolation was complete. We could neither receive nor write any letters, nor were we allowed any newspapers. The only thing which reached us was a copy of the Government of India's communiqué justifying their policy of wholesale repression. No communication of any kind with the outside world was permitted, but some sounds floated on the air from Poona city, and we guessed and knew that there must be disturbances in every city of India.

On the third day our guarded gates opened to let in Ba accompanied by Sushila. How good! "What's the news? How were you arrested? What's going on outside?"

But they could not tell us very much, because they, along with Pyarelal, had been arrested on the evening of the same day as we had, when planning to go to a protest meeting in Bombay at which Ba was to have presided. This much they could report, that all meetings and processions had been banned, but that the public turned out regardless of the police, and lathi charges, tear-gassing and arrests were going on. Poor Ba was considerably shaken, not by the upheavals and her arrest, but by the anxiety she had gone through as to where Bapu was, and whether she would be taken to him or not. Once she had reached the Aga Khan's Palace she quickly recovered.

There was no doubt that the country was in a tremendous turmoil. Wholesale arrest of all its beloved leaders before they had launched any movement, or given any instructions or guidance, was bound to throw the nation into confusion and drive the masses wild with anger.

242

Bapu now dictated to Mahadev a letter for the Viceroy:

> The Government of India were wrong in precipitating the crisis. The Government resolution justifying the step is full of distortions and misrepresentations . . .
>
> . . . I had publicly stated that I fully contemplated sending you a letter before taking concrete action. It was to be an appeal to you for an impartial examination of the Congress case. As you know the Congress has readily filled in every omission that has been discovered in the conception of its demand. So would I have dealt with every deficiency if you had given me the opportunity.

Bapu went on to analyze in some detail the Government communiqué, then pointed out that:

> . . . The declared cause is common between the Government of India and us. To put it in the most concrete terms, it is the protection of the freedom of China and Russia. The Government of India think that freedom of India is not necessary for winning the cause. I think exactly the opposite.

And he ended by reaffirming his true friendship for the British people.

We had listened in suspense lest Bapu should mention the possibility of his fasting, and though he had not done so, yet we had no feeling of security because from the look of things a fast would be sure to materialize sooner or later. This was the one thing of all others that Mahadev dreaded, for he feared that if Bapu went on a long fast at this juncture, he would not survive. The letter was handed over to Mr. Kateley for dispatch, and we awaited the Viceroy's reactions.

The next day when Mahadev and I happened to be sitting in the same room reading, he looked up at me and said, "What a grand opportunity this would be for writing. I have at least six books in my mind which I would like to get down on paper, but the intolerable thought of Bapu's probable fast hangs over me like the Sword of Damocles, and I can't get my mind onto anything."

I knew Mahadev's most ardent wish was not to survive Bapu. Such was his attachment, that he simply could not face the idea of outliving him, and at various times in the past I had heard him passionately express this sentiment. So I could well understand the intensity of his feelings in the situation in which we now found ourselves placed. Indeed what could I say that would be reassuring? We had to put our faith in God and await the future, whatever it might be.

The next morning as I passed through the small room between Bapu's and Sarojini Devi's, I found Mahadev sitting on the floor shaving. He looked up and said, "You've got some nail scissors, I think. I want to trim my nails."

"Yes," said I, and fetched them.

"And a bigger pair, if you have them, for trimming my mustache."

I fetched those also, and while I was watching him finishing up his toilet, someone came running to say that the Inspector-General of Prisons had come, and was talking to Sarojini Devi in her room.

"You go along," said Mahadev.

"No no, you go, you know him much better than I do," I replied, and giving him a little push on the back, got him to go into the next room. I then went to the veranda where Sushila was giving a massage to Bapu, who was lying in his bed. I told them of the Inspector-General's arrival. Suddenly I heard Ba's voice calling, "Sushila, Sushila." We thought Ba was calling her in connection with the visitor, but Ba's voice came again in an agonized tone: "Sushila, Mahadev's got a fit, come, come!"

Sushila rushed, and I waited behind to help Bapu off his bed. We hurried along the veranda, and as we entered the room, we saw Mahadev stretched on the bed, his eyes shut and his face red with the effort of a terrific struggle which passed through his whole being. Bapu put his hand on him and called him by name, but he did not open his eyes. Ba cried out, "Mahadev, Mahadev, Bapu has come." But no, he remained locked in an inner battle that he seemed to be rapidly losing. "Fetch a hot-water bottle, quick, quick!" someone said and I dashed to the bathroom. By the time I came back, it was all over. Mahadev had gone, and only the empty body lay there.

Everyone was speechless. Not only the passing away of such a

244

noble and devoted soul, but the thought of the irreparable loss it would mean to Bapu rent our hearts. That was the first thought that Ba gave voice to as she cried, "Bapu has lost his right hand, and his left hand! Both his hands Bapu has lost!!"

But as was always the way in Bapu's presence, all outward expressions of violent emotion were quickly overcome. Bapu remained almost completely silent, as if passed into a world of prayer. He spoke only to give a few instructions.

"Clear all the furniture out of the small room, for laying out the body."

The body was first taken to the bathroom, and there he himself assisted in the washing and the wrapping in a white khadi sheet. I saw to the preparation of the room.

The Inspector-General rushed to give orders for a priest, and firewood for the pyre. But where was the funeral to be? The Government had to be consulted. Bapu said at all cost he must attend to the funeral rites, for Mahadev was for him a son, and more, but the Government would not dream of allowing Bapu to go outside. After a very tense period of suspense, with the telephone continually in use, the Government finally agreed that the cremation should take place just outside the wire fence at the back of the enclosure, where it adjoined open rough ground stretching far away toward the river and the hills. Here there were no roads, and no other houses to overlook the scene.

Mr. Kateley had given orders for flowers to be brought up from the garden, and by the time the body was ready for laying out on the floor—the floor of that very room in which Mahadev had been barbering himself in preparation for death, though he knew it not —there was a glorious pile of flowers ready. It fell to my lot to decorate the body. I covered it with flowers of every color, and around the head and face I placed a halo of beautiful big yellow blossoms. All this time Bapu sat on the ground near the head, reading from the Gita.

The priest came, the ceremonies were carred out, Bapu doing everything with his own hands. Now the body was lifted, and here again Bapu lent his hand. Across the garden we went and out through the wire fence, where a gateway had been hurriedly made.

A few yards away the pyre stood ready, the body was placed on it, and more and more wood was piled up. Then Bapu took the burning torch and set the fire blazing that swept away all remnants of the familiar form that only a few hours ago had been invested with Mahadev's spirit, and living among us.

Silently we passed back to the house. Long, hard and heavy were the days that followed. Gradually we readjusted ourselves and the Government sent Pyarelal to help Bapu in his writing work.

CHAPTER LVII

THOUGH Bapu became his normal self, and we all cheered up and avoided any gloomy atmosphere, the depth of his feeling over Mahadev's death could be seen by the absolute regularity with which he went each morning with flowers to the site of the cremation, where verses from the Gita were recited. A mound of stone and mud plaster was made to mark the spot, then on its flat top I molded the sacred letter ओं (the mystic letter OM), and according to Bapu's special wish added a cross beneath it. The star and crescent of Islam I molded in the four corners. At the time of placing the flowers, it was always the little cross on which Bapu placed them, making the complete outline with tiny blossoms. The rest of the decorations we used to see to. As I watched Bapu, I would remember the crucifix in Rome, which had so held him, and it seemed to me that that symbol of supreme sacrifice represented for him the most fundamental urge of his being.

It was at this time that Bapu's choice of Christian hymns gradually changed from "Lead Kindly Light" to "When I Survey the Wondrous Cross," which now became the one hymn that he asked for on all special occasions.

After we had been shut up tight for over a fortnight, the Gov-

246

ernment permitted Bapu to have what newspapers he chose, including back numbers. A list was made out. When the bundle came it disclosed an overwhelming amount of news. Throughout the country there had been demonstrations, meetings and marches, with accompanying lathi charges, tear-gassing and arrests by the Government. Nonviolence had been widely observed, but in some cases, maddened by the Government's precipitate action, people had taken to cutting telegraph wires, pulling up railway lines, attacking police stations, etc.

We watched Bapu as he read through the newspapers, wondering what his reactions might be. He remained calm and a little grim. When he finally spoke, it was to say that the wonder was there had not been more violence, seeing the way the Government had acted.

In a little less than a fortnight there came a cold and curt reply from the Viceroy to Bapu's letter, expressing his inability to accept Bapu's criticism of the Government communiqué or his suggestion that the Government should reconsider its policy. Bapu undoubtedly felt the utter lack of human touch in this formal letter, and the shadow hanging over us deepened. But we kept up our spirits, and in this effort Sarojini Devi was indomitable.

When the birthday of Lord Krishna* came around, she said: "Now we must do something. All the world outside is celebrating the day, and here, as prisoners, is there not an even greater significance for us seeing that he was born in prison?"

I remembered that someone had once given me a tiny ivory carving of the infant Krishna lying on a leaf. I hunted in my box and found it. At that season the garden was full of magnificent dahlias, and I gathered some of every color and made a cushion of flowers on a little table, placed the tiny ivory Krishna in the middle, and lighted incense. No one was more pleased than Ba, who stood with folded hands before the table, lost in prayer. From that day I kept the table decorated. Each morning I brought in flowers from the garden and made a new design, and each day when Bapu came along the veranda on his way to his morning walk, he would turn into my room and look at the flowers. He noticed that I was

* Incarnation of Vishnu (God as Preserver).

247

making a different pattern every day, and said, "You must go on like that, and always make some new design."

Thanks to the wonderful variety of flowers in the garden, I was able to.

It now became a regular habit with Ba to come daily to worship and pray at the little shrine. It was profoundly touching to see the concentration of her thought at such times, and the visible depth of her faith.

When October 2nd, Bapu's birthday, came, Sarojini Devi again said something special must be done, and we devised gaieties of various kinds. Then came Divali, the Hindu Festival of Lamps, and good Mr. Kateley made no objection to our illuminating the verandas and the windows with little open lamps of vegetable oil.

None of us, not even Bapu, had realized up to this time of incarceration together in the Aga Khan's Palace the full richness of Sarojini Devi's nature. Of course we all knew of her poetic genius, her amazing oratory, and her sparkling wit, but it was only now, through direct experience, that we came to know of the bigness of her motherly heart, and the strength of her character in moments of suffering and sorrow. Her large room, and its back veranda, became our dining room and kitchen, over which she presided. No outside help being permitted, a batch of convicts with a Jamadar and two sepoys in charge were sent every day to work in the garden, look after the goats and keep the place clean. One of these sepoys, a quiet young man, used to help Sarojini Devi with her cooking. We also helped, but it was her domain, over which she ruled like a benign empress. She would sit there on the back veranda on a stool, little charcoal stoves on the floor in front of her, and stir the pots with a long spoon. Though she would be dressed in an old silk dressing gown with her long hair falling loosely over her shoulders, yet she would never for a moment lose her royal aspect. She thought of everybody's needs. She would make us—Sushila, Pyarelal and myself—sit down as if we were her children, and serve us with her own hand. And on one occasion when I was ill she insisted on cooking me special dishes and bringing them to my room. Yet she was sixty-four, and none too well in health.

248

As the year drew to an end Bapu's restlessness increased, and we felt the shadow of the fateful fast spreading over us. He now said he wanted to go into three days' silence for meditating on a letter he intended writing to the Viceroy. It soon transpired that he was contemplating taking a twenty-one days' fast if he could get no response. That there would be any response he knew was most unlikely, and from that moment we saw the ordeal rising up before us as a certainty.

I asked Bapu if he would like to have in front of him on the wall during his three days' silence the sacred ओ and if so I would draw it for him. He said:

"Yes, and under the ओ put *Hey Ram*."*

This I did, drawing them on a big piece of cardboard. And from that time Bapu always kept the symbols before him, even after his release.

The three days' silence over, Bapu started drafting the letter. It was to go off on New Year's Eve. Bapu wrote: "I must not allow the old year to expire without disburdening myself of what is rankling in my breast . . ."

Why did not the Viceroy regard him any longer as a friend and try to understand his meaning? Though he did not agree with the Government by what he was able to make out from inside prison, yet his mind was always open to conviction. He had given himself six months to wait in patience. That time limit was now up.

> The law of Satyagraha as I know it prescribes a remedy in such moments of trial. In a sentence it is, "Crucify the flesh by fasting." That same law forbids its use except as a last resort. I do not want to use it if I can avoid it.
>
> This is a way to avoid it. Convince me of any error or errors, and I shall make ample amends. You can send for me or send someone who knows your mind and can carry conviction. There are many other ways if you have the will.

So there was still a thread to hold on by. The days of waiting for the reply seemed interminable. It came in a fortnight, and was much longer and more frank than the previous one. There was

---

* *Hey Ram*—O God.

still no vestige of acceptance of Bapu's reasoning, but only an attempt to read in Bapu's letters a meaning that was not there:

> . . . If I am right in reading your letter to mean that in the light of what has happened you wish now to retrace your steps and dissociate yourself from the policy of last summer, you have only to let me know and I will at once consider the matter further. . . .

Then followed the words that gave again one glimpse of hope:

> And if I have failed to understand your object, you must not hesitate to let me know without delay in what respect I have done so, and tell me what positive suggestion you wish to put to me.

Bapu again wrote a full reply, the central point of the letter being that if the Viceroy wanted him to make some positive suggestion, he might be able to do so if he were put among the members of the Working Committee.

The Viceroy's reply to this left no more room for hope. Bapu's suggestion to be placed with the Congress Working Committee for consultations was not even referred to, and the final argument was the same as ever—"repudiate or dissociate yourself from the resolution of the 9th August."

So Bapu in his answer gave a definite date for the commencement of his fast, and added:

> Usually, during my fasts, I take water with the addition of salts. But nowadays, my system refuses water. This time therefore I propose to add juices of citrus fruits to make water drinkable. For, my wish is not to fast unto death, but to survive the ordeal, if God so wills. The fast can be ended sooner by the Government giving the needed relief.

There followed a long letter from the Viceroy, but no hope of compromise. To this Bapu replied in another long letter, and that ended the discussion.

It was now February 7th. Over five torturing weeks had passed, and at the end we found ourselves within three days of the commencement of the fast, which ultimately started on February 10th.

The Government, as usual, made businesslike arrangements. Dr. Gilder, former Congress Health Minister in Bombay and a well-known heart specialist, who had often attended on Bapu in the past, was transferred from Yaravda Jail to the Aga Khan's Palace. In spite of the seriousness of the occasion we all had a laugh, including Bapu, at Dr. Gilder's beard which he had grown in prison. We said it suited him and made him look quite French, but he removed it in a day or two and returned to his full mustache, which again made him look like the cultured Parsee that he was.

Within three days of the commencement of the fast Bapu began to suffer a lot, and after a little persuasion the Government agreed to allow Dr. Dinshaw Mehta, the Nature Cure specialist, to come for regular attendance, as this was the treatment in which Bapu had the greatest faith, especially during fasts. There was a general feeling that Bapu was not going to survive the ordeal, and the Government agreed to permit visits by relatives and friends. Dr. B. C. Roy, later Chief Minister of Bengal, of whose judgment Bapu had a high opinion, arrived from Bengal and stayed in Poona during the critical days, so as to be able to visit Bapu daily. Some political moderates and mediators were also allowed, no doubt with the hope of influencing Bapu.

One important visitor, with whom Bapu had special talks, was Rajaji. Bapu had so deep a regard for Rajaji's knowledge and insight that he had, for years, loved to call him "The keeper of my conscience." The problem which they now had under discussion was how to deal with Jinnah and his rapidly developing demand for the division of India.

When the fast began I was on duty for any jobs required of me more or less during eighteen hours a day. After some days I suddenly came down with a violent attack of malaria. I was told I must have quinine injections, as they were the surest way of checking the disease, and, with malaria in the house, mosquitoes might carry the fever to Bapu, which would be fatal. Dr. Roy, knowing my great dislike of injections, came to cheer me up, and in his deep booming voice said, "Don't you know they used to give injections in Vedic times?"

"Did they!" I said in the midst of my fever.

251

"Oh yes, they used to administer them with the tip of a cow's horn."

Anyway I had them—with a needle of course—one on each side, and felt awful. But the malaria disappeared, for which I was most thankful.

When I returned to Bapu's room the twenty-one days were drawing to a close, and Bapu's strength had almost ebbed out. If it had not been for the clause in his vow allowing for a little fruit juice if absolutely necessary, he would never have survived.

The Government had gone so far (so we learned afterwards) as to collect the sandal and other wood for the cremation, and to arrange by which route the funeral procession should pass. At the same time they had given detailed instructions to their officials throughout India for extreme vigilance, and the immediate suppression of any disturbances on news of Bapu's death.

But God spared India the sorrow and England the shame. Bapu survived.

After the fast was broken, visitors were stopped by Government. If I remember rightly, Devadas was allowed to continue coming for some days, and Bapu's nephew, Kanu Gandhi, a young, athletic man, full of energy and very devoted to Bapu, who had been sent to help in the nursing, was not removed immediately. Dr. Gilder, it was agreed, should remain.

CHAPTER LVIII

THOUGH the fast did not melt the Government's heart, it burned like hot iron into the flesh of the nation, and gave the last touch to the people's detestation of British oppression.

It took Bapu time to recover. The physical strain was bad enough, but the mental strain was even worse. Nevertheless he pulled himself out of it.

Now Sarojini Devi contracted a very bad case of malaria. She could not throw it off, and became terribly weak. This caused general alarm. Mercifully the Government took action, and released her unconditionally before it was too late. An ambulance was brought, and she had to be carried down to it on a stretcher. How much we missed her, especially myself! But we were all thankful to think of her out of a house already haunting in its associations.

All this time Ba was in very indifferent health, and it was evident that her condition was slowly and steadily deteriorating. Mental depression also wore her down.

Mr. Kateley offered the distraction of a few games, and Bapu willingly agreed. So badminton and table tennis were introduced for the younger members, and carrom (a kind of shuffleboard) for the older ones.

Sushila persuaded Bapu and Ba to perform the "opening ceremony" of the badminton court in the garden. The plan was for Bapu to hit the shuttlecock over the net to Ba and for her to return it. I don't think the shuttlecock got over the net properly even once, but it caused much amusement, and lightened the atmosphere.

Dr. Gilder and Mr. Kateley sat down to the carrom board and played away solemnly every afternoon. One day, as I was passing by the table, they said, "Come along and join us."

"Then you two become partners," I replied, "and I'll play against you both, moving from side to side for my turn."

I had played this game in the old days in England, and used to enjoy it because there was much more skill than luck in it. I took my first side and we started off. I think we turned out about even on that first day, but the next day I began to beat them. After they had been beaten continually for some days they said, "Look here, we are going to give you a handicap."

"All right," I replied, "what shall it be?"

"You must stay on one side only, and take both your shots from there."

It certainly became much more difficult to beat them now, but I did succeed, and too often to satisfy them. Just as they were trying to think of some further handicap, one came to hand quite unexpectedly.

For some days Ba had been coming on and off to watch the game, and evinced quite a keen interest in it. One day, as she was looking on, Bapu happened to pass, and he laughingly told her she should join in. At first Ba protested, but Bapu became quite earnest in his suggestion, and finally she agreed. I was to be her partner. Of course dear Ba had never in her life played any such game, and we all coached her. It became a merry party, and with luck, when Ba's shots did not go too much astray, we used to win. Bapu, every now and then, would come to have a look, and was delighted to see Ba was getting some distraction.

He then said to her, "You should do some practice on your own, so as to get good at it."

The next day in the morning I found Ba at the carrom board seriously practicing all by herself. After that I used to help her with lessons whenever she felt like it. And before long we used usually to win at the afternoon game.

But alas, Ba's health was steadily failing. She became more and more depressed, and used to say she was sure she was going to follow Mahadev. She developed a very bad cough, sometimes she got terrible palpitations of the heart, and day by day her strength diminished. To make matters worse, there was distressing delay in getting the Government to permit the doctors she desired. At last it was agreed that Dr. Dinshaw Mehta should come regularly to give her treatment. As her condition grew worse, she felt a strong desire for an Ayurvedic doctor. Again there was painful difficulty and delay, but ultimately Dr. Shiv Sharma was sent. To help in the nursing, Bapu's niece Manu Gandhi and also Prabhavati ben were sent.

By this time her condition was becoming serious, and her sons and other relatives were permitted to come daily.

It was over a year since her health had begun to give way, and by now she was completely worn out with the torturing struggle. On the 22nd the last crisis came. Bapu held her in his arms. As the breathing began to change he said to her gently: "What is it?"

And she answered in a sweet clear voice, with a tone of wonder in it, as if she were experiencing something totally new and wonderful: "I don't know what it is."

There was no fear, no worry. A few more breaths and she passed from the body, while those of us standing around had begun chanting the sacred strains of Ramdhun.*

Bapu remained silent and simply signed for the body to be laid flat.

The women relatives took the body to the bathroom for bathing, and once more I prepared the room for the laying out of a corpse. From the garden glorious flowers were again brought, and I placed them all around and over the little body. Incense was lighted, and the reciting of the Gita was begun.

It was already evening, so the cremation had to be put off till the next day. Again the question arose as to where it should take place. Bapu told the Inspector-General, "The body should be handed over to my sons and relatives, which would mean a public funeral without interference from Government."

But the Government fought shy of this, and so it was decided that cremation of Ba's body should take place on the same spot where Mahadev was cremated.

All-night watch was kept over the body with incense and chanting. For hours Bapu sat looking at the remains of her who had been his faithful and undaunted companion for sixty years. He seemed to be in silent commune with her. At one moment Sushila even heard a murmured soliloquy, as if he were talking to Ba.

In the morning relatives and friends poured in with more and more flowers. By the time we went down to the cremation ground Bapu was tired out, but he kept himself going, and remained by the pyre till it burned down to a pile of ashes.

When the day came for us to collect the bones, we found Ba's bangles intact among the ashes. I remember well the thrill that passed through all of us, and how the Jamadar, who was standing on guard, burst out with the assurance that it meant Ba had gone straight to heaven.

* The chanting of God's names.

255

CHAPTER LIX

LIFE in the Aga Khan's Palace was becoming more and more difficult to bear, but we just had to make the best of it, for there was no sign in view of any change in the situation outside regarding the Government's attitude toward Bapu and the Congress.

Another stone and mud mound was made alongside Mahadev's and I molded designs on it in the same way. Bapu's daily visit with flowers continued without fail, but his health was much pulled down, and after a month or so his weakened frame was seized by malarial fever. It was a very bad attack, and his condition became serious. The fever went down with quinine, but the weakness persisted. Dr. Dinshaw Mehta was again called in. A long and painful convalescence now seemed to be ahead. A haunting feeling got hold of everyone, including even the Jamadar and the sepoys, that this Palace had something deadly about it, and at all cost Bapu should be transferred.

Bapu had himself been pleading with the Government for some time, asking to be put in a less expensive place than a big palace, though with little hope.

As the days went by, however, we got the feeling that perhaps some kind of transfer was being considered, and we speculated among ourselves whether we should remain together or be divided up into regulation jails, with men and women in different prisons. One day at the beginning of May, when the Inspector-General visited our camp, he asked, as casually as he could, as if nothing were behind it, whether, in the opinion of the doctors, Bapu was fit to travel a hundred miles in a car or train. Obviously something was being planned. Now we began calculating what places were about a hundred miles from Poona. But still nothing actually happened for the next day or two. I suggested to the others that we might as well sort out our things and pack up what we could in advance. After staying nearly two years in one spot, a lot of clutter collects, even in a detention camp, and Bapu would be sure to expect us to leave the rooms in perfect order without any rubbish lying about. The others preferred to await developments, but I started sorting and packing up my own corner.

On the evening of the 5th, when I was sitting by Bapu's bed reading aloud, the Inspector-General suddenly walked in. I jumped up and placed a chair for him near Bapu. He sat down and said, "Mahatma *ji,* you and your party are to be released unconditionally tomorrow morning at eight o'clock."

"Are you joking?" Bapu asked, restraining his wonderment.

The Inspector-General answered Bapu that he was quite serious, and that he had received the orders that day.

The others had come running in from the farther room, where they were having their evening meal.

The Inspector-General went on to explain that Bapu would be permitted to stay on at the Palace for some time if his convalescence required it, but that the guard would be removed at 8 o'clock sharp in the morning.

Once the guard was removed there was no question of Bapu staying any longer in that deadly place. So he told the Inspector-General he would go to Parna Kuti, the Poona residence of Lady Thakursay, where he had often stayed in the past.

Now the packing and clearing up began in real earnest, and went on practically all night. Bapu, the while, lay awake on his bed plunged in thought. There was the personal thought of going out of prison without those two who were nearest and dearest to him, and there was the thought of the frustrated nation which would turn to him in eager hope. What could he do? Would God give him back bodily strength? Would he be alone or would the Congress Working Committee members be released also? Or if not, would he be allowed to contact them? It was all so sudden and unexpected.

Early in the morning we went down with Bapu to place a last tribute of flowers at the cremation ground. It was a hard moment as we turned away to go out into the world without those two.

Punctually at 8 o'clock the Inspector-General passed us out through the barbed-wire gates. Only those immediately concerned had been previously informed, so the drive to Parna Kuti was quite peaceful. But in no time the news spread—spread like wildfire throughout the length and breadth of India, nay, the whole world. Visitors came rushing, and cables and telegrams came pouring in from far and near. It was not in Bapu to hide himself away. He greeted everyone and listened to all the written messages, dictating many of the replies himself. What little strength he had was soon used up, and within five days it was decided that a halt *must* be called. Bapu was persuaded to go away to Juhu, where the whole party was put up in the bungalows of Gandhigram, near the beach.

Now strict control was put on the amount of work and number of visitors. The limiting of the visitors was the most difficult task, needing both firmness and tact. Sarojini Devi, in spite of her delicate state of health, had joined us at Juhu, and she volunteered to undertake this arduous job. Adding wit and good humor to the required firmness and tact, she managed the callers as no one else could have done.

The problems facing Bapu would have been enough to oppress him even if he had been in the best of health. Ordinance Rule was in full swing, the press was gagged, thousands, including the Congress Working Committee members, were in jail, and starvation stalked the land. The moderates had tried hard to break the deadlock, but all their attempts had failed. Now everyone looked to Bapu, and slowly and surely he began. He wrote to the Viceroy, Lord Wavell, saying that since there was a general expectation that now, as a free man, he should "make some decisive contribution to the general good," he would once more plead for permission to see the members of the Congress Working Committee, as without that he could do little or nothing. At the same time, if the Viceroy wished to see him before granting the permission, he would gladly come for discussion. This letter received a negative reply, but Bapu patiently went on preparing the ground in his own way. The misery of the country was so great, and the obstinacy of the British Government so palpable, that practically all shades of public opinion had consolidated behind Bapu.

After a month in Juhu, it was recommended that Bapu should move to Panchgani, a hill station in the Western Ghats.

CHAPTER LX

EVEN while still in the Aga Khan's Palace my mind had been busy with the idea of starting a little center of my own somewhere in the North of India when once we were released, and now the time had come. I discussed it with Bapu, and he agreed. I was to be given a lump sum of money and to plan out the whole thing myself. There was one hitch when Bapu said he would like me to have trustees. I felt this would ruin my freedom of self-expression, which was what I was really seeking, though I had not analyzed it to myself in so many words. The trustees would know little about agriculture and animal husbandry, which were the two things which appealed to me most in rural development, and their ideas in so many matters would be totally different from mine. Finally Bapu let me go *free,* and my heart expanded.

Though I wanted to have fields and cattle, yet the old background of khadi work, and the knowledge that it was that which appealed to Bapu most, led me to seek an area where khadi could be developed. At the same time the Himalayas were calling, but there no cotton grows, and khadi work, as I visualized it, would not be possible. So I sought a compromise. Let me be in a spinning and weaving area with the snows of the Himalayas in sight.

I went to Roorkee where friends gave me every assistance in scouring the countryside for the right spot. Between Roorkee and Hardwar there is a fine stretch of agricultural land, intercepted

259

with small rivers and dotted all over with villages, where spinning and weaving has gone on from time immemorial. When the weather is clear, from many of these villages one gets a distant but glorious view of the Great Himalayan Range. Here was the compromise I was seeking.

After considerable searching I chose a spot about halfway between Roorkee and Hardwar, one mile from the motor road, on the lands of a little village called Muldaspur. The neighboring village was a Moslem village, and in the whole region it was a mixed Hindu-Moslem population, with about two hundred weavers within a radius of five miles. I managed to procure ten acres of land, and on this I set about building little cottages of sun-dried mud bricks, with thatched roofs. The local Harijans, as usual, were the house builders, and they carried out the whole construction.

By this time two workers had joined me—a young intellectual, Dharampal, who was interested in the idea of rural development, and a Vaidya (Ayurvedic doctor). With these two I camped on the land while the construction work was going on. We had two huts for ourselves, and a third one we used as a cowshed. Into this we introduced our first cow, Jamuna, with her week-old calf, both of them white and very charming to look upon. Jamuna, however, did not take to me at once. She had never seen anyone but villagers before, and therefore regarded me with strong suspicion. As she had long horns, and was very active in her movements, this attitude of hers was rather embarrassing. Day by day I made gentle advances, and after about a week she decided to let me groom her, and finally to milk her. Up to then we had had to have a man from the village for morning and evening milking.

It was by now the middle of winter, and in the first week of January, rain began. It rained and rained and rained, while we in our little grass huts shivered with cold, for there could be no heating, and the wind blew right through the thin grass walls. When at last the weather cleared, we beheld the whole Himalayan Range right down to the lowest foothills all gleaming white with freshly fallen snow. The villagers said that there had not been such a snowfall in living memory.

260

Now the sun shone brightly, and our construction work progressed apace. By the time it was finished we had a cowshed, a store, a kitchen and my *kutia* on four sides of an open space where the cattle were tied in the daytime, and to the west of my *kutia*, a line of three more cottages—two for workers, and one for Bapu, who planned to visit the Ashram at the first opportunity.

There came at this time a blow which struck deep into my being —Romain Rolland had passed away. I had been cherishing the hope that I should see him again someday after the war, but it was not to be.

The Ashram now had to be given a name, and I wrote to Bapu saying my idea was to call it Kisan Ashram, as it was especially for the service of the *kisans* (farmers). Bapu wrote back on February 27, 1944:

> You can have Kisan Ashram but if that, why not Mazdur [laborer] or its equivalent? A *kisan* can be a millionaire, not so a working man, a labourer. But I do not mind Kisan, if you prefer it.

I stuck to Kisan, because the kisan is essentially a countryman, but not so the mazdur, who is usually a city laborer. Also, the kisans in that area were far from being millionaires.

The winter passed, the spring came, and still there was no chance for Bapu to come to the little Ashram. He was continually tussling with the resistance of the British Government to any agreement. If Bapu's pleading and arguments showed signs of becoming irresistible, then new obstacles would be created, and of course the trump card was Jinnah and his demand for Pakistan.

Divide and rule had always been the strength of the foreign power, and now it was the only hope left for being able to keep a controlling influence over the valuable subcontinent. So, when Jinnah actually agreed to have talks in the autumn of 1944 with Bapu on the question of an agreement between the Indian National Congress and Moslem League, there was serious alarm in British circles; and to offset the possible achievement of Hindu-Moslem solidarity, the bogies of the Depressed Classes and the Princes were immediately displayed again with fresh vigor.

261

The talks were, of course, a failure, for it appeared that Jinnah had never had any intention of coming to a reasonable agreement. His criterion for nationality was religion. According to this reasoning, all the Moslems of India were of one nationality and all the Hindus of another. That countries like China and Russia contained millions of Moslems who nevertheless considered themselves Chinese and Russian, had no effect on him whatever. But what made his demands even more incongruous was that he maintained that the Moslems as a separate nationality had the sole right to decide, in the areas he chose to describe as Moslem-majority Provinces, whether to separate from India or not, regardless of the opinion of the rest of the population which, except for the North-West Frontier regions, formed only a little less than half of the total population.

Bapu, however, remained unruffled and patient. Not so others. And if Jinnah's real object was disruption, he was already making headway.

Living as I was in a mixed Hindu-Moslem region, where the two communities had dwelt together for centuries and where the Moslem peasants were, if anything, better off than the Hindu peasants, all this Pakistan talk had, for me, a most unhealthy and unnatural ring.

After the fruitless Gandhi-Jinnah talks, there followed efforts by others at a *rapprochement* between the Indian National Congress and the Moslem League, but that also failed. With all the Congress Working Committee members still shut up in jail, nothing substantial could be hoped for. Though the war in Europe was drawing to an end, the Japanese threat in the East remained, and with India sullenly anti-British, the situation was anything but satisfactory for the Western Powers. The Viceroy, being a military man, fully realized the need to win the good will of the Indian people, and his opinion was beginning to tell on the politicians in London. In March 1945 Lord Wavell went to England for urgent consultations, and on his return announced his intention to try to bring about a settlement, for which purpose he called a conference of all parties at Simla, which opened on June 25th, just after the war in Europe had come to an end. Now at last the

262

members of the Congress Working Committee were released. Bapu agreed to attend the Conference as an observer.

I had been watching the march of events from my mud cottage in Kisan Ashram, and when Bapu arrived in Simla, I wrote and suggested coming to him. He wrote back: "Do come," and I immediately set out. This was the first time I had left the Ashram since starting it, and the chief problem was Jamuna, who disliked anyone else milking her. I made the best arrangements I could, and hoped for the best, but she looked dissatisfied and restless.

When I reached Simla and joined Bapu at the home of the Rajkumari Amrit Kaur, where he and his party were staying, I found a whirl of political excitement. The Congress Working Committee members, decidedly jail-worn after thirty-four months of confinement, were trying hard to size up the situation, and kept coming to have consultations with Bapu. Representatives of all the different communities and groups were also busy, and Jinnah was there casting his shadow of negation on all efforts at a reasonable settlement.

The Conference dragged on till July 14th, and ended without reaching any solution.

Everyone dispersed. Bapu went away to Poona, and interested himself in the setting up of a simple Nature Cure clinic near there, where poor people could get treatment. I, of course, returned to Kisan Ashram.

My first concern was Jamuna. I was told she had become almost impossible to milk. When milking time came around, I approached her. For a few minutes she accepted me quietly, and I thought all was going to be well, but before I had finished milking, one of the men to whom she had taken a violent dislike foolishly came and spoke to me. She was furious, and from then on to the end of that lactation I could not succeed in milking her without having two or three men to hold her. Next time she calved she was all right, but one had to be most careful to ensure perfect quiet at the time of milking.

CHAPTER LXI

KISAN ASHRAM developed rapidly. Our livestock increased to four cows and calves, two bullocks, and a pony for me with which to get around the countryside. More workers were also added. One of them, an expert in carding and spinning and an excellent social worker, Ramjibhai, instructed the village children in reading and writing, and also gave them physical drill.

Our cloth production was now increasing steadily and the next question was to introduce design and color into the weaving, and to organize sales. For this an old and experienced worker joined us. He possessed artistic taste, and soon began to turn out a large variety of cloth. Naddaji looked an artist too, with his long, gently curling hair and expressive clean-shaved face.

Though the winter climate at Kisan Ashram was quite cold, the summer heat was intense, and I began to realize for the first time the extremes of the North Indian climate. Even when I was younger the heat had always told on me, and now I found it still harder to bear, but the cold winter gave me strength to pull through the rest of the year.

Although I was continually busy with the work around me, I nevertheless kept an eye on the world scene, which was rapidly developing. Now that the war in Europe was over, the British Coalition Government came to an end, and with the general elections the Labour Party swept into power. The Viceroy again visited England, and announced on his return that there would be elections in India both for the Central and Provincial Assemblies.

As the preparations for the elections went on, the people got more and more restive and displayed in unmistakable ways their antipathy to the British for the bleeding of the nation in support of the Western Powers' war effort without consulting anyone but themselves, for the long-drawn-out repression, and withal, for the absence of any definite promise of freedom from the detested foreign yoke. The most startling of these manifestations of dissatisfaction was a mutiny in the Royal Indian Navy in February 1946. There was also marked unrest in the Indian Air Force and the Police. Lord Wavell continued to emphasize the necessity for immediate conciliatory action, and on March 15, 1946, Attlee, who had become the Labour Prime Minister, announced the British Government's decision to send out to India a Cabinet Mission.

In the meantime the elections had taken place and ministries had been formed in the various Provinces. The United Provinces, in which Kisan Ashram was situated, now had a strong Congress government, headed by the veteran leader Pandit Govind Vallabh Pant. In the new atmosphere created by the conclusion of hostilities on the Eastern Front, and the commencement of the withdrawal of foreign troops from India, there was a general urge to resuscitate the Province and make an all-out drive for increased food production. Quite a lot of good agricultural land had been requisitioned for military airfields and camps, and the sooner these were put back into cultivation the better. A large piece of excellent land near Kisan Ashram was held by the military as an emergency landing ground, and I began to look into the possibilities of getting this returned to the villagers. Once I started investigating this problem of requisitioned lands I could not rest satisfied with the handling of just one emergency landing ground, so I went to Bapu and discussed the matter with him. He, in turn, had a talk with Pandit Pant, and the outcome was that I was appointed as Honorary Special Adviser to the U. P. Government in connection with the newly launched "Grow More Food" campaign.

I went to Lucknow to take over my new job from the Agriculture Minister, and to make myself acquainted with the workings of government machinery. Here was an entirely new world. Up to now I had lived among Indian Indians, but now I came in

265

direct contact with the Anglicized bureaucracy. All the officers and clerks were dressed in European or semi-European clothes, and called one another "Mister."

Dharampal was appointed as my secretary, and I was also given a stenographer, two peons, a driver, and a big blue motor van which could contain the whole staff and luggage. In this we set out on a tour of the Province. I inspected a number of disused air-fields and camps, visited General Auchinleck, the Commander in Chief, in Delhi, and also a number of other English generals in Lucknow, Roorkee and Dehra Dun.

I remember when I went to see the General in Command at Lucknow it was the middle of the hot season, and the army had been given instructions to "strip to the waist." The result was I found the General sitting at his office table with a bare torso, and, as all other officers and orderlies around also had bare bodies to the waist, there was no telling who was what, for every sign of rank had disappeared with the removal of the upper garments. As the instructions had just recently been issued, everyone was feeling a bit awkward, especially when an outsider, and a female at that, suddenly turned up in their lines.

Here were the Englishmen casting off their clothes, while in the civil departments the poor Anglicized Indians sat sweltering in shirts, and coats over shirts, in order to be correct!

As in the past, I found the military considerate in their attitude and quick to take action. Not so the civil administration. As the days went by, I became more and more aware of the terrible machine we were taking over from the British, and counted on its being completely altered once we got full control.

Kisan Ashram remained my headquarters, but after the tour in the blazing heat of summer, I went to Mussoorie for a short spell and anxiously watched from there the political scene, around which were gathering dark and ominous clouds.

The British Cabinet Mission had come and gone, having recommended the immediate setting up of an Interim Government with the co-operation of the Congress and the Moslem League, to be followed by a Constituent Assembly, with elaborate safeguards and guarantees to satisfy Jinnah. But he managed to be dissatisfied

266

whatever happened, and he seized on the nationalist Moslems in the Congress as his target. He said they were traitors—traitors to his two-nation theory—and that therefore he would not have anything to do with an Interim Government which had a Moslem Congress nominee. This in turn upset the Congress, and they expressed their inability to join in a coalition in which their choice of nominees would be restricted to non-Moslems. Complicated discussions and maneuvers followed. The Moslem League, on Jinnah's express advice, made a move which seemed to be going to give them the Interim Government without Congress, but the Cabinet Mission outmaneuvered them, and added that further efforts for the formation of an Interim Government would be made after a short break during the period while the elections for the Constituent Assembly were in progress. Jinnah was angry, and said under these new circumstances the elections should be postponed, but the Cabinet Mission turned down his demand.

Bapu was distressed at the way things had gone, and said that the Cabinet Mission should not have dealt with Jinnah "in that legalistic manner." The Moslem League now withdrew all co-operation and announced its intention of taking to "Direct Action." On the closing day of the Moslem League's session Jinnah declared amid wild cheering that "today we bid goodbye to constitutional methods." And he added, "We have also forged a pistol and are in a position to use it." August 16th was announced as the day in which "Direct Action" was to begin.

The Moslem League having removed itself from the picture, and having declared its intention of starting "Direct Action," the Viceroy saw no other course than to invite the National Congress to form an Interim Government, which he did on August 12th. The Cabinet Mission had already returned to London. Jawaharlal, who was again President of the Congress, once more approached Jinnah for co-operation, but to no avail. So he formed his Government independently, and was sworn in along with his colleagues on September 2nd.

In the meanwhile the Moslem League's "Direct Action" had begun. Bengal, where a Moslem League ministry, under the Premiership of Suhrawardy, was in power, was chosen, and Calcutta was the starting point. Jinnah's pistol proved to be nothing more or less than the unleashing of hideous hooliganism. Never in history had such terrible communal riots burst forth, and the streets of Calcutta were soon strewn with dead and dying. The police were markedly inactive. Suhrawardy, in order to achieve this objective, even went so far as to install himself for a time in the control room of the police headquarters. But by the third day the tide began to turn against those who had started the conflagration, and then the military was called in. When they took over, the officer in command reported that up to then the police had not fired a single round, and only used tear gas in one or two cases.

After the first stunning shock of August 16th, the Hindus, who were in the majority, had quickly organized themselves, and revenge being the spirit that stirred them, there was soon little difference left in the ghastly doings of both sides.

Day after day in Mussoorie news of these terrible happenings kept coming, and a wave of horror and agitation spread through the populace.

Though the holocaust in Calcutta subsided, there was no truce. Both sides remained seething with suppressed fear and rage, and stray acts of violence were continually being reported.

Bapu was at this time in Sevagram. What would his reactions be? People waited anxiously. They were stern and calm. Writing in the *Harijan,* he said:

> We are not yet in the midst of civil war. But we are nearing it. . . . If the British are wise they will keep clear of it. Appearances are to the contrary.

He saw clearly the danger in the British hand, and said the time had come for the people of India to choose between Pax Britannica and Freedom. If they wanted the latter, they must not turn to the foreign power for protection, but settle this matter themselves.

> Whoever wants to drink the ozone of freedom must steel himself against seeking military or police aid. He or they must ever rely upon their own strong arms, or what is infinitely better, their

268

strong mind and will which are independent of arms, their own or others.

Of the actual killings in Calcutta he wrote:

> If through deliberate courage the Hindus had died to a man, that would have been deliverance of Hinduism in India and purification of Islam in this land. As it was a third party had to intervene.

CHAPTER LXII

MY health having improved with the fresh mountain air, I now returned to Kisan Ashram. To be back in country surroundings and among the animals was a consolation. Work was going on well. The little dispensary had become very popular, drawing anything from 40 to 80 patients a day according to season, and the khadi work had increased considerably. Now that they had become efficient carders (teasers of cotton), the villagers found themselves able to spin enough strong, even yarn for sale. Another thing which helped them economically was that they were now able to prepare all their cotton quilts, etc., for the cold winter weather. These subsidiary occupations of carding and spinning fitted into their agricultural life with perfect ease and naturalness, while at the same time, the yarn thus provided gave whole-time occupation to the village weavers, who happened to be mostly Moslems. Living in the midst of this balanced, busy rural life, I realized as never before the significance of Bapu's economics. The villagers were in control of the production of the raw materials and the means of manufacture of both the vital necessities of life, food and clothing. They grew their own grain and cotton, the food grains they ground and pounded by hand, and the cotton they carded, spun and wove by hand. They were therefore masters of their fundamental needs.

On day when I was sitting working in my room an old Harijan came to the door. I told him to come in and sit down. He was small and thin, with a gentle face.

"Well," I said, "where have you come from?"

"From Bichpuri," he replied, "the little village down there by the Patri Rao. Do please come one day and look at the place. Our fields are disappearing under the sand which the river brings down, and soon our mud cottages will be washed away. Nobody listens to our tale of sorrows. You must come to see for yourself."

There was something very charming about the simple old man's voice and manner, and I felt he was sincere in what he said, so I went.

As a result of the war and the repression, India was in those days on the brink of nation-wide famine, and these people, being at the very bottom of the social scale, had all but gone over the edge.

On my return to the Ashram I sat down and wrote a description of the village and sent it to Bapu for publication in the *Harijan*. A little while after this, Bapu forwarded me a check for five thousand rupees from an anonymous reader, who had sent it with the request that the money should be used for the betterment of the poor people I had described.

I thought of the parable of the sower who went forth to sow "and it came to pass, as he sowed, some [seeds] fell by the wayside . . . and some fell among thorns . . . and other fell upon good ground and did yield fruit." And what fruit! It enabled me ultimately to get the whole village moved to a new site on higher ground with a good, clean well and other advantages.

In order not to rouse the envy of Harijans in the neighboring villages, who, though slightly better off, were nevertheless nearly all in difficulties for good drinking water, I used a little of the money for supplying them with hand pumps.

Now another, and equally unexpected, help came to me for the villagers. About two miles from the Ashram there was a training center of the military Sappers and Miners. Mrs. Duke, the wife of a British military officer, whom I had first met at the time of the

Simla Conference in 1945, knew the Brigadier in command, and she brought him out to see Kisan Ashram.

"This is Brigadier Williams," she said, introducing him, and added in her frank and direct way, "Down there in his school he is busy teaching his men to make roads and then to destroy them again so as to be able to make them afresh. Is not that really a pity!"

"Yes," I exclaimed. "Why should not he make roads that are badly needed. I could give him lots of practice for his men."

I looked at him inquiringly. He was tall and quiet, and had a friendly smile. My hopes were roused, and not in vain. He said he would like his men to have this realistic practice, and before he and Mrs. Duke returned to Roorkee it had been decided that he would send out his people to look at the alignment of the road I had in mind.

I spoke to the villagers, and they were thrilled.

In a few days two huge bulldozers and a road-grader arrived. If I had entered into discussions with the villagers concerned as to how many feet, or even inches, of this or that man's land should be cut into, or whether this tree or that bush should be removed, there would have been endless argument. Now, with the excitement of the bulldozers' arrival, the villagers did not stop to worry about details. I rode on my pony Tulsi and they came along with me, leading the bulldozers up the alignment. Once the first line had been cut the matter was settled, and in this way we marked out the road in one day right up to the village without any arguments or quarrels.

These powerful military machines cut and rolled the soil about with amazing speed, and within a short period, I forget now exactly how many days, we had an excellent earth road of over a mile in length. As a result, the local attitude toward the military underwent vast improvement, and everyone was overflowing with delight and gratitude.

CHAPTER LXIII

WHILE I had been busying myself with all this work at Kisan Ashram, the political scene had steadily worsened.

After the declaration of "Direct Action" by the Moslem League, Lord Wavell had called on the Congress to form an Interim Government, not because of his own inclination, but because of advice from London. His heart was not in it. Constitutional methods did not come naturally to him and his officials. From the very start he began interfering with the affairs of the ministry, and his anxiety to please Jinnah and somehow to get representatives of the Moslem League into the Cabinet was quite evident. And this in spite of the fact that the League would enter the Cabinet in order to carry on "Direct Action" inside the Government. The Moslem League, seeing the way the land lay, went ahead with their worst form of "Direct Action," and on October 10th started "reprisals" for Calcutta by wholesale slaughter of Hindus in the villages of Noakhali district in East Bengal.

Five days later it was announced that the Moslem League had agreed to enter the Interim Government at the invitation of the Viceroy. The Congress anxiously asked: "On what terms?" The Viceroy gave assurances that the League would fall in line, but no written assurance from Jinnah was forthcoming. Bapu was full of doubts, but the Congress, which was going its own way more and more, decided to accept the Viceroy's assurance. In a little over a month Jinnah issued a directive that no representative of the Moslem League should participate in the Constituent Assembly, and that the Moslem League resolution of July 29th, in which they had withdrawn their acceptance of the Cabinet Mission Plan, should after all stand.

272

Bapu's worst fears had now come true. As long ago as June 13th he had written to Lord Wavell:

> You are a very great soldier—a daring soldier. Dare to do the right. You must make your choice of one horse or the other. So far as I can see, you will never succeed in riding two at the same time. Choose the names submitted either by the Congress or the League. For God's sake do not make an incompatible mixture and in trying to do so produce a fearful explosion.

Regardless of that advice, Lord Wavell had at last managed to concoct that "incompatible mixture," and not one but a long series of explosions had been set in action.

Bapu advised, and warned, and did his best to help the Congress leaders, but he saw clearly how difficult they were finding it to share his outlook and methods. Politically the whole scene was moving away from his line of approach. But there was another sphere of action, in which he was still free to function in his own way, and that was the fearless, nonviolent approach to riot-torn areas.

So, at the end of October, he set out for Noakhali via Calcutta. In that battered city, which was still smoldering with suppressed rage, he set himself to win over the Moslem League Chief Minister, Suhrawardy. A friendly, outspoken, frontal attack brought immediate results, and within a few days an agreement was reached for communal harmony in Calcutta, and only then would Bapu agree to start out on his tour of the shattered villages of Noakhali.

But just before leaving Calcutta, information reached Bapu of rioting in the neighboring Province of Bihar. News having spread there of the hideous doings in Noakhali, a sinister cry of "Revenge!" was heard, and Hindus began slaughtering Moslems. This cut Bapu to the heart, for he had always looked on the Biharis as some of the kindest and most devoted people that he knew. In his Prayer Speech of November 3rd he said:

> I am pained beyond measure. The cry of blood for blood is barbarous. You cannot take revenge in Bihar for the happenings in Noakhali.

273

Jawaharlal with other Cabinet Ministers had rushed to the scene of rioting, but it was not easy to quell the storm all at once. Three days later Bapu issued an "Appeal To Bihar":

> I regard myself as a part of you. Your affection has compelled that loyalty in me. And since I claim to have better appreciation than you seem to have shown of what Bihari Hindus should do, I cannot rest till I have done some measure of penance. . . .

It was a long statement, and Bapu ended up by announcing that he would undergo a partial fast of twenty-one days on fruit juice only, and if the Biharis did not come to their senses he would after that taken on a total fast unto death. The result was electrifying. The Bihari nature could not but respond to Bapu, for the people adored him as perhaps in no other Province.

Bapu in the meantime set out on his wanderings in Noakhali district. In one of the first letters I received from there, dated December 1, 1946, he wrote:

> I am not likely to leave this place for some time to come, if ever.

And three days later:

> Don't worry about me. Put your faith and trust in God. I am in His safekeeping. He will make or mar me. For Him it will be all making, never marring.
>
> . . . My *ahimsa* is on its trial. More of this another time. This is only to relieve you of all anxiety on my behalf. I am now taking or trying to take the usual diet but it may take some time after the twenty-one days' denial to get used to it.

This referred, of course, to the twenty-one days of fruit juice and water that he had just been through in penance for the Biharis.

I felt in every letter I received from Bapu, and from all news I heard from others, that he was passing rapidly into an advanced state of detachment. In order to cope with the appalling violence, fear, and hatred with which masses of Indians had been overtaken, he was striving to divest himself of everything but a sense of God's presence. From Noakhali he again wrote, in January 4, 1947:

274

Do not even worry how I am faring or what I am doing here. If I succeed in emptying myself utterly, God will possess me. Then I know that everything will come true, but it is a serious question when I shall have reduced myself to zero. Think of "I" and "O" in juxtaposition and you have the whole problem of life in two signs. In this process you have helped me considerably for, though at a distance, you seem to be doing your duty to the fullest extent possible in your field of work.

After four months in Noakhali, Bapu went to Bihar, again soothing and encouraging the afflicted, and admonishing those who had wrought the havoc. But, along with the guiding words, he gave every ounce of his strength to inquiring, investigating, and advising both the official and nonofficial organizations on practical steps for relief.

All this while the political struggle was continuing. On February 20, 1947, the British Government had announced their intention to complete the transfer of power to Indian hands not later than June 1948. Both the Congress and the Moslem League hailed this decision, each feeling they saw hope for the fulfillment of their cherished goals. But those goals were diametrically opposed. The Congress wanted an undivided India, and the Moslem League wanted Pakistan. But the Pakistan of their dreams was such a fantastic thing that the British themselves could not in decency approve, for it would have meant, in some cases, handing over large areas with even a Hindu majority to the Moslem League. The Leaguers, realizing this, tried to achieve their ends again by "Direct Action" and organized communal riots in Punjab and Assam. The Punjabi Unionist Government fell under the impact, and large-scale migration of Hindu refugees began, but the Assam Government managed to bring the situation under control.

Militant groups, which had been slowly developing in India for a long time, had steadily increased communal friction, chief among which was the Hindu Mahasabha and the Rashtriya Swayam Sevak Sangh, commonly known as R.S.S.

The Hindu communal groups were, of course, strongly opposed to Bapu's ideals. In fact it was they who, in the old days, had violently attacked Bapu on his Harijan tours, and on one occasion had even thrown a bomb at the car in which they thought he was traveling. Now their hostility to Bapu was becoming more and more evident. There had been picketing of Sevagram by them as far back as 1944, at which time their remarks had been dark and ominous. At another time, during one of Bapu's train journeys, big stones had been put on the railway line, which very nearly derailed the train. Now just next to Bapu's quarters at the Bhangi Colony (Sweepers' Colony) in New Delhi, where Bapu had taken to staying each time he went to the capital, the R.S.S. had for some time a camp, where they were busy drilling young men.

In order to facilitate the transfer of power, the British Government decided to send out a new Viceroy, and they made the brave choice of Lord Mountbatten, who, though not of the Labour Party, had the all-round capacity for the job and could at the same time win the confidence of the Conservative Party. He arrived in India on March 22, 1947, and immediately sent a message to Bapu in Bihar expressing the wish to talk things over with him.

Bapu, who was busy in the riot-wrecked villages, came as soon as he could disengage himself. His first interview with the new Viceroy took place on March 31st, after which they met at frequent intervals.

CHAPTER LXIV

NOW that Bapu had come to Delhi at last, I went to be with him for a little while, but I did not stay very long because new work was calling me at the other end.

It was becoming clear to me that the scope for work in the Kisan Ashram area was much more than could be carried out with limited personal funds. As the U.P. Government had recently started a Rural Development Department, and I myself was working within the Government machinery in the capacity of an Honorary Advisers, I thought it best to put this whole area under the new department. Just while these ideas were working in my mind, I was asked by Government to help in the supervision of two big cattle schemes which were being planned near Rishikesh, at the foot of the Himalayas. This decided me. I placed the Kisan Ashram work in the hands of the Rural Development Department and, taking the cows with me, moved on to the new area.

The schemes I was to look after were so far only on paper, but funds had been sanctioned, half from the U.P. Government and half from the Central Government, and a skeleton staff had also been appointed. My first job was to select a suitable area. In those days there had been very little clearance, so I had to investigate the forests with their open patches of pampas and other tall grasses. If one walked or rode on horseback, one could not get a clear idea of one's surroundings because of the tremendous jungle growth. The pampas was often fifteen feet high. So I went on an elephant with the Forest Department officials and surveyed the three forest blocks nearest to Rishikesh. These blocks run into thousands of acres. I finally selected the Virabhadra block, of nearly three thousand acres, which stretches for about four miles down Ganga's bank starting two miles below Rishikesh. Here there was more open grassland than in the other blocks, and it had the great advantage of the long river frontage.

The wild beauty of those great forests, and their wealth of animals and birds, stirred in me new strength. There is a vast vitality in untrammeled Nature which communicates itself to those who live with her. And this was the first time that I had come to live in a real jungle. Here were tigers, leopards, sambar (Indian elk), spotted deer, hog deer, wild pigs, jackals, foxes, and numbers of smaller animals, while every now and then there would come visiting herds of wild elephants. The birds were equally numerous, from peacocks and eagles to tiny tits, and also water birds of all kinds. In my joy I wrote a full description to Bapu, and said I proposed naming the place "Pashulok" (Animal World). He replied: "Your describing the Ashram as 'Pashulok' is a magnificent idea. It is poetic."

So Pashulok it became.

The Government schemes were for two cattle centers, one for the comfort of old and disabled animals, and the other for cows during their dry period, which in India, among ordinary cattle, is much longer than in the West, sometimes amounting to eight or nine months.

The first of these schemes was to be taken up immediately and the second at a later date. I camped in the Ramnagar Guesthouse of Kali Kamli Wala Charitable Trust, which was situated on Ganga's bank just where the Pashulok lands began. It was the middle of the hot weather, and my health was none too good, so, after laying out the site for the cattlesheds and demarcating the area to be fenced, I decided to make a trip into the mountains, to which Pashulok was, indeed, the gateway.

I had had to leave my pony Tulsi at Kisan Ashram, because she would have been too small for the rough jungle work at Pashulok, and I was wondering what to do about a new horse when I happened, one day, to look out of the window and see two Gujars (nomadic Moslem herdsmen) passing by with two horses, one of which struck me as being just the animal of which I was in need. I ran out of the house and stopped the Gujars. A talk ensued. It seemed they would sell for a reasonable price. As for the little horse, or what would be called a pony in the West, I altogether fell in love with him at close quarters. The final outcome was that I purchased him. I brought him into the garden and tied him up under a tree, and from that day our friendship began. I named him Mana, fitted him out with saddle and bridle, and told him we would now start out on a trip into the interior valleys of the Himalayas.

Dharampal, who was still working with me, joined the party with two or three of his friends, and my stenographer Krishna Murti also came along. All were much younger than I was, but I had Mana. The plan was to go to Uttarkashi, a little holy place lying on the way up to the source of the Ganga, where a friend had offered me his house for our stay. I had fondly imagined that the climate would be pleasantly cool, but it was quite the contrary. The bridlepath, after passing along a ridge at seven to eight thousand feet altitude, dropped down into the valley of the Bhagirathi Ganga (above the confluence with the Alaknanda at Devaprayag, Ganga is called Bhagirathi), and we stewed in stuffy moist heat.

All along the way I was dreaming of Bapu ultimately coming to the Himalayas, for the same dream was evidently with him. Just before setting out on the trek, on June 15, 1947, I had received a letter from him in which he said:

> I am myself thinking of going to Uttarkashi but it is all in the realm of dreamland. Therefore take no thought of it. You may however send me every detail about it [the place].

As far back as the autumn of 1945 thoughts of getting away from the crowd and bustle of Sevagram had been with Bapu, and the news spread that he was actually leaving. At that time he wrote in answer to my inquiries:

> I am not leaving Sevagram, must not having founded a home for so many institutions. I must now contradict and correct the report.

But at the end of the letter he added:

> Let us trust in God guiding us. He may so compass that ultimately I may have to live with you. Wish nothing except to do His will. . . .
>
> (29-10-45)

Now in May and June of 1947 it was the feeling that he had no place in the India of the day which weighed on Bapu, and this feeling he had begun to express in so many words. Not only the thought of the approaching partition of the country oppressed him, but the spectacle of India being industrialized and militarized by her own people who, in his conception of free India, should have taken her on to the road of decentralized village industries and demilitarization. "I am looked upon as unpractical," he would say. And again: "My word carries no weight today."

As we journeyed up the Bhagirathi valley I eagerly watched the landscape and the climate, but how great was my disappointment when I found that right up to Uttarkashi there was no view of the snows, but only of the river and the steep wooded slopes

279

on both sides. As for the climate, at that time of year, June, it was intolerably stuffy and hot.

Regretfully I wrote to Bapu a full description. In his reply, dated June 29th, he said:

> My going to Uttarkashi you have knocked on the head. . . . However I am in God's hands. I shall wish neither one way nor the other. Sufficient unto the day is the good thereof. I must not think of the evil. No one knows what is really good or really evil. Therefore let us think of nothing but good.

For some days after reaching Uttarkashi I was very exhausted, for I had had to walk a good deal of the way, and seeing that I could not pick up my health in that climate, I decided to move elsewhere. The young men who were on short leave left for various destinations, and the party was now reduced to Dharampal, Krishna Murti and myself, with Mana and the boy who looked after him and also cooked my food.

Friends in Uttarkashi recommended Pratapnagar to me, situated on a mountain ridge above Tehri at a height of over 7,000 feet. The Maharaja of Tehri-Garhwal was good enough to put his guesthouse up there at my disposal, so off we went.

Once we reached the top of the ridge there was no more stuffy heat. The air had become fresh and cool, and a glorious view spread out before us. The great snow range which we used to see from Kisan Ashram was there right in front of us. It looked so near, yet we were told it was still several days' journey away. The clouds of the coming monsoon were already wreathing the peaks, but every now and then the summits would show clear.

I had brought along with me to Uttarkashi, and now up here, all Bapu's letters, which I had from the beginning collected and kept safely in a box. Last time I had been in Delhi I had consulted Bapu and he had agreed to my suggestion of publishing a selection. So now I settled down to the job, and by the time we left Pratapnagar, I had sorted and arranged, and Krishna Murti had typed out copies of over 350 letters.

Though it was the rainy reason, yet there were fine intervals when one could get out for a short while. But Mana did not get much exercise. He spent his time grazing the lush grass, and nosing around even into the rooms. When he discovered where I used to take my food sitting on the floor, he came to the door and watched. For the first day or two he did not come farther than the veranda. But the smell of the freshly cooked *rotis* was so tempting that before long he began advancing through the door. I warned him that he should not come right inside, so he was very discreet. However, when I was not looking, he would shift his hoofs forward about one inch at a time. Finally of course he got his whole body inside the room and his nose close to my food. How could I resist his sweet requesting expression! I gave him some bread, and then explained to him that he *must now* go out of the room, which he did.

One day when the boy had gone for something, the kitchen door had been left open. This was an opportunity not to be lost. When the boy came back he found Mana standing on the veranda, licking his lips. Inside the kitchen, the dough for making the bread had vanished, and two mango stones, well sucked, were left on the plate where there had previously been two ripe mangoes. The kitchen door was not left open again!

CHAPTER LXV

ALL the while I was at Pratapnagar I was contemplating how to find a place where Bapu could come to stay in the Himalayas. But the news from the plains grew worse and worse, and the chances of Bapu getting away were rapidly fading.

At Delhi, Lord Mountbatten, the Congress and the Moslem League were carrying on endless discussions. India was going to be divided, that was now certain, but how and when had still to be settled. Bapu had all along been against partition, but if it was inevitable then, he pleaded, let it be only after rioting had been brought to an end, and after the British had withdrawn their controlling hand. If the country was cut up under the pressure of lawless disturbances, there would be no end to the demands of the communal factions, and consequently no end to the rioting, and if the partition was made while the British held sway, on their handing over power there would be a fresh outburst.

Both Lord Mountbatten and the Congress ministers appreciated this reasoning, but the legacy handed down through Lord Wavell had queered the pitch. So the details for partitioning the country were carried on in spite of mounting communal friction and the presence of a British Viceroy. Even the date for transfer of power was fixed. It was to be August 15, 1947. The day was approaching and everyone felt nervous. The first bout of "Direct Action" in the Punjab had not brought the Moslem League control over the whole Province, but it had nevertheless so shaken the populace that wholesale migrations were now taking place. When the army was divided on a communal basis, Moslems for Pakistan and Hindus for India, it was the last straw, and the minorities on both sides lost all sense of safety.

Many people expected Bapu to start a campaign against the Congress for having agreed to partition of India. But he did no such thing. He realized clearly that the Congress ministers, harassed by the presence of the Moslem League "Direct Action" group inside the Interim Government, and oppressed with the fear that even the mutilated India of the partition plan might slip through their fingers if they did not seize it, could not do otherwise than they did. So from the day the decision was announced and the date for handing over fixed, Bapu began advising the people to accept the situation, and make the very best of the freedom they were about to obtain.

Now that the British had won a comparatively safe ally in Pakistan, they did not seem to mind being a little generous to India, so the independence was real. But though Bapu counseled acceptance by the people of a divided India, he could never reconcile himself to the idea of wholesale transfer of communities. Why should people leave their ancestral homes? Moslems in India had as deep roots in the soil as the Hindus, the vast majority of their

282

families had been Hindus a few generations before. Neither the Moslems of India nor the Hindus of Pakistan should leave their motherland, and moved by this fundamental urge Bapu wished to spend the whole of his time in the riot-torn areas, consoling, guiding and steadying the people. However, neither the Viceroy nor the Congress ministers could let him go altogether. Though it was becoming less and less easy for them to follow his advice, yet they must have him with them as much as possible. The result was that Bapu kept moving between Delhi, Bihar and Bengal.

While I was in Pratapnagar, Bapu was most of the time in Delhi, having been urgently called from Bihar for consultation. From there he made two short trips, one to Kashmir and one to Lahore.

My intention was to spend the rest of the rains in Pratapnagar, and then return to Pashulok to continue the construction work which had had to be suspended during the wet season. But I found myself unable to stand the high altitude owing, apparently, to having overstrained myself during the long treks in June. So I decided to come down early in August.

Riding down mountain paths being unpleasant both for the horse and the rider, I walked all the nine miles to Tehri. It began to get oppressively hot and stuffy as we neared the bottom. A little way above the bridge over the Bhilangana River some letters and a newspaper were handed to me. Opening the paper was always an anxious job in those days. I unfolded it, and there in large letters on the front page was the rumor that Bapu had decided to spend the rest of his days in Pakistan. I knew one had to be prepared for any such shocks, but this news set the mind working furiously.

We reached the bridge, Mana was led over in front and I followed. Just as I was stepping onto the other bank, I felt myself going. I saw some sacks placed by the side of the path, and hurrying to them, fell in a dead faint. The first thing I remember was hearing Mana calling *"Hm hm hm!"* He had turned around and was anxiously inquiring what was the matter with me. I asked for some water, but before I could drink it, the glass fell out of my hand, and again I lost consciousness. Next time I came around I

283

found that people from a nearby cottage had brought a bed and some almond tea. Very soon I felt wonderfully better. Mana was standing nearby watching, so I mounted him and rode up to the house of the Judge with whom we were going to stay.

I wanted to start off the next day on Mana, but my host would hear of no such thing, and insisted that I should rest for two or three days. Mana thought this was an excellent plan, as he had the Judge's grass lawn to graze on, and—since the dining room veranda adjoined the garden, he soon found his way to the door, where he would stand calling out for *rotis* at lunchtime. I remonstrated with him, and said we were guests here, and horses should not come indoors. But nothing doing! Mana began advancing inch by inch toward the back of the Judge's chair, until our kindhearted host got up and relieved him.

The Maharaja, having heard about my illness, very kindly sent a car to fetch me to Narendranagar, his capital, which is beautifully situated on the mountains just above Rishikesh, at an altitude of about three thousand feet. Mana followed with the boy.

The 15th of August was approaching when power was to be transferred to India, and I did not want to go down to the plains until the celebrations were over, for one did not feel like rejoicing in the prevailing atmosphere.

From the guesthouse where we were staying there was a wonderful view of the plains below, and on the evening of the 15th we could see Rishikesh, Hardwar and Dehra Dun, all glittering with illuminations. So Freedom had come! But what more was coming? Hundreds of thousands of refugees were already on the move or crowded into relief camps. Thousands had been killed in riots, and thousands more might be killed any day.

The news had come that Bapu had already gone to Calcutta and was staying with Suhrawardy in the Moslem slum quarters.

There was nothing for it but to go on steadily with one's work, but before returning to Pashulok I thought it best to go to Delhi and get my heart examined. On arrival at Birla House I heard of the extraordinary risks which Bapu was undergoing in Calcutta. How the Moslem home where he was staying had been attacked by Hindu communal gangs who shouted, "Gandhi go back!" . . . "We don't want Moslems here!" then searched for Suhrawardy, smashing windows and banging on doors, and how Bapu, by quiet and fearless handling of the situation had brought the crowd to their senses, and thereby sanity to the whole of Calcutta. A hideously ugly situation on the eve of August 12th had been transformed, as if by a miracle, into wild rejoicings and intercommunal fraternization. Congratulations poured in to Bapu from all sides, and Lord Mountbatten wrote that celebrated letter to Bapu in which he called him the One-Man Boundary Force under whose charge there were no riots, whereas in the Punjab, where they had 55,000 soldiers, there was large-scale rioting.

But Bapu was not at ease. He felt danger of a reaction was still in the offing. In a letter to me he wrote: "The joy of the crowd is there, but not in me. . . . Hindu-Moslem unity seems too sudden to be true."

My heart had been passed as sound by a specialist, the only trouble being frequent missing of the beat owing to overstrain, both physical and mental. I was planning to get back to my work at Pashulok as soon as I could, when suddenly I came down with a severe attack of malignant malaria.

In Punjab widespread rioting was uprooting whole masses of people. The Sikhs, who were the bravest and most fiery community in the Province, had been severely hit by the partition, as their area became cut in two, an area which their industry as farmers had turned into the granary of India. This added to the violence of the riots. As a result of all this, Delhi, which lies on the borders of the Punjab, with a mixed Hindu-Moslem population, became crowded with refugees, whose pitiable plight and tales of horror created a more and more tense situation.

In the midst of my fever I heard that rioting had broken out in the city. Next came the news that it had broken out in Calcutta also, and that Bapu had narrowly escaped being hit first by a brickbat and then by a lathi when his house was again attacked. This was followed by the news that Bapu had gone on a fast to stop the rioting. My head reeled with the fever and the news. "God is our only hope" was the one thought to which I clung.

Though Birla House was some distance from the riot area, I could clearly hear the sound of rifle shots as I lay on my bed. My condition being rather bad, a well-known physician, Dr. Joshi, was called in. He came again the next day, but the third day he did not turn up. In the evening we heard that he had been shot dead in the street near his home.

Through the darkness now came a gleam of light. Communal peace had been restored in Calcutta and Bapu had broken his fast.

Before the outbreak of riots in Delhi, Lord Mountbatten and Jawaharlal had already been asking Bapu to come to the Punjab, for they had realized that through the police and military they could never achieve what his steadying and calming influence could do. But after news of the Calcutta disturbances and the fast which had left Bapu very weak, no one could hope for his coming soon. I was lying in my bed thinking of these things when some-one came into the room with a radiant face. "Bapu is coming!" I sat straight up. The house was already in a buzz of preparation. Eager voices could be heard in the passages. Every now and then someone would look in with a beaming smile. Before the day was out I was up myself and moving about, though absurdly shaky after the malarial fever.

There was no question of Bapu's being able to stay at the Bhangi Colony, because the place was overflowing with refugees. So the familiar corner room at Birla House looking over the garden, a place where we had often stayed in the past, was got ready.

Cars were sent to a small station outside Delhi, and from there they brought Bapu in order to avoid the crowds, which would have been uncontrollable at the Delhi main station.

Frail and emaciated, Bapu seemed all spirit as he entered the house. Beaming with the irresistible good humor which always swept away tension and strain, he greeted the eager, anxious faces that surrounded him. As soon as he had bathed and taken food, the talks and consultations began. Bapu's reactions were calm, clear and firm. He decided to stay in the capital till it returned to sanity, and only go on to the Punjab when Lord Mountbatten

286

(now the first constitutional Governor-General in Free India) and the ministers were ready for him to proceed.

No sooner had the news spread through the city that Bapu had arrived than the rioting began to subside. A sense of shame came over the people.

Bapu lost no time in setting about his task of healing, and from the first day proceeded to visit the refugee camps one after another. Each one was a smoldering fire, in which he had to face angry, distracted, and desperate people, be they Hindu, Sikh or Moslem. But his calm, brave approach, and patient love for all alike, stilled their rage and encouraged them to put before him their endless troubles and hardships. These were very real, for the authorities and others, do what they would, could hardly keep pace with the needs of the never-ending influx of uprooted people. This meant that though large-scale rioting had stopped, Delhi was anything but peaceful. It was, indeed, a simmering caldron liable to boil over at any moment.

Under these circumstances it was evident that Bapu would have to remain in the capital for an indefinite period. Though he resigned himself to the prospect, the thought of getting on to the Punjab and Pakistan was continually in his mind.

CHAPTER LXVI

BEFORE long news came of rioting having broken out in the North-West of the United Provinces. This meant that the Kisan Ashram area would be affected. I expressed to Bapu my wish to go there, but he flatly refused on account of my health. In like manner he never took me out with him on his visits to the camps. He said an invalid would only get in the way, and my first and foremost duty was to get well. So I remained behind. But each time Bapu went out, I would accompany him to the front

287

door and stand watching the car as it carried him away into the unknown. If God wished, Bapu would return alive, otherwise . . . The same feeling hung over me at the time of the Public Prayer, which used to be held at the upper end of the Birla House garden. Owing to my missing pulse, I used to feel faint if I sat upright in the Prayer for any length of time, so I would stroll in the vegetable garden beyond the trellised walk, from where I could listen.

I sent Dharampal to report on conditions around Kisan Ashram, and he came back with the good news that in the surrounding villages there had been no disturbances, though rioting had taken place not far away. The inmates of the Ashram had continually moved about unarmed, even without sticks, from village to village, and this seemed definitely to have calmed the atmosphere. On one occasion they got an SOS in the middle of the night from a Moslem village about half a mile off. Straightaway they went there, and the situation was saved simply because of their presence.

Any little bits of news like that gladdened Bapu's heart. Some day, of course, the madness would subside, and people would again live together in peace. But there was a greater sorrow than the riots which weighed on Bapu. Never before had I seen him so inwardly sad. When left alone between talks and interviews his face would take on a profoundly pensive look, and the suppressed sighs, and murmured tones of "O God" (*Hey Ram*) seemed to speak of a deep suffering of the spirit.

One day when I suggested to Bapu that I might go to discuss matters with the Military, as I had in the past during the war, Bapu scribbled on a piece of paper, being in his Monday's silence:

> These are not the old days. Now there are wheels within wheels. You can't do any useful service by seeing these military men except as friendly faces who will give you a warm welcome but nothing more. That is my reaction. The thing is beyond me except in my own way which has no vogue today.

The same suffering I seemed to see in Bapu regarding Kashmir, which was just now ruthlessly invaded by tribesmen from the Pakistan side. That he did not object to the use of the military was

288

not because he liked that method, but because he realized that the Government could handle the situation in no other way. Just as preparatory training is necessary if you are going to use military methods, so is it necessary if you are going to use nonviolent methods. But the will to keep up that training had left the Congress leaders now that they had inherited the fighting services from the British.

Bapu did not complain. He knew that, in the days of the Satyagraha battle, his chief colleagues had accepted nonviolence only as a policy. Yet he must have hoped, in view of its extraordinary success in dislodging the British rule, that it would still hold a place in Free India. One thing Bapu made perfectly clear was that whichever defensive method they used, there should be one hundred per cent bravery, and he would be prepared to see the military die to a man. For him fearlessness was the first attribute in all endeavor.

The other and more fundamental aspect of nonviolence, namely, decentralized rural economy, was also being neglected. In 1938, when the Congress set up a National Planning Committee, it was clear that they hankered after the Western type of industrialization, and now it appeared they were going to go the whole hog.

In addition to all this—and I suppose it was a natural corollary —the Congress leaders had, as to the manner born, all taken up residence in grand Government bungalows, and even the Viceroy's House was not discarded.

Bapu's long and calm vision had seen a simple, healthy and happy India showing the way to stability and peace. But now the India that was emerging into view was one in which, it seemed, he would rather not remain alive.

"I don't know what you think of this freedom," I heard him say one day to someone, "for me it is a disillusionment."

He carried on with his untiring work of healing, but the zest had gone out of his life. Formerly he had expressed the wish to live to one hundred and twenty-five years, so as to be able to put India on the true path. But now, what was the good?

It was heart-rending to watch Bapu in those days. And what haunted me was the thought that once he lost interest in living, he would not remain in this world. How often he had said, "God will guard me so long as there is use for me, but the moment that time is past, no human effort will be able to protect me."

"Can anything be done to hold Bapu's interest and pleasure in life?" I kept saying to myself. Thinking along these lines I one day said to Bapu:

"Let me build you a mud cottage and a cowshed on the golf course of the Viceroy's House. There is lots of land going to waste, and if you start living there right under the noses of the new rulers, they will be bound sooner or later to come down from their palatial dwellings and live humbly too. In this way the atmosphere might gradually change."

Bapu smiled and said, "Let me first finish the tour on foot through the Punjab, which I have in mind, before thinking of anything like that."

The future looked dark.

A few days later I happened to ask Bapu if he would come to open the Pashulok cattle center when it was ready, and all he said was, "What is the good of counting on a corpse?"

My heart sank within me. To others also he had made strange references to what seemed to be a premonition. But one had to keep up hope and remain outwardly cheerful.

In spite of this inner sadness Bapu retained much of his old cheerfulness, and everyone around him was at pains to avoid any gloomy atmosphere.

CHAPTER LXVII

IT was now December. Over three months had gone by since Bapu's arrival in Delhi, but still the situation was such that people begged him to stay on a little longer, as otherwise things might again get out of control. As my health had somewhat improved, I felt it was my duty to go back to Pashulok. So, hard though the wrench was to leave Bapu at this juncture, I tore myself away. That was December 18th.

In less than a month came news of some communal trouble in Delhi, and then a letter from Bapu saying he had undertaken a fast. At the end of the letter he wrote:

> Don't rush here because I am fasting. The *yagna* [sacrifice], as I have called it, demands that everyone, wherever he or she is, should perform his or her duty. If an appreciable number do this, I must survive the ordeal. Trust God and be where you are.

(16-1-48)

So I waited, and prayed, and went on with my work.

Within three days the sacrifice had its effect, communal peace was restored in Delhi, this time on a much firmer basis, and on January 19th Bapu broke his fast.

I received a postcard from Bapu on January 19, 1948, saying: "All anxiety is over."

But no sooner had this postcard arrived than there came news of a bomb explosion on January 20th behind the Prayer Ground at Birla House during the evening Prayer, not more than twenty-five yards from where Bapu was sitting. No one was hurt, but what did this mean? Reports were confusing. The next evening Bapu's after-Prayer speech, which was reported by friends from Rishikesh who had heard it over the radio, left no doubt as to the meaning of the bomb. Bapu had explained, they said, that he did not realize till after the Prayer that the explosion had been from a bomb and was meant for him, and that the composure he had shown, therefore, deserved no special praise. That would be deserved only if he fell as the result of a bomb with a smile on his face and no malice in his heart against the assailant. Bapu had then gone on to say that no one should harbor resentment or anger against the thrower of the bomb, who probably thought himself an instrument of God for removing one whom he considered to be an enemy of Hinduism. He had then appealed to the police not to harass the young man but to try to convert him, and finally he had told the audience that the lesson for them to learn from the incident was that in future they should be able to go on with the

Prayer though there were more bomb explosions or even a shower of bullets.

I buried myself in my work, and there was plenty of it. The first group of cattlesheds was complete and the site for the other group had to be chosen in another part of the Pashulok lands. Living quarters for the staff were under construction, and my own *kutia* was nearly half finished. I had to be continually on the move in order to supervise everything. During those days I was still living in the Kali Kamli Wala Guesthouse by the bank of the Ganga.

On January 30th an officer from the Central Government came to see the place I proposed for the second group of cattlesheds. In order to show him the whole area and make it clear why the site I had selected appeared to me the best, I took him out on an elephant. We rode all around the jungle and through the tall pampas grass down to the riverbank, where I pointed out the exact spot I had in mind. He liked it very much, and, as evening was now drawing in, we returned to the Guesthouse, where I got off and he went on to Rishikesh.

The food was ready, so I sat down to my evening meal. Shortly afterwards I went onto the back veranda. A jeep was racing down the rough road, and when it came to a stop at the gate, the Delhi officer and some members of the Pashulok staff flung themselves out and rushed toward me. I caught the sound of stifled sobs, and, before I could think, one of the party, throwing himself for support against the wall, convulsively cried: "Bapu has been assassinated! Shot dead on the Prayer Ground!"

I stood silent and still. A vast emotion held me as in a trance. The only thought that came to me was Bapu, Bapu, so it has come! I looked up into the heavens and there, through the boughs of the trees, the stars were shining in peaceful splendor far, far away. They told of Bapu's spirit released and at peace, and as I gazed on them it was as if Bapu was there—yes, there and with me too. It all became one.

And surely Bapu's spirit was with me, for I did not weep when I came back to earth. I remember asking only one question: "Was it instantaneous?"

"Yes, absolutely," they said, and my heart thanked God.

292

I went into the house and sat upright in meditation. The body trembled unceasingly, perhaps for hours, but the mind was clear, strangely clear and calm.

The long-drawn-out crucifixion of Bapu's spirit was over, completed and consummated in the crucifixion of the flesh. It might take years, it might take centuries, but this last sacrifice, willingly given for the love of humanity, would conquer where all else might fail. My mind went back to the Crucifix in the Vatican at Rome. Yes—Bapu knew that was the gateway to the thing he was seeking. In knowledge, humility and love he had to be ready to give all. Now he had given it, and the words he had written me after his last fast kept coming to my mind as in a chant: *All anxiety is over.*

In the early part of the night people came to me from Rishikesh saying, "Come, come! We will take you to Delhi. Many buses and trucks are going, and we shall get there at daybreak before the cremation."

Again Bapu's words came to me:
Trust God and be where you are.

And those written over seven years before:
There is no meaning in having the last look. The spirit which you love is always with you.

"I will stay where I am," I said, thanking all the kind friends very much.

The next morning I went about my work as usual—outwardly as usual, but inside there was a new and unknown world to which I was trying hard to adjust myself. So closely had Bapu been interwoven in all the thoughts and actions of my daily life, that at every turn I had to pull myself up and remember that Bapu in the flesh was no longer there. Now there would be no more letter-writing, no more building of cottages with the hope of Bapu coming to stay in them. The very cottage that was then growing up on the sacred bank of the river Ganga I had pictured being a perfect spot for Bapu to come to for rest from time to time, and it was hard to bear that morning when I went to supervise the construction work which was going on.

Tempting as it would have been to turn to Bapu in thought,

seeking him and asking him to help and guide, something within me peremptorily forbade any such thing. "Bapu must be left in perfect peace, and you must stand on your own legs." From the very first hour this feeling possessed me.

So the day passed, and yesterday seemed years away.

That evening news poured in on the Rishikesh radios of the amazing scenes in Delhi, and friends came out and told me. From all sides people had converged on the capital, till the mass of humanity became so vast that it was with the greatest difficulty that the funeral procession reached the cremation ground.

Wild rumors had been circulated in the beginning as to the assassin having been a Moslem, then a refugee, but finally came the cold clear truth—it had been a deep-laid, long premeditated plot of fanatical Hindus. The actual deed had been done by an R.S.S.* man, and some Hindu Mahasabha people had also been party to the crime. Thus had the forces of darkness once again shattered themselves against the forces of light. So powerful was the wave of revulsion which passed through the country that riots became a thing of the past.

During the next few days most touching stories kept coming in of what happened when people first heard the news of the assassination. The officer in charge at Kisan Ashram told me he was traveling with his wife in a crowded bus when someone shouted the news to the driver, who at once stopped the bus.

"We all leapt out onto the road," he said, "and started weeping and wringing our hands as if each one of us had lost his or her own beloved father."

Reports even came in of people having died of shock, and others who tried to commit suicide. In Pakistan it was said that the masses wept most bitterly.

When the messages, tributes and press comments began to come in from other parts of the world, it became evident that people of all races had felt a personal loss, and everywhere there was a sense of a true and fearless guide in a darkening world having left us.

* A political organization later declared illegal.

294

Even a great military officer like General Douglas MacArthur reacted spontaneously to this feeling when in his tribute he said:

> In the evolution of civilization, if it is to survive, all men cannot fail eventually to adopt his belief that the process of mass application of force to resolve contentious issues is fundamentally not only wrong but contains within itself the germs of self-destruction.

According to the Hindu rites, Bapu's ashes were to be immersed on the thirteenth day after the cremation. A special train was to run from Delhi to Allahabad where the immersion was to take place on the 12th in the holy confluence of the Ganga and Jumna rivers. Again I was pressed to go, but the same conviction held me, and I declined. This time there was a further reason for me to stay where I was. A small quantity of the ashes was being brought from Delhi, and I had been asked by the local people to perform the immersion ceremony at the sacred ghat at Rishikesh, where the Ganga races past fresh and young from the mountains.

When the ashes arrived in a little copper urn, they were brought to me with the request that they should be divided into three parts, the main portion for Rishikesh, and two tiny portions, one for the Bhagirathi Ganga at Uttarkashi, and the other for the little river that flows by the villages in the Kisan Ashram area.

A strange and ethereal feeling came over me as I carried out the division of the ashes with friends standing round chanting *Randhun* (repetition of God's names). I lost any feeling of the body, and when I walked with the little urn in my hand to the ghat, I did not sense the ground beneath my bare feet.

Ganga's pure and sparkling water was swirling by the wooden platform that had been built out over the stream. As I cast the ashes into the swift blue current I felt, as never before, the glory of Nature who takes our earthly remains back to her bosom in all-embracing love.

CHAPTER LXVIII

BEFORE the end of the February I went once to Delhi. The recollection has remained with me as a still, gray space in time—Jawaharlal pale and haggard, Vallabhbhai steeped in silent gloom. There was nothing to be said, nothing to be done. We could only sit together and think of Bapu. Any words that were spoken seemed trivial and far away. As for Delhi, it was like a city of the dead, with everyone walking in the shadow of his own sorrow. I went to Birla House, I went to the cremation site at Rajghat, everywhere the same gray, still blankness. "Let me go," I cried to myself, "back to the life and light of the fields and forests, where Nature knows no such thing as mourning for the dead, because in her there is no death. For me Bapu is there, not here." And I hastened back to Pashulok.

The glory of spring was in the air.

"Work, work, let me work in harmony with this great drama," was my one thought.

I laid out the new cattlesheds and saw to the finishing of the others. My own cottage was completed along with a few buildings nearby as living quarters for my personal staff, and a stable for Mana. More land was cleared of rough scrub and grass, and put under cultivation.

As usual I had the construction work done with the local materials, and I took pains to see that the buildings should blend with the natural beauty of their surroundings. Thick mud walls and thatched roofs were not only pleasant to look upon, but pleasant to live in, being cool in summer and warm in winter.

When the new cattlesheds were ready, the old pensioners were shifted there, and the dry cows were kept in the first sheds. A new problem now had to be tackled. A large number of wild and semi-

296

wild bulls roamed in our three thousand acres. They harassed our cows, but no one could catch them or drive them out. So I arranged with a young man who was already dealing with the wild cattle in the Meerut district to come to see what he could do with these bulls. He arrived with two horsemen, two horses, and two runners with long ropes. They set to work without delay, and by the time they had finished the job there were over forty bulls in the taming camp, who nearly all turned into quite good bullocks for the plow.

The wild bulls could be coped with, but not so the wild elephants. They only came occasionally, but when they did, they had it their own way. They would walk through our fences as if they weren't there, and eat any crops that took their fancy.

One full-moon night in the middle of May, just after I had gone to bed in my solitary *kutia,* I heard in the distance that unmistakable vibrating sound mixed with strange roarings and squealings which meant elephants! I jumped up and went to the open room on the roof from where I could see all around. The sound was coming from the jungle on the opposite bank, but some wild squeals seemed much nearer. I could not make out from where they came till I noticed some round, black things passing down the middle of the river. These were the heads of elephants, submerged up to the eyes and with just the tips of their trunks above water, from which they emitted squeals and yells of sheer delight as they sailed along in the moonlight. And now the rest came into view on the opposite bank, thirty to forty of them, of all sizes from mighty tuskers to little babies.

There happened to be big stacks of freshly cut bamboos placed along the bank ready for transport by water to Hardwar. Here was a bit of fun for the elephants, who were obviously out on a spree. They flung the bamboos in all directions and trampled into the middle of the stacks. The woodcutters, who had been camping nearby, fled up the bank and started lighting fires in the brushwood, but the elephants were quite unconcerned. They played with the bamboos till they were tired of them, and then passed on down the riverbank, carefree and gay.

It was not only the wild elephants that delighted my heart at

Pashulok, but the domesticated ones also. When I first came there I used to obtain one from the Forest Department for special occasions, but she was rather mischievous and would give little whistling squeaks in the hope of attracting the elephants in the jungle across the river. Her mahout (driver) told me that she had escaped once and joined the wild herd, but had returned thoroughly beaten up. The other elephants would have nothing to do with her because she smelt of human beings, and had thereby lost caste. Nevertheless, whenever we were passing near the river she would start giving little calls. The mahout would scold her each time, but no, she could not resist the temptation, and once or twice she actually got a distant answer.

Later on I was fortunate enough to get the use of the State elephant belonging to the Maharaja of Tehri-Garhwal. State functions having come to an end, the elephant was more or less idle. Rampyari (Beloved of Ram) was her name, and she was most discreet and intelligent.

The idea occurred to me that we might train her to help in our agricultural operations. I designed the harness and took her exact measurements. The saddler had to be reassured, when the order was given, that the harness would not be too big. I did my very best to get a special plow made, but the Government workshop did not rise to the occasion, and so I had a big wooden roller prepared and a tree trunk shaped for pulling over the newly plowed fields to break up the clods of earth.

When we showed Rampyari her harness, she looked doubtfully at it and pushed it away with her trunk each time we tried to put it over her head. The mahout cajoled her with all the sweetest words in his elephant vocabulary, but to no avail. Finally I fetched some *gur* and held it out in such a way that she had to put her trunk through the collar band to take it. That did the trick, and once the harness was over her head she made no more objections. In fact within a few days she had begun helping the mahout by lifting up the harness with her trunk.

We went very cautiously the first day, with only men holding onto the traces, who could let go if Rampyari got excited. But she seemed to understand the whole affair, and within a day or two was working away in the fields as if she had been a farmer all her life.

CHAPTER LXIX

THE cattle schemes, which had been set up on an experimental basis, were beginning to prove too top-heavy. The hierarchy of Government servants was an intolerable burden. There was a manager, a veterinary doctor, two or three stockmen, *kamdars* (farm hands) and sweepers. I watched with painful amusement the way this machinery worked. The manager would give orders to the doctor, who would in turn pass them on to one of the stockmen, the stockman, if it was at all possible, would hand on the job to a *kamdar,* who would look about him to see if by chance a sweeper was around, in which case he would fling the instructions onto this last and lowest division of the hierarchy, from which it could go no further.

Then things which might suddenly be needed, but did not fit in exactly with the red-tape regulations of the setup, could not possibly be attended to unless, of course, I broke the rules, which, for the sake of the cattle, I sometimes did to the horror of the bureaucracy. And deeds which should never be done were perpetrated without the slightest compunction, such as when an officer arrived in a truck with three breeding bulls who were heavily infected with hoof-and-mouth disease, and unloaded them in the middle of our cattle yard without a word of warning regarding their condition. He had been giving instructions from the Animal Husbandry Department to deliver bulls at Pashulok, and he had done it. So that was that. The result for us was that we soon had some two hundred head of cattle down with the disease.

I became more and more fed up, and felt strongly that better service to the public and their cattle could be rendered through a nonoffical organization. I discussed the matter both in Lucknow and Delhi, with the final result that the Government schemes were wound up, and an institution, which we named the Pashulok Seva Mandal (Pashulok Service Association), was formed. The object of the Association I described in the following words:

> To develop an area or areas where men and animals combine with Nature in the formation of a decentralized society demonstrative of Bapu's ideals for World Peace, where man in his own village will, along with his cattle, be self-sufficient, healthy and happy.

In pursuit of this objective the following activities were planned:

1. A co-operative village on seven hundred acres.
2. Upgrading of local cattle by keeping over one thousand acres open to them for grazing, and providing them with good Hariana breeding bulls.
3. Development of village industries suitable to the area, such as oil pressing, canework, bee-keeping, etc.

Dr. Rajendra Prasad, who had now become the first President of the Republic of India, attended the inauguration, and such was the host of visitors, guards, and attendants who camped all around that for twenty-four hours not a wild animal was to be seen. True, there was rustling in the tall pampas grass as usual when I went back and forth between the Ashram and my *kutia*, where the President was lodged for the night. But instead of it being wild pigs, it was security men.

I had hoped that this nonofficial organization would be much easier to work through than the bureaucracy with all its red tape. But I soon discovered I had made a big mistake.

The first difficulty that developed was funds. A Gandhi National Memorial Trust had just been formed in those days, to which millions of people had made donations, and the result was that very few private individuals were ready to give money for independent schemes connected with Bapu. They said the Memorial Trust and the Government should support me. But the Memorial

300

Trust was not very keen on my project, and what aid they did give was as tied up in red tape as any Government money. As for the Government itself, it now said that since the Gandhi National Memorial Trust was there, that was obviously the right source from which my main support should come, so it gave only a little aid.

After the first year things began to get very difficult, and just as I was wondering how on earth to keep the place going, an offer of substantial financial aid, along with proffered assistance in running the scheme, was made to me. It seemed too good to be true, but the connecting circumstances made it impossible for me to doubt the honesty of the offer, and so I accepted it. Before long, however, I began to sense trouble. It was not love of the Pashulok ideals which had inspired this aid, but desire to get control of the place and the rich natural resources lying dormant in it. A long struggle ensued. I was determined not to let the beautiful Pashulok area get into the hands of exploiters, even if it meant having to give up the project, and the ultimate end of it all was that I requested the Government to take the land back under their own protection.

During this painful period my health had become very bad owing to repeated attacks of malaria. Each year, and even twice in the third year, the fever reduced me to a wreck.

I remember one particularly bad attack which laid me up inside my room for over a week. When my legs became steady enough to carry me, I came outside and began slowly walking up and down. Mana, who used to graze around the cottage, had apparently noticed that I had been ill, so, when he saw me outside, he came and rubbed his head against my arm and proceeded to walk up and down with me as if wanting to cheer me up. And he certainly did. The animals and birds, both tame and wild, were my constant solace, without whom I should have been in a bad way during that trying time.

My idea now was to get away on my own, where nobody would be tempted to try to exploit me and my surroundings, but where I could, in a small way, still do something for the villagers and their cattle. At the same time the Himalayas were ever calling.

This led me far into the interior valleys in search of a spot where I could settle down. With three or four companions, Mana and some pack animals, I wandered in that way about two hundred miles, staying here and there to "try on" the surroundings.

The bottoms of the valleys in the Himalayas are hot and often malarial in summer, even when they are four or five thousand feet in altitude. So it was necessary to search on the higher slopes between six and seven thousand feet, but there flat land and water were both difficult to find. Wherever these two things happened to be present in one place, the spot was invariably occupied by the local inhabitants. Then I wanted an additional thing—a view of the Eternal Snows. These three things were impossible to find together in any reasonably available place.

At last, far up the valley of the Bhilangana and twenty-six miles beyond the motor road, which then ended at Tehri, I came upon a small piece of tolerably level ground with a wonderful view up the thickly wooded valley, over the top end of which rose the mighty twenty-two-thousand-foot mountain of Kedarnath. Water was absent, but it was not too far away and could be brought in a little channel made of hollowed-out tree trunks.

This then should be the place. It was Forest Department land, and they leased me about two acres. I said to myself: "People may cast covetous eyes on three thousand acres, but with only two I should be quite safe.

The site of the Ashram being in the midst of a pine forest, a certain number of pine trees had to be cleared away, which, at the same time, gave us timber on the spot. Stone was also present. So it did not take long to construct a tiny cottage for myself, a cowshed, and a separate building with kitchen and living quarters for others. When it was finished the place looked quite in keeping with its surroundings, and I named it Gopal* Ashram.

* Cowherd, one of the names of Lord Krishna.

302

CHAPTER LXX

CHANGES had recently taken place regarding my co-workers. Dharampal had been to England, married an English girl, and taken to a line of his own, and Krishna Murti had joined the staff of the Gandhi National Memorial Trust. I was not now in need both of a secretary and typist, there being no more Government work, so I was on the lookout for someone who would combine secretary, typist and all-round assistant. Two or three people came and went. Either they were no good at typing or they were good at typing and no good at anything else, and none of them were the sort of people for living in Gopal Ashram.

One day Dharampal arrived with a young man and said, "Here is someone who will suit you."

"That's very good," I said, looking at the newcomer with interest.

He was young, slight of build, and possessed a reticent nature, but what little he said made good sense. So Jagdish stayed. He proved to be the all-round combination for which I had been looking, and more, for he was a bit of an artist, and an avid reader of the best in Indian and Western literature, especially philosophy. At the same time being himself of the Himalayas, he felt quite at home in the mountains.

For the cattle and other jobs I had two good assistants, one a young ascetic from Rishikesh, Swami Yoganand, who devoted all his time to the animals and the garden; the other we called Bhramachariji, and he looked after my food and milked the cows. The one was a Bengali, clean-shaved, well-built, handsome and eager, and the other a son of the Himalayas. A simple villager by birth, he had run away from home as a boy in order to study Sanskrit, and later on had wandered over all the Himalayan pilgrim routes visiting Kedarnath, Badrinath, and even Gomukh, the mouth of the glacier from which the Ganga emerges. He shaved only once or twice a year, and when he had his black beard he looked exactly as if he had stepped out of a painting of the Apostles.

For fetching the triweekly post from the post office ten miles down the valley, collecting wood and grass from the jungle and taking grain for grinding to the water mill, we had two local village boys.

The animal members of the family were Mana, three cows and their calves, a young bull for service of the local cattle, and two powerful watchdogs to keep off leopards.

Now, for the first time, I was in the very heart of Himalayan rural life, far away from the influence of the plains. The villagers were hardy, self-reliant and diligent, especially the women, who did much of the field work as well as the household jobs. The men did the plowing, and were experts in building up and keeping in repair their little terraced fields dug out of the steep mountainsides and held in place by strong stone walls. In some cases the height of the wall would be greater than the breadth of the terrace it held up. Both in this terracing, and the digging of small irrigation channels, the villagers showed a perfect instinct for contours and levels, without, of course, any artificial aids whatever. Most of the men were also good lumbermen and went off at intervals to work for Forest Department contractors.

The Harijans of these parts, who were of aboriginal stock, were usually singers and dancers with a drum as their sole accompaniment. Whenever they passed by the Ashram on their way from village to village, they would come in and give a performance.

When there was anything wrong with the weather, which adversely affected the crops, these people would be in great demand for supplicating the gods, and when the drum of the invocation sounded, its vibrating rhythm could be heard for miles across the deep valley. Some of these invocations are quite remarkable, and echo back to Vedic times.

Our dogs, Bholanath and Shakti, were a continual source of interest to me. They were far superior to human beings as night watchmen, for they kept alert all the time; and if a leopard came, instead of running away they made a furious attack on it, chasing it right off the Ashram's land.

When Shakti had puppies it was delightful to watch how the parents behaved. Shakti was all motherly patience and affection, whereas Bholanath considered discipline an essential part of puppies' education. Sometimes while he was resting, the puppies would come romping over him. He would immediately rebuke them with a sharp thrust of his head, as if he were going to bite, and they would rush off squealing to their mother, who would anxiously gather them together with her nose, as if saying, "Never mind, never mind, don't cry. But really you should not disturb Father like that when he is sleeping." And with that she would trot off with them to a little distance so as to avoid any further annoyance to Bholanath.

When the puppies grew bigger, Bholanath took to playing with them, and even the games had an educational value. He used to give a tremendous rough and tumble to the male puppies, but with the female puppies he was infinitely more gentle. These educational games Shakti also used to play with the puppies, especially racing and throwing one another on the run.

When we started making a terraced vegetable garden in the middle of that endless pine forest, our most troublesome neighbors proved to be porcupines—big, strong ones with black and white quills. They, like the leopards, used to come after dark. One night before our watchdogs had arrived I heard the rustling sound of porcupine quills just outside my window, so I jumped up and went out with a lantern to drive the marauder off before he ate up our precious vegetables. But I could see no sign of him, so I went back to bed. In the morning I found porcupine quills scattered all along in the grass, and about thirty yards away at the end of the enclosure were lying his mangled remains—nothing but quills and feet. What I must have heard was a leopard dragging him past my window, and when I went outside no doubt the meal was going on just along there by the wall.

CHAPTER LXXI

THOUGH I had buried myself away in the Himalayas, I continued to watch with keen interest developments in the rest of the country, and they made me feel terribly restless. Huge industrial and other projects were being planned, for which gigantic sums of money had to be borrowed, or accepted as gifts, from other countries. This was all so different to what one had pictured for free India. The more I thought about it the more wound up I became, and finally I started a little monthly paper all on my own, which I called *Bapu Raj Patrika*. It was addressed in very simple language to the peasantry of India. My object was to try to explain to the villagers the kind of self-reliant economy that Bapu had visualized for them, and to urge them to get together in a common demand for a simple decentralized society.

It was, of course, a fantastic venture. Living in those faraway mountains, I had to write all the articles myself, and the financial side of it was equally dependent on my lone effort. The little paper did get a certain number of subscribers, and it appeared in five languages—English, Hindi, Gujerati, Tamil, and Telugu—but it never paid its way and ultimately left me penniless.

In the meantime, not satisfied with merely writing, I decided to go down to the plains in the winter and tour the villages on horseback. The experiences that I gained in this way added to my conviction that the Congress Government was not in real touch with the peasantry, and that the growing corruption of the bureaucracy was eating into the vitals of the nation. But other things also were brought home to me, especially the impracticability of my efforts, and the dangers into which I could fall. The object for which I had been aiming had been so to impress upon the Congress ministers the true state of affairs in the countryside, that they would move toward Bapu's economic principle as the only sure way of ameliorating the lot of the masses, at the same time coming down with a heavy hand on corruption. But friends, who now thought of joining me in my campaign, wanted to develop a frontal attack. Their argument was that sooner or later we must dislodge the ministry and run the Government ourselves if we wanted to achieve a Gandhian regime. Their way of thinking, speaking, and writing was quite different from mine, and if they joined me, I knew everything would develop in such a way as to make it impossible for me to co-operate. Yet if I went on alone on my own line, what would it amount to? I must find some other way of working.

At that time community projects for rural development were being started, and it seemed to me that if one could have a simplified experimental project, orientated toward Bapu's ideals, it might be possible to make it into a clear demonstration of what one was driving at; and what from one such living example the methods should spread. Just then I happened to meet Jawaharlal at a gathering near Wardha, and I put the suggestion before him of starting such a project in the Gopal Ashram area, which was particularly suitable. He readily agreed, and with his blessings I went to Delhi. There in careful consultations with the Central Organization for Community Projects I worked out a complete and detailed scheme on simplified lines, with more local interest and control than in the orthodox pattern, and with objectives all orientated toward Bapu's ideals. The Central Government approved, and I took the scheme to Lucknow. There the trouble began, because it is the State machinery that has to run the Community Projects, and the officials sensed danger to their all-controlling power. However, as the Central Government was prepared to sanction over 1,200,000 pounds for the project, it was too tempting to let go. So after a good deal of argument, I was told to return to Tehri and work out the final details and full budget with the local authorities.

The Tehri-Garhwal public took a keen interest, and we formed an excellent committee of workers. My hopes ran high. The date for the opening ceremony was fixed and we returned to Gopal

Ashram to make preparations for the occasion, and to send invitations to the farthest mountain villages.

On the appointed day villagers turned up from far and wide, most of them dressed in their own homespun and woven woolen clothes—hardy, simple people who had covered miles of rough mountain paths without turning a hair.

Next the Government officials, who were duty-bound to attend the function, began to arrive. The District Planning Officer had fallen off his mule and been taken back to Tehri hospital. The Divisional Forest Officer had fallen off his horse and arrived with a bandaged head, and afterwards the District Magistrate, on return to headquarters, spent a week in bed. Our project was not popular.

Before many days had passed we began getting information and instructions from Lucknow which showed that the bureaucracy was not going to let go its hold on our scheme. I hurried back to Lucknow and had further lengthy talks. Once more I was assured that everything would be all right, but no sooner did I get back to Gopal Ashram than the same thing began all over again.

If this was, after all, to be just an ordinary orthodox project, and not the simplified, decentralized experiment that we had planned, then it was better to hand the whole thing over to the Government to run their own way. And that was what I did.

This meant leaving Gopal Ashram, for I could not contemplate living in the middle of an area where all my hopes had been thwarted, and the kind of official project in which I did not believe was going to be developed.

Many Gandhians at this time had joined the *Bhoodan* (land gift) movement of Acharya Vinoba Bhave, and I was pressed to join also, but I did not feel drawn toward it.

Before making a final decision as to what to do and where to go, I went to Delhi to talk things over. A series of coincidences now brought me in touch with Kashmir. For cattle development it seemed to hold out great possibilities. These tempted me very much, the ministers were ready, and it was decided that I should go there for work.

Back I went to Gopal Ashram, and within ten days packed

up everything, distributed the animals and left. The one thing that really pained me was having to bid farewell to Mana. He had been aging rapidly, and for the last year or more I had been using another horse for riding. So I pensioned him off with the Gujars from whom I had originally bought him and who had a real affection for him. They agreed that he should graze along with their cattle and horses, and not be given any work. But it was hard to part with him. No horse had even been so close and devoted a friend.

CHAPTER LXXII

DURING the second of my visits to Delhi, while working on the setup of the Bhilangana Project, I was one evening sitting in my room when a gay and charming woman walked in. Her cheeks were fresh and pink and her hair golden. She looked at me with a smile which seemed familiar. "Nilla!" I exclaimed. Yes—there was Nilla, the sprite who had danced in and out of Wardha Ashram years ago. She was older of course, yet just the same. That evening we could not get far in recalling and recounting our various experiences of twenty years, and even several more meetings did not cover them all. Much of her time had been spent in the Middle East, and never had she forgotten Bapu's wish that she should work through her art for better and broader understanding between the various world religions and cultures. Just at present, she said, she was devoting herself to translations of Kashmir poetry in which there was a unique blending of Hindu and Moslem thought and mysticism. I began to realize more fully now the qualities that Bapu had realized so long ago. Next time I came to Delhi we met again, and when the question of my going to Kashmir arose, she was all for it.

Of the little Gopal Ashram family, Jagdish, now with a pretty young bride, and Brahmachariji accompanied me. After the grueling journey through the plains we played like children with the snow that we found on the north side of the nine-thousand-foot Banihal Pass.

None of us had ever seen Kashmir before, and we gazed in wonder at the totally new world spread out before us four thousand feet below, for Kashmir is a world complete in itself, not a valley in the ordinary sense. At that season all the surrounding mountains were covered with snow and it looked most impressive.

On our arrival in Srinagar we were conducted to the house of Bakshi Gulam Mohammad, the Prime Minister, who, with characteristic Kashmiri hospitality, put us all up for the night. The next day we moved on to a Government Dairy Farm at Shaltain, five miles outside the city. Several of the houses were pitted with bullet marks.

"How is this?" we asked looking at the walls.

"Did not you know?" they replied. "The Tribal raiders came up to here before they were stopped."

We were lodged in an attractive little house near a grove of beautiful Chenar trees. I began to look about me with intense interest. Trees, flowers and grasses were all different from those on the other side of the Banihal Pass. They bore a look of the northern climes, and I felt reminiscences of childhood as I recognized the daisies and buttercups.

The plan was for me to propose a scheme to the State Government, and to select a site which I thought suitable for cattle development. There was a free-and-easy atmosphere, even in official circles, and red tape could be overcome in a way impossible in Delhi or Lucknow, so it was not difficult to get straight to work.

In the Animal Husbandry Department I found there was already a scheme afoot for importing Jerseys, so I thought it better for me to try another breed in my scheme, as two or three different breeds could advantageously be experimented with in Kashmir. My desire was to work for the higher regions, and if possible, do some cross-breeding with the yak, as this cross is very highly thought of along the Himalayan frontier. The cattle in these higher regions being mostly small and black or blackish in color,

310

I decided on the Dexter breed, and made out my scheme accordingly. Within a month the Government had sanctioned it, and now I had to choose a site for the center.

Nilla, who was busy with her studies of Kashmiri poetry, came to my aid with a little car in which she drove me to look at various places. All were beautiful, so beautiful indeed that one felt carried away by the scenery, but I had to take many points into consideration, and it required time to decide. Finally I fixed on the little valley leading off the Sind Valley, where a road turns up toward Gangabal. The obtaining of the land and the construction of the buildings was quite a job, and it all had to be done quickly as the snows of winter were coming, and the cattle must arrive in time to cross over that great Pass before it became blocked. Again the military were most helpful. The local stone was very hard and had to be blasted, so they came with all the necessary equipment and made it possible to complete in less than three months what would otherwise have taken six. All the construction work was done by local village craftsmen, and when it was completed, with its shingle-covered roofs, it looked thoroughly Kashmiri. I called the little place Gaobal—the place of the cow.

In October, when the first cowshed was just ready, the Dexters arrived in Bombay by sea from England and I went to receive them. I broke the journey at Delhi, and stayed with the President, Dr. Rajendra Prasad. Though he was living in that huge Viceroy's House, he occupied the smallest rooms at the top of the building, and his food and style of living had remained just as simple as they were in the old days. Before going on to Bombay I arranged with the aides-de-camp to have fresh green grass from the Viceregal grounds sent to the railway station when the Dexters were due to pass through Delhi, for I knew how much they would relish it on their long journey in a strange land.

At Bombay it was still very hot, and the poor little Dexters were panting heavily when they landed. One of the heifers had died of heat on the Red Sea, and I looked with alarm at the breathless condition of the others. I was thankful that I had arranged with the railway authorities for horseboxes instead of cattle trucks so that they could be attached to a passenger train, and that I had also had electric fans fixed for them. Though they could not say "thank you," the way they immediately lay down and relaxed under their fans was enough to tell how grateful they were.

I went ahead by air, so as to be able to arrange the trucks at Pathankot for taking them over the high Pass, and the Veterinary Officer, who had gone with me to Bombay, traveled by the train.

In order that they should be quite comfortable, I gave them four trucks and traveled myself in one, carrying the heifer who was in advanced pregnancy. The first night we halted at Udhampur in the foothills, and the next day went over the Pass. The second night we halted in Srinagar, and the third day the precious little animals arrived safe and sound at their destination. How thankful I was, and how tired too!

The next thing was to look about the villages for good local cows suitable for crossing with our Dexter bulls. It was not easy to find many, as practically all that were worth anything had become concentrated in the Srinagar Dairies. However, we collected six, and informed the surrounding villages that our bulls were at their service also.

This time I was myself the manager, so there was no standing about with hands in pockets for anyone. The staff consisted of a stock assistant, an accountant, a storekeeper, and *kamdars,* these last being all taken from the nearby villages.

In the mountains, if cattle are to flourish, they must be taken up to the higher altitudes in summer, and preferably this should be done in two stages. So as soon as spring came, and the snows began to melt, I started looking for good pastures above our farm. Gaobal was situated at about 6,000 feet, and the next stage which I fancied was at 7,000 feet, on the edge of a great forest in which there was some good grazing. The Forest Department sanctioned for our scheme over thirty acres, and we managed to obtain also a few fields adjoining the forest. Here we built Gaopatri, and the third year we built the topmost cattlesheds in an open sweeping grassland of sixteen acres, at 8,600 feet. And what a place that was! On one side there was a clear view right down the Sind Valley, and on the other three sides there was a vast untrammeled forest of firs and pines intermixed with rich undergrowth.

Our scheme was now in full swing. Though we had had rather bad luck with our first calvings, the second calvings which were then in progress were turning out very well. Besides our pedigreed Dexters and local cows, we had a yak, two zos and two zomas, as the first cross between the yak and cow are called in Kashmir— *zo* male and *zoma* female. These five animals I had obtained from the Kargil area, which lies in the high mountains at an altitude of ten to twelve thousand feet on the way to Leh, capital of Ladakh.

Cross-breeding among Dexters, Kashmiris and yaks was at last materializing, but by this time the Animal Husbandry policy of the Government had undergone a complete change and foreign breeds were no longer wanted, as the plan was now to have only Kashmiri cattle. The importation of the Jersey herd from England, which I had thought to be a certainty, was canceled, as well as the visit of the Jersey-*cum*-Organic Farming expert, Newman Turner, which I had all but arranged through the Colombo Plan.

The Central Government policy, however, was to import foreign breeds for the Himalayas, as the best Indian breeds were only suited to a hot climate. So I went to Delhi and suggested to the Animal Husbandry people there that, since they were keen on foreign breeds and Kashmir was not, it would be good to transfer the Dexters to an area where there would be scope for their propagation.

The idea was agreed to, and the Dexters went across to the Simla area of Himachal Pradesh while I, with my little party, returned for the time being to Tehri-Garhwal.

But what to do? I had no place in which to live, and very little money left. Kisan Ashram, Pashulok, Gopal Ashram and Gaobal had all passed out of my life like dreams.

No more Government projects, that at least was clear.

CHAPTER LXXIII

ALL these ten years since Bapu's departure I had been intensely active outwardly, but deep down inside it had been a period of suspension, a kind of hibernation. Now the inner being had begun to stir. "Whatever it is," I said to myself, "God's guidance will come."

The restlessness went on increasing. By remaining far away in the mountains, was I trying to escape this new world, divided against itself and trembling in fear of its own inventions? The thought of going out came to me, but the way was not clear. I could not find my bearings, or rather, myself.

So I just went on living and waiting. But the body has to be kept somewhere, and therefore I began to look about for some quiet nook in the mountains where I could build a cottage. Such a nook was not easy to find, and I kept on wandering for some time.

One day the post brought me a parcel from Paris. I opened it to find a book of Romain Rolland sent by his widow.

"I'd love to read it," I said to myself, "but I've forgotten all my French." So I placed it on a shelf. Then I thought, Let me see if I cannot make out one or two of the letters day by day.

I picked up the book, and when I put it down I found I had read and enjoyed at least three letters. Now I read the book daily, and when I had finished it I began reading it all over again.

In the meantime, without quite knowing how it had come about, I had begun writing my life's recollections. People had been pressing me to do this for many years, but I had flatly refused.

"Until it comes of its own accord I will never write," I told them.

314

Now this had happened, hesitantly at first, but day by day the impetus increased. Then suddenly it came to a stop.

"What am I, where am I? To what has my life led?"

As I contemplated the past I realized clearly how I had never been able to give Bapu full satisfaction, for there had always been something suppressed that caused the tension which Bapu noticed and against which he had warned me time and again. I realized too that the ceaseless activity of the past ten years, though an outlet, had yet left me with an unfulfilled feeling. I felt overwhelmed with a blinding melancholy, and for several months did not write another word.

The wandering continued till at last I found a little piece of land, and I said to myself: "Then let me settle here." As it was devoid of any buildings, I stayed in a farmhouse nearby with Jagdish and Brahmachariji, from where I could go daily to supervise construction of a small cottage and cowshed.

This place that I had found was extraordinarily beautiful, something I could hardly have expected to discover. There were miniature grasslands, a deodar grove, and a glorious view of the mountains. Of an evening, after the laborers had gone home, I would stay behind on the grass slopes and gaze upon the Great Range spread out before me—Bandarpunch, Kedarnath, Badrinath, on and on right around to Nanda Devi and Trisul, mountains rising from twenty to twenty-five thousand feet. As the sun set, the Eternal Snows would turn from gold to orange and finally take on a brilliant rose-colored glow till the shadow of the night mounted slowly up to the summits. It was a vision of peaceful strength, but also it stirred the spirit within, and I would return to the farmhouse as in a dream, for the restlessness had not subsided.

On one such evening when I entered my room I said to myself: "Have I not any other book of Romain Rolland which I could read, now that I have been through those letters twice?"

And I remembered that long ago I had packed away in the box containing Bapu's original letters, the volumes that Romain Rolland had given to me in Villeneuve when Bapu had stayed there in 1931—*Beethoven—Les Grandes Époques Créatrices*.

315

In those early days of stress and turmoil I had had no quiet time for reading, and later on I had got it into my head that I could not remember any French. So the volumes had remained unread.

Now I went to the box, took them out and sat down to read, and as I read something began to stir—something fundamental. I shut my eyes. Yes—it was the spirit of him from whose music I had been separated for over thirty years that I heard and felt, but now with new vision and inspiration. I became conscious of the realization of my true self. For a while I remained lost in the World of the Spirit, and when I finally came back the former tension and restlessness had passed out of me. The third and last chapter of this present birth had begun. Not a finishing, but a preparation.

316

APPENDIX

Viceroys of India between 1921 to 1948

Lord Reading, 1921–1926
Lord Irwin, 1926–1931
Lord Willingdon, 1931–1936
Lord Linlithgow, 1936–1943
Lord Wavell, 1943–1947
Lord Mountbatten, 1947–1948

Important dates

1921–1922 Weingartner concert during London season
1923 First meeting with Romain Rolland
Nov. 3, 1927 Simon Commission—Royal Commission for assessing the constitutional needs of India
Dec. 31, 1929 Resolution of the Indian National Congress declaring its aim as Complete Independence
1930–1931 Civil Disobedience Movement
March 1931 Gandhi-Irwin Pact for a truce between the Indian National Congress and the British Government
Autumn 1931 Round Table Conference in London—Second Session, to which Mahatma Gandhi went
February 1935 Government of India Act, 1935, by which a limited measure of self-rule was granted to India
March 22, 1940 to April 12, 1940 Mission of Sir Stafford Cripps to India to seek a compromise with the Congress and to enlist their support for the war effort, which proved fruitless
1942 Japanese invasion and occupation of Burma and penetration into Assam borders

317

July 14, 1942   Quit India Resolution of the Indian National Congress

August 9, 1942   Quit India movement and wholesale arrests of all Congress leaders

June 25, 1945 to July 14, 1945   Simla Conference called by Lord Wavell shortly before which Gandhi and Congress Working Committee members had been released

March 24, 1946 to June 29, 1946   Cabinet Mission for negotiating transfer of power

Sept. 2, 1946   Interim Government

December 9, 1946   Constituent Assembly

August 15, 1947   Transfer of power

January 31, 1948   Assassination of Mahatma Gandhi

May 6, 1952   Dr. Rajendra Prasad elected first president of the Republic of India—which he remains today

Jawaharlal Nehru has been Prime Minister of India since August 15, 1947

CPSIA information can be obtained
at www.ICGtesting.com
Printed in the USA
BVHW041800170119
538094BV00010B/201/P

9 781163 819036